OECD Public Governance Reviews

Improving ISSSTE's Public Procurement for Better Results

OECD

BETTER POLICIES FOR BETTER LIVES

Please cite this publication as:
OECD (2016), *Improving ISSSTE's Public Procurement for Better Results*, OECD Public Governance Reviews, OECD Publishing, Paris.
http://dx.doi.org/10.1787/9789264249899-en

ISBN 978-92-64-24988-2 (print)
ISBN 978-92-64-24989-9 (PDF)

Series: OECD Public Governance Reviews
ISSN 2219-0406 (print)
ISSN 2219-0414 (online)

Photo credits: Cover © Khakimullin Aleksandr/Shutterstock.com

Corrigenda to OECD publications may be found on line at: *www.oecd.org/about/publishing/corrigenda.htm*.

Foreword

OECD countries are increasingly attempting to control healthcare spending and reduce fiscal strains caused by an ageing population, the rise of certain chronic diseases and public savings targets which, as a result of the global financial crisis, often imply significant spending cuts. Since 2009, total health spending per capita has fallen in 11 out of the 34 OECD countries. Mexico devotes around 6% of its gross domestic product to health, which makes it one of the OECD's lowest per capita spenders on health.

In this context, healthcare procurement is receiving increasing attention in OECD countries. Efficient healthcare procurement can provide high-quality goods and services for a competitive price and reinforce citizens' trust that their tax contributions are put to good use and that their well-being is a priority.

The State's Employees' Social Security and Social Services Institute (*Instituto de Seguridad y Servicios Sociales de los Trabajadores del Estado*, ISSSTE) in Mexico is committed to achieving these goals. Following substantial work to implement the recommendations on efficiency, integrity and fighting bid-rigging resulting from an earlier comprehensive assessment of its procurement system conducted with the help of the OECD, the ISSSTE identified further areas to be improved. With targeted OECD support to enhance performance in healthcare procurement, ISSSTE is seeking to benefit from good practices in planning and designing procurement processes, increasing competition for contracts and improving the supply of medical services.

Based on the *2015 Recommendation of the Council on Public Procurement*, the OECD assesses national and sectorial public procurement systems. It supports governments in achieving public spending targets and preventing the misuse of funds, ensuring that what is needed is delivered to the right place on time, at the right price and in a fair and open manner.

This report is the outcome of extensive stakeholder dialogue and incorporates advice from leading OECD healthcare procurement peer experts. It also recognises ISSSTE's recent achievements, some of which are remarkable, such as the MXN 260 million savings obtained through consolidated purchases and renegotiation of medical services contracts. It further makes recommendations to enhance ISSSTE's procurement practices in the four key areas analysed: improving data collection, advancing procurement co-ordination, engaging in dialogue with suppliers and increasing competitive tendering.

Through concrete action plans and recommendations sequenced by order of priority, the report recommends a hands-on approach to advancing procurement reform. Taken together, the recommendations form a comprehensive view of what constitutes good approaches to health procurement for ISSSTE. Highlights include the importance of good-quality data and performance analysis, institutionalising good practices, the role of market intelligence and the advantages of competition and contract management. Good practices on transparent interaction between public officials and suppliers in public procurement processes are also identified as an area of priority action in Mexico. These form a central part of the currently ongoing executive actions to prevent corruption and avoid conflicts of interest in public administration.

Under tight financial constraints, ISSSTE is on a path of evolving its management and transparency of the procurement process while recognising that quality procurement has a price: it is a complex process, for public entities as much as for the private sector. This report reaffirms the value of investment in public procurement as a strategic function and will help ISSSTE address the fundamental challenges that are present in the procurement of healthcare. Through more efficient and effective delivery of healthcare services to citizens, Mexico can demonstrate quality governance worthy of citizens' trust and engagement, delivering better health for better lives.

Angel Gurría
OECD Secretary-General

Acknowledgements

This Public Procurement Review of the State's Employees' Social Security and Social Services Institute (Instituto de Seguridad y Servicios Sociales de los Trabajadores del Estado, ISSSTE) was prepared by the Public Governance and Territorial Development Directorate of the OECD headed by Rolf Alter. Work on public procurement is carried out by the Public Governance and Territorial Development Directorate as part of its mission to help governments at all levels design and implement strategic, evidence-based and innovative policies to strengthen public governance; respond effectively to diverse and disruptive economic, social and environmental challenges; and deliver on government's commitments to citizens.

Under the direction of János Bertok and Paulo Magina, this review was led by Despina Pachnou, with contributions by Emma Cantera of the OECD Secretariat. Chapters 1-4 were written by Despina Pachnou, with inputs from Heidi Sada. Chapter 5 was written by Emma Cantera. The action plans for the Procurement Co-ordination and Market Intelligence Units, annexed to Chapters 2 and 3 respectively, are based on drafts prepared by Steve Graham of Hadley Graham Ltd, advisors to the Department of Health, United Kingdom. Heidi Sada conducted research and contributed to the collection and analysis of information and data. Ken Kincaid and Jennifer Allain edited the manuscript. Jennifer Allain also prepared the manuscript for publication, with support from Sophie O'Gorman, Anaisa Gonçalves and Julie Harris. Gilda Moreno Manzur translated the report into Spanish and Angela Marcela Martínez Montealegre reviewed the translation and English-Spanish alignment with contributions from Jacobo Garcia Villarreal from the OECD Secretariat. The OECD Mexico Centre for Latin America, under the leadership of Roberto Martínez Yllescas and, formerly, of Eugenia Garduño, provided local support.

Peer reviewers for this project were Marjorie Ramírez, former Head of Division of Framework Agreements at the central purchasing body ChileCompra in Chile; Dorthe Bartels, Head of the Procurement and Tendering Department at Amgros, the pharmaceutical procurement service for regional authorities in Denmark; Steve Graham of Hadley Graham Ltd, advisors to the Department of Health in the United Kingdom; and Joana Candeias, Senior Officer at the Direction of Central Purchase of Health Goods and Services of SPMS, the shared services body of the Ministry of Health in Portugal. This Review incorporates the peer reviewers' insights and advice, as well as good practices they shared during the OECD workshop on "Improving Public Procurement Practices in ISSSTE", which took place 2-4 September 2014 in Mexico City. This Review includes good practice examples provided by Kenza Khachani, Economic Performance Manager at the French central purchasing body, the Union of Public Purchasing Groups (Union des groupements d'achats publics, UGAP); Angela Russo, Head of International Cooperation Projects at the Italian central purchasing body (Concessionaria Servizi Informativi Pubblici, Consip SpA); and Anne Kristin Reinsve, Internal Control Special Advisor at

Vestre Viken Hospital Trust in Norway. It also benefited from valuable comments by Matthieu Cahen, Antonio Capobianco and Marian Lemke of the OECD Secretariat.

The OECD expresses its gratitude to the ISSSTE for its fruitful co-operation and leadership, in particular the Director General, José Reyes Baeza Terrazas;the Secretary General, Juan Manuel Verdugo Rosas; the Director of Administration, Minerva Castillo Rodríguez; the Deputy Director of International Relations, Salua Quintero Soda, and their teams. The OECD acknowledges all of the interlocutors from the ISSSTE for the quality of the discussions and the richness of the information provided during this Review. Special thanks go to the Deputy Director of Planning and Institutional Performance Evaluation, Antonio de Cabo Gómez; Executive Co-ordinator José Saturnino Medésigo; the Deputy Director of Medical Supplies, Pedro Lurueña Caballero; the Deputy Director of Infrastructure, Adrian Golzarri Arroyo, the Deputy Director of Material Resources and Services, Francisco Javier Ortiz Villanueva; the Deputy Director of Conservation and Maintenance, Georgina Meade Ocaranza; the Head of Audit for the Development and Improvement of Public Management at the ISSSTE's Internal Control Unit, Iliana Judith Pérez Pacheco; the Administrative Co-ordinator of the Finance Directorate, Rigoberto Mendoza Javier; the Administrative Co-ordinator of the Delegations Directorate Mayte Márquez Ramírez; the Head of Technical Support Services at the Medical Supplies Sub-Directorate, Lucía Ríos Nuñez; the Head of the Department of Analysis of Strategic Programs, Victor Manuel Negrete Fernández; and the Head of Co-operation Services with International Organisations and Bilateral Agencies, Maria del Rosario Guadarrama Martínez. Numerous other ISSSTE staff members provided valuable information and comments. OECD missions were made possible with the co-ordination of the Administration Directorate under Minerva Castillo Rodríguez and the Deputy Directorate of International Relations under Salua Quintero Soda. The peer review team had enlightening discussions with representatives of the National Chamber of the Pharmaceutical Industry (CANIFARMA), Mexico's Supreme Audit Institution (*Auditoría Superior de la Federación*, ASF) and Alejandro Luna Ramos, Head of the Public Procurement Policy Unit at the Ministry of Public Administration (*Secretaría de la Función Pública*, SFP), as well as with several of the ISSSTE's suppliers. Ambassador Dionisio Pérez-Jácome Friscione and Maya Alejandra Camacho Dávalos, Second Secretary at the Permanent Delegation of Mexico to the OECD, were instrumental in facilitating the carrying out of this review.

This Review was discussed and approved by the Public Governance Committee's Working Party of Leading Practitioners on Public Procurement during its session of 28 April 2015, where the Deputy Director of Planning and Institutional Performance Evaluation of the ISSSTE, Antonio de Cabo Gómez, presented the ISSSTE's initiatives to build procurement capacities and monitor performance. The Review benefits from the insights provided by senior experts who participate in the Working Party of Leading Practitioners on Public Procurement.

Table of contents

Tables

Figures

Boxes

Acronyms and abbreviations

ANDIS	National Association of Health Supply Distributors *Asociación Nacional de Distribuidores de Insumos para la Salud*
ASF	Supreme audit institution of Mexico *Auditoría Superior de la Federación*
CAAS	Goods, Leasing and Services Committee *Comité de Adquisiciones, Arrendamientos y Servicios*
CANACINTRA	National Chamber of Transformation Industries *Cámara Nacional de la Industria de Transformación*
CANIFARMA	National Chamber of the Pharmaceutical Industry *Cámara Nacional de la Industria Farmacéutica*
CAOC	Chief Acquisition Officers Council (United States)
CFC	Federal Competition Commission *Comisión Federal de Competencia*
COG	Item spending codes *Clasificador por objeto de gasto*
COMPRANET	Mexico's electronic procurement system *Sistema Electrónico de Información Pública Gubernamental*
CPEUM	Mexican Constitution *Constitución Política de los Estados Unidos Mexicanos*
CUCoP	Unique Classifier of Public Procurement *Clasificador Único de Contrataciones Públicas*
FOVISSSTE	Housing Fund of the State's Employees' Social Security and Social Services Institute *Fondo de la Vivienda del Instituto de Seguridad y Servicios Sociales de los Trabajadores del Estado*
IMSS	Mexican Institute of Social Security *Instituto Mexicano del Seguro Social*
ISSSTE	State's Employees' Social Security and Social Services Institute *Instituto de Seguridad y Servicios Sociales de los Trabajadores del Estado*
LAASSP	Law on Acquisitions, Leasing and Services of the Public Sector *Ley de Adquisiciones, Arrendamientos y Servicios del Sector Público*
MAAGMAASSP	General Procurement Manual *Manual Administrativo de Aplicación General en Materia de Adquisiciones, Arrendamientos y Servicios del Sector Público*
NAFTA	North-American Free Trade Agreement

NHS	National Health Service (United Kingdom)
NICE	National Institute for Health and Care Excellence (United Kingdom)
OFFP	Office of Federal Procurement Policy (United States)
OIC	Internal Control Unit *Órgano Interno de Control*
PAAAS	Annual Procurement Programme *Programa Anual de Adquisiciones, Arrendamientos y Servicios*
PCU	Procurement Co-ordination Unit
PEMEX	Mexican Petroleum *Petróleos Mexicanos*
PENSIONISSSTE	National Pension Fund for State Workers *Fondo Nacional de Pensiones de los Trabajadores al Servicio del Estado*
PHARE	Hospital performance for responsible procurement *Performance hospitalière pour des achats responsables*
POBALINES (ISSSTE)	Policies and guidelines on acquisitions, leasing and services (ISSSTE) *Políticas, bases y lineamientos en materia de adquisiciones, arrendamientos y servicios (ISSSTE)*
PPIRS	Past Performance Information Retrieval System (United States)
RADS	Council for the Use of Expensive Hospital Medicines (Denmark)
RCB	Purchase request *Requisición de compra de bienes o servicios*
SAIM	Sub-Directorate of Medical Supplies *Subdirección de Abasto de Insumos Médicos*
SCM	Sub-Directorate of Conservation and Maintenance *Subdirección de Conservación y Mantenimiento*
SEDENA	Ministry of National Defence *Secretaría de la Defensa Nacional*
SEMAR	Ministry of the Navy *Secretaría de Marina*
SFP	Ministry of Public Administration *Secretaría de la Función Pública*
SHCP	Ministry of Finance and Public Credit *Secretaría de Hacienda y Crédito Público*
SI	Sub-Directorate of Infrastructure *Subdirección de Infraestructura*
SIEDI	Internal System for Institutional Performance Evaluation *Sistema Interno de Evaluación de Desempeño Institucional*
SRM	Sub-Directorate of Materials and Services *Subdirección de Recursos Materiales y Servicios*
SuperISSSTE	ISSSTE's supermarket and pharmacy branch

	Sistema de Tiendas y Farmacias de los Trabajadores al Servicio del Estado
TURISSSTE	ISSSTE's tourism branch *Sistema de Agencias Turísticas del ISSSTE*
UNAM	National Autonomous University of Mexico *Universidad Nacional Autónoma de Mexico*
UNSPSC	United Nations Standard Products and Services Code

Executive summary

Public health accounts for around 9% of GDP in OECD countries and is a spending area facing increasing challenges from ageing populations and difficult socio-economic environments. At the same time, reforming public procurement is often an important part of government efforts to improve transparency, integrity and effectiveness in the use of public funds. In public health in particular, improved procurement practices can both contribute to the control of healthcare spending and also help improve provision of high-quality healthcare.

The provision of a wide array of healthcare services imposes complex medical and budgetary challenges on the State's Employees' Social Security and Social Services Institute in Mexico (*Instituto de Seguridad y Servicios Sociales de los Trabajadores del Estado*, ISSSTE). Following the successful implementation of peer review recommendations issued by the OECD in 2012, a multi-stakeholder follow-up review of ISSSTE by the OECD focussed on four key aspects of its procurement system: procurement planning and co-ordination, market intelligence activities, the supply of medical services and the level of competition for ISSSTE contracts through an analysis of direct awards. The OECD also developed action plans for the creation and implementation of both a Procurement Co-ordination Unit and a Market Intelligence Unit within the ISSSTE. This review details the OECD's findings and recommendations and incorporates ISSSTE's actions to address them.

Key findings

- ISSSTE has reinforced the central management of its procurement resources and activities. A 2014 organic statute groups all sub-directorates involved in procurement under the Administration Directorate. The new statute also prioritises the structures and processes, giving the Secretariat General the responsibility to drive improvements.
- The importance of procurement is thus acknowledged at ISSSTE's central level (Director General, Secretary General and the Administration Directorate). However, there is no single, explicit, non-legal procurement strategy that defines the long-term vision for procurement and identifies priorities, timelines and targets as well as the main ways to achieve them.
- ISSSTE has different data collection tools, but no single comprehensive database covering both central and decentralised ISSSTE units and giving accurate information on who buys what, when and on which terms, and which goods are in stock. However, ISSSTE is in the process of developing concrete measures to improve the collection of procurement data through the establishment of a procurement database.
- At the central level, the ISSSTE has procurement co-ordination processes such as CONCERTA, which links the Administration Directorate, the Medical

Directorate, the 35 delegations and the 15 hospitals. CONCERTA has helped streamline acquisition planning. There is still room for better planning and co-ordination, in particular with the ISSSTE's regional delegations, by consolidating information about purchases.

- ISSSTE has internal good practices to measure the performance of its procurement activities, but no integrated system with developed and standard monitoring arrangements.
- ISSSTE's market intelligence activities meet the legal requirements. However, results usually do not feed into the design of the procurement strategy on what to buy, how, and under what terms. Thus, ISSSTE may miss opportunities to buy strategically, secure innovative goods or services, lower prices or increase quality.
- Officials, in particular in delegations, will benefit from tailored support and training in market research.
- A thorough cost-benefit analysis guides the procurement of ISSSTE's comprehensive medical services provided by external contactors.
- Competition for comprehensive medical services increased as a result of efforts in 2013 and 2014 by ISSSTE's Administration Directorate to broaden the supply base and lower prices, resulting in savings of MXN 262.40 million in 2013.
- ISSSTE is taking steps to improving contract management of comprehensive medical services to improve the buyer-seller relationship and prevent disputes.
- Direct awards at ISSSTE are largely explained by inadequate planning, inconclusive market research, the complexity of rules or budget transfer delays.

Key recommendations

To help ISSSTE prioritise actions, recommendations are ranked by order of priority and feasibility, from immediate/short-term to medium-term and long-term actions, and are accompanied by a corresponding action plan whenever applicable.

Strengthening planning and co-ordination

- Develop an explicit, performance-focused procurement strategy, containing a long-term vision for procurement, sequencing actions and timelines, and detailing monitoring and adjustment strategies.
- Building on current initiatives to build a reliable patients' census for high-specialty medicines and a dataset for procurement contracts in central units, establish a comprehensive procurement database that allows the generation of reports on past spending and the extraction of information for forecasting future purchases.
- Institutionalise internal good practices throughout ISSSTE and reinforce communication between central and decentralised areas.
- Establish procurement performance indicators measuring efficiency and outcomes.
- Create a Procurement Co-ordination Unit with the proper human and financial resources and approvals.

Improving market intelligence

- Develop a market intelligence methodology and plan, assessing the available human and material resources and including method variations according to the degree of critical importance or complexity of procurement.
- Formalise the Market Intelligence Unit in the Medical Supplies Sub-Directorate depending on available human and financial resources.
- Work with other healthcare providers and healthcare experts to pool knowledge.
- Select people with the appropriate skills to create an informal network of market research specialists from among the ISSSTE's procurement officials.

Enhancing the procurement of comprehensive medical services

- Consider consolidating the procurement of comprehensive medical services with other healthcare providers, such as the Mexican Institute of Social Security (IMSS).
- Involve more medical areas in contract performance management.
- Design evaluation criteria to accurately measure a bidder's capacity to respond to medical needs and risks.
- Train and support small and medium-sized enterprises to increase their participation in procurement.

Boosting competition for contracts and limiting direct awards

- Start in-house and on-the-job training by experienced ISSSTE procurement professionals on securing competition for contracts.
- Implement standard data collection tools all procurement units as a step towards a comprehensive ISSSTE-wide procurement database.
- Educate medical and procurement units in the strategic relevance of advance procurement planning.
- Regularly examine the use of exceptions to competitive tendering in order to understand sources of constraints and develop standard documents.
- Tailor training developed by Mexican public bodies and institutes to ISSSTE to strengthen internal capacity.
- Consider implementing a standardised classification model for identifying products.

Chapter 1.

Healthcare procurement at the ISSSTE

This chapter provides an overview of the scope and methodology of this public procurement review. It explains the role of the State's Employees' Social Security and Social Services Institute (ISSSTE) in the Mexican healthcare system. It presents the challenges as well as recent initiatives by the ISSSTE to improve its procurement structures, optimise human and financial resources, and improve healthcare results.

The statistical data for Israel are supplied by and under the responsibility of the relevant Israeli authorities. The use of such data by the OECD is without prejudice to the status of the Golan Heights, East Jerusalem and Israeli settlements in the West Bank under the terms of international law.

A fundamental part of the Mexican healthcare system

The ISSSTE is a decentralised public organisation of the Mexican federal government, with its own legal personality and assets.[1] Established on 30 December 1959 and one of the largest bodies of its kind in Mexico, the ISSSTE provides healthcare, social security services and financial benefits to federal public servants.[2] It is the third social security system in Mexico, after the IMSS and the States Social Protection Healthcare Systems.

The Mexican healthcare system forms part of the social security system. It is built on three pillars that serve different swathes of the population according to their employment status and economic capacity (Table 1.1):

- Pillar 1 is a voluntary private insurance system. Individuals pay to a health insurance provider premiums that are determined by their risk profiles and which buy mutually agreed packages of health services.
- Pillar 2 is the social security system. It is mandatory for all employees in the formal economy and is divided into two types according to employment relationship:

1. Employees in the private sector and their families receive healthcare services from the IMSS.
2. Employees of the federal public sector and their families receive healthcare services from the ISSSTE. The national oil company, Petróleos Mexicanos (PEMEX), the Ministry of National Defence (Secretaría de la Defensa Nacional, SEDENA), and the Ministry of the Navy (Secretaría de Marina, SEMAR) have healthcare systems covering their own employees. States' (federal regions) employees are covered by the social security system of the individual State for which they work.

- Pillar 3 caters only to citizens not covered by any other scheme. It is the *Sistemas de Protección Social en Salud Estatales* (the States Social Protection Healthcare Systems).

Table 1.1. **Mexican healthcare system, 2012**

System	Percentage of the population served
Private insurance	1.8
Social security	
– IMSS	52.1
– ISSSTE	10.6
– PEMEX, SEDENA, SEMAR, states (federal regions)	1
Social Protection Healthcare System	44.9

Note: The sum of the beneficiaries of the healthcare system is greater than 100% because of duplication in some of the services received. For example, some beneficiaries of the States Social Protection Healthcare System are also recipients of the IMSS "Oportunidades" programme".

Source: Based on information in: Panopoulou, G., U. Giedion y E. González-Pier (2014), "The Universal List of Essential Health Services and the Catastrophic Health Expenditure Fund", in Giedion, U., R. Bitrán and I. Tristao (eds.) (2014), *Health Benefit Schemes in Latin America: A Regional Comparison*, Chapter 4, Inter-American Development Bank, http://publications.iadb.org/handle/11319/6484.

The ISSSTE covers approximately 12.6 million beneficiaries (ISSSTE, 2013a), who are federal public servants,[3] pensioners and the families of both (Table 1.2). This is more than the total population of many OECD countries.

Table 1.2. **ISSSTE beneficiaries, 2013**

	Direct		Families	Total
	Workers	Pensioners		
Federal District	717 530	258 381	2 271 282	3 247 193
31 states	2 052 842	650 215	6 680 319	9 383 376
Total	2 770 372	908 596	8 951 601	12 630 569

Source: ISSSTE (2013a), *Anuario Estadístico del ISSSTE 2013*, www2.issste.gob.mx:8080/index.php/mdir-inst-finanzas-anuarios-anos/100-instituto/finanzas/2355-dir-finanzas-anuarios-capitulos2013 (accessed 17 February 2015).

The Institute is the country's eighth largest workforce (Alejo, 2014). It employs more than 100 000 workers, about 80% of which are unionised (ISSSTE, 2013a).

Table 1.3. **ISSSTE personnel by type of appointment, 2013**

	Unionised	Non-unionised	Medical residents	On fee contracts	Interns	Total
Federal District	24 809	7 135	1 062	253	408	33 667
31 states	53 888	10 527	410	285	1 228	66 338
Total	78 697	17 662	1 472	538	1 636	100 005

Source: ISSSTE (2013a), *Anuario Estadístico del ISSSTE 2013*, www2.issste.gob.mx:8080/index.php/mdir-inst-finanzas-anuarios-anos/100-instituto/finanzas/2355-dir-finanzas-anuarios-capitulos2013 (accessed 17 February 2015).

ISSSTE's procurement structure

The ISSSTE's structure is defined in an organic statute (*Estatuto Orgánico*). In April 2014, the Board of Directors, the ISSSTE's highest governance body, adopted a new statute which entered into force in June of the same year with the purpose to establish a procurement function more transparent and eficient.[4] This statute gives the ISSSTE's Secretariat General the responsibility to drive institutional co-ordination and the improvement of systems, structures and internal processes, and to measure the quality and appropriateness of rendered services and benefits. The statute also clarifies and streamlines functions, including those related to procurement functions, of the central and decentralised units of the ISSSTE. It formalises and reinforces the central management of the ISSSTE's procurement by the Administration Directorate, which now groups all of the sub-directorates involved in procurement, including the Infrastructure and the Planning and Budgeting Sub-Directorates. The Administration Directorate is thus entirely in charge of planning, awarding and monitoring procurement. Figure 1.1 shows the units that are involved, in one way or another, in the procurement activities of central ISSSTE and delegations (excluding FOVISSSTE, PensionISSSTE, SuperISSSTE and TURISSSTE, the National Medical Centre 20 de Noviembre, hospitals and schools).

Figure 1.1. **ISSSTE's organisational structure**

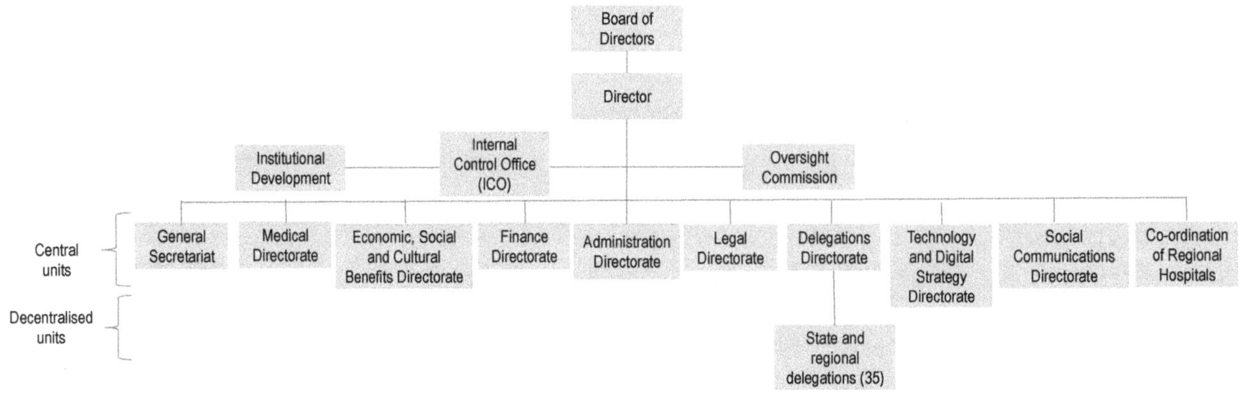

Source: ISSSTE (2014), "Acuerdo 57.1344.2014 de la Junta Directiva, relativo a la aprobación del Estatuto Orgánico del Instituto de Seguridad y Servicios Sociales de los Trabajadores del Estado" (Organic Statute of the ISSSTE), *Diario Oficial de la Federación*, 18 June, available at: http://normateca.issste.gob.mx/view.asp?sesion=201502041031452225&infocard=201406181050098504&d=Y.

The Board of Directors is the ISSSTE's highest authority and is in charge of strategic planning, setting priorities and designing programmes, structures and institutional frameworks. It is also responsible for evaluating, controlling and supervising the activities of the other ISSSTE governance bodies and administrative units. The Board is comprised of 19 members from the federal public administration and trade unions:

- General Director of the ISSSTE
- General Director of the IMSS
- three members of the Ministry of Finance and Public Credit, one of whom is the minister
- Minister of Health
- Minister of Social Development
- Minister of Labour and Social Protection
- Minister of Environment and Natural Resources
- Minister of Public Administration
- nine representatives of workers' organisations.

The ISSSTE's Director General is its legal representative and is responsible for managing and executing its operational activities.

The ISSSTE provides medical services through 1 189 medical units across the country (Table 1.4), which includes one Temporary Centre in the capital for patients from the regions.

On a typical day, the ISSSTE provides for more than 100 000 visits to healthcare professionals and over 3 000 responses to emergencies (Table 1.5).

Table 1.4. **ISSSTE's medical infrastructure, 2014**

Delegations in charge of medical units	35
Medical units by level of service	1 189
First level	1 066
Family medicine units	379
Family medicine clinics	87
Specialised family medicine clinics	15
Family medical attention consultancies	499
Medical attention in work centres	85
Temporary residence for ill persons from the states (regions)	1
Second level	110
Specialty clinics	12
Hospital clinics	71
General hospitals	27
Third level	13
Regional hospitals	14
National Medical Centre "20 de Noviembre"	1

Source: Based on information provided by the Medical Directorate of the ISSSTE.

Table 1.5. **Daily healthcare activities in the ISSSTE, 2013**

Indicators	Total
Number of ISSSTE beneficiaries	12 630 569
Population assigned to family medicine units (including family medicine units, family medicine clinics and specialised clinics)	10 094 425
Daily medical services	**Daily average**
Total medical consultations, including:	100 581
Family medicine consultations	67 032
Specialty consultations	27 455
Dental consultations	6 094
Emergency care	2 986
Hospital discharges	1 044
Patient days	4 872
Surgical interventions	1 012
Child births	104
Clinical tests	155 504
Radio-diagnostic studies	9 327
Other services	**Total**
Pensions paid at the end of the year (all pensioners)	908 596
Number of children attending day-care centres daily (average)	17 790 (own) 8 259 (outsourced)

Source: Based on infromation provided by ISSSTE, Health insurance Sub-Directorate, Finance Directorate and ISSSTE (2013a), *Anuario Estadístico del ISSSTE 2013*, www2.issste.gob.mx:8080/index.php/mdir-inst-finanzas-anuarios-anos/100-instituto/finanzas/2355-dir-finanzas-anuarios-capítulos2013.

The ISSSTE has recently created programmes to respond specifically to the medical needs of patients with chronic diseases. Table 1.6 shows 11 of the most recurrent and costly diseases for 2013.

Table 1.6. **Medical consultations, hospital discharges and estimated medical cost per component, 2013**

Illness	Cases (thousands)		Medical cost (MXN millions)		
	Estimated consultations	Hospital discharges	Cost of consultations	Hospital costs	Total
Cancer	518	36	2 151.30	2 422.40	4 573.70
Cardiovascular diseases	1 205	18	1 375.50	2 357.60	3 733.10
Chronic kidney failure	1 608	16	1 553.10	1 073.60	2 626.80
Arterial hypertension	2 388	3	2 245.80	160.2	2 406.00
Type 2 diabetes	2 104	13	1 978.90	386.9	2 365.80
Fractures	156	16	146.50	908.50	1 055.00
Cholelithiasis and cholecystitis	134	19	125.70	649.20	774.90
Childbirths and caesarean sections	134	27	125.70	563.70	689.40
Osteoarthritis	360	4	338.50	203.40	541.90
Appendicitis	15	8	14.20	421.60	435.80
Hernias	67	11	62.90	310.00	372.90
Total	8 689	171	10 118.10	9 457.10	19 575.40

Notes: 1. Cancer consultations include chemotherapy and radiotherapy sessions. 2. Cardiovascular illness consultations include consultations for haemodynamic sessions. 3. Kidney failure consultations include peritoneal dialysis and haemodialysis. 4. All amounts have been rounded up to the hundreds of thousands.

Source: ISSSTE, Finance Directorate, Sub-Directorate of Health Insurance, 2013.

In 2013, the ISSSTE registered heart diseases as the most important cause of fatalities, with 2 156 deaths, 15.23% of the total number of fatalities of the ISSSTE's beneficiaries, followed by malign tumours (1 923 deaths, 13.58%) and diabetes (1 754 deaths, 12.39%; ISSSTE, 2013a, 2013b).

One the Mexican federal agencies that buys more goods and services

Public procurement accounts for approximately 24% of total government spending in Mexico. This share is lower than the Latin American average of 26% (Figure 1.2) and the OECD average of 30% (Figure 1.3).

Figure 1.2. **Government procurement as a share of total government expenditure in Latin America, 2011**

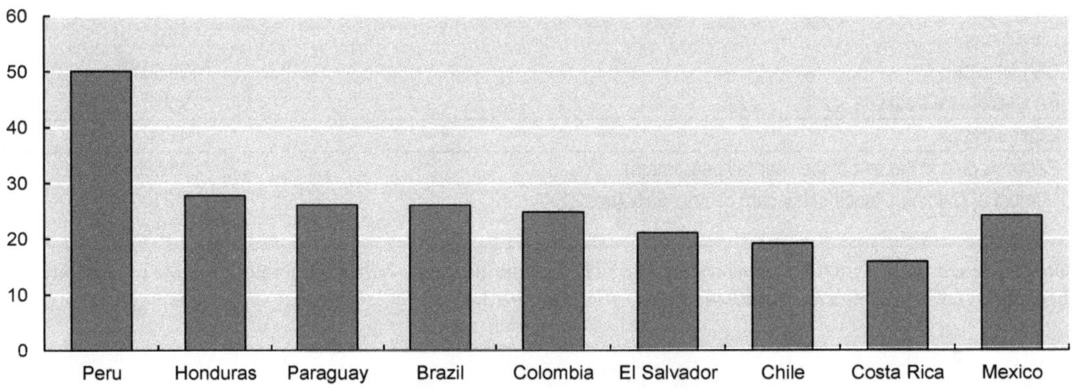

Notes: Data for Brazil, Paraguay and Peru are recorded on a cash basis. Costs of goods and services financed by general government are not included in government procurement because they are not separately identifiable from social benefits, according to IMF Government Finance Statistics, from which data used in the above figure are taken. The share of government procurement related to investment is measured as acquisitions less disposals of fixed assets (the consumption of fixed capital has not been taken into account).

Source: OECD/IDB (2014), *Government at Glance 2014: Latin America and the Caribbean: Towards Innovative Public Financial Management*, OECD Publishing, Paris, http://dx.doi.org/10.1787/9789264209480-en.

Figure 1.3. **General government procurement as a share of GDP and of total government expenditure in the OECD, 2011**

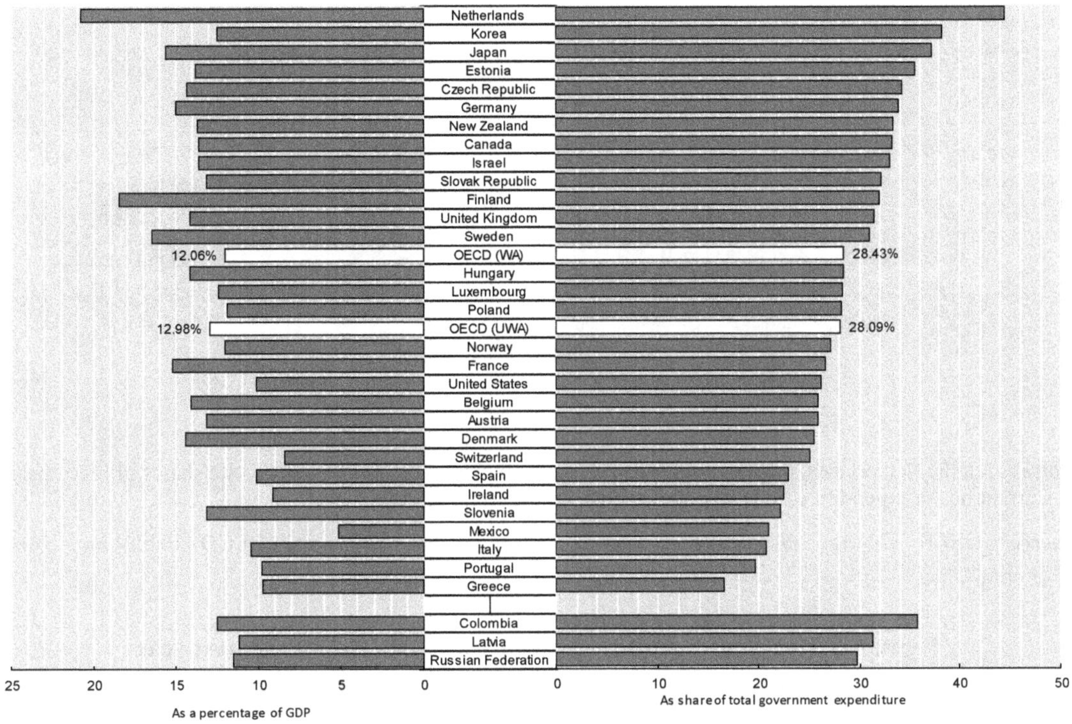

Notes: Data for Australia are based on a combination of Government Finance Statistics and National Accounts data provided by the Australian Bureau of Statistics. Data for Chile are not available. Data for Canada and New Zealand refer to 2010.

Source: OECD National Accounts Statistics, http://dx.doi.org/10.1787/na-data-en.

Providing a wide array of preventive and curative services foists complex medical and budgetary challenges on the ISSSTE as it seeks to improve the quality of healthcare while controlling or lowering medical costs in a context of budgetary discipline. Mexico is one of the lowest per capita spenders on health in the OECD at less than two-third of the OECD average (Figure 1.4). Along with Estonia and Turkey, it devoted only around 6% of GDP to health – two-thirds of the OECD average (Figure 1.5; OECD, 2013a).

In 2014, the ISSSTE was allocated a budget of around MXN 205 billion (Alejo, 2014). It spends 20% of its annual budget on public procurement (OECD, 2013b).

Figure 1.4. **Health expenditure per capita, 2011 or closest year**

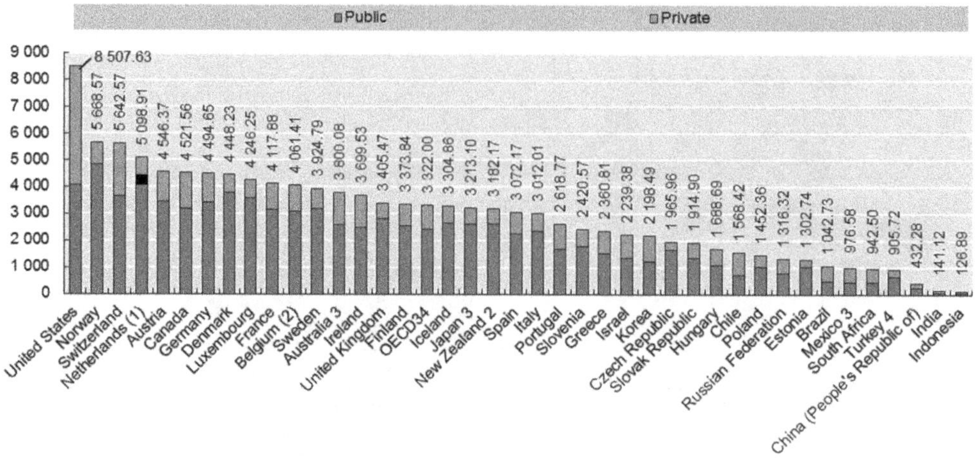

Notes: 1. In the Netherlands, it is not possible to distinguish clearly the public and private shares of investment. 2. Current health expenditure. 3. Data refer to 2010. 4. Data refer to 2008.

Source: OECD (2013c), *Health at a Glance 2013: OECD Indicators*, OECD Publishing, Paris, http://dx.doi.org/10.1787/health_glance-2013-en.

Figure 1.5. **Health expenditure as a share of GDP, 2011 or nearest year**

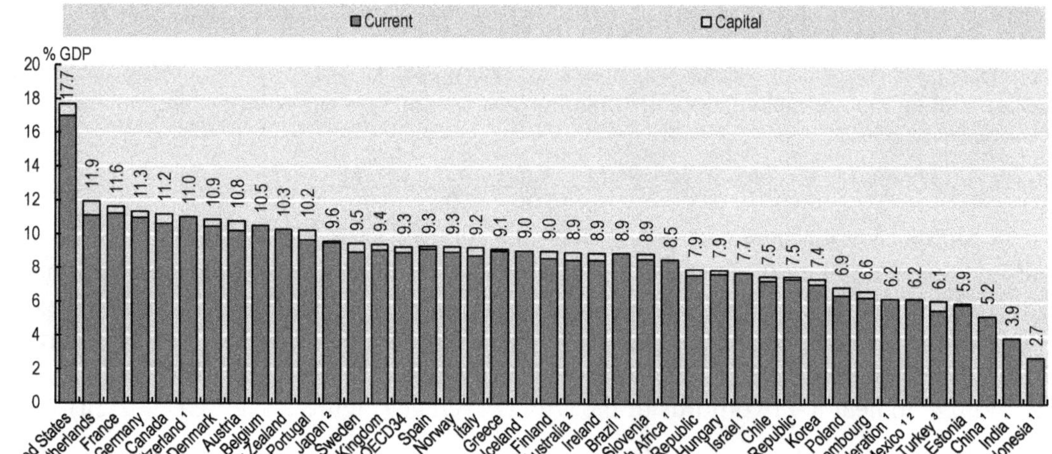

Notes: 1. Total expenditure only. 2. Data refer to 2010. 3. Data refer to 2008.

Source: OECD (2013c), *Health at a Glance 2013: OECD Indicators*, OECD Publishing, Paris, http://dx.doi.org/10.1787/health_glance-2013-en.

Table 1.7 outlines the value of total purchases that the ISSSTE made to cover its needs between 2010 and 2013 and the values of those purchases as percentages of its annual budget (ISSSTE, 2013a; OECD, 2013b).

Table 1.7. **ISSSTE's purchases of goods and services, 2010-13**

	Goods (MXN thousands)	Share of total budget (%)
2010	12 590 740.5	8.5
2011	17 868 645.30	10.67
2012	12 405 598 400.30	7.06
2013	8 173 854 056	4.33
	Services (MXN thousands)	Share of total budget (%)
2010	7 420 219 811.17	7.28
2011	12 951 597 190.82	8.9
2012	8 748 221 453.28	4.98
2013	9 144 729 510	4.84

Source: Based on information provided by the ISSSTE and CompraNet. The share of total budget is calculated against the budget used every year.

To meet its goal of providing high-quality healthcare that meets beneficiaries' needs at the same or lower cost, the ISSSTE is taking measures to improve the efficiency and effectiveness of its medical goods and services procurement. This OECD peer review is part of that effort.

Public procurement reforms are already undertaken with support of the OECD

OECD countries are increasingly asked by their citizens to improve transparency, integrity and economy in the use of public funds, so as to serve the public interest and ensure good governance. In this context, public procurement, which is a major spending area accounting for approximately one-third of total general government expenditures in OECD countries (Figure 1.3), attracts citizens' and governments' attention. It is frequently a key reform target of governments, in particular in countries with tight public spending targets. The OECD, as the leading forum where public procurement policy dialogue takes place and good practices are shared, is called upon more and more often by countries to undertake public procurement peer reviews to propose improvements and help countries focus reforms.

The OECD public procurement peer reviews assess national, sub-national or sectorial procurement systems and their capacities to develop, steer and implement policies. The analysis in the reviews sets the assessed systems in an international comparative context, and makes use of OECD data, lessons learnt in the development of the *OECD Recommendation of the Council on Public Procurement* (OECD, 2015) and good practices developed in the context of the OECD Public Governance Committee's Working Party of Leading Practitioners in Public Procurement and the G20. The focus of the reviews is developed together with the country or public entity that is being reviewed, to maximise impact and relevance and support targeted reforms. Over the last decade, the OECD has reviewed public procurement systems in member countries (for example, Greece, Korea, Mexico and the United States) as well as non-member countries (for example Brazil, Colombia and Morocco). The OECD has provided proposals for improvements and helped build consensus for reforms among national stakeholders.

Against this context, in 2012 the Mexican State's Employees' Social Security and Social Services Institute (*Instituto de Seguridad y Servicios Sociales de los Trabajadores del Estado*, ISSSTE) asked the OECD to review the effectiveness and integrity of its procurement system. At the same time, the ISSSTE requested the OECD's support in fighting bid rigging in public procurement. The OECD's public procurement peer review of the ISSSTE (OECD, 2013a) and the Secretariat's report on fighting bid rigging (OECD, 2013b) assessed the ISSSTE's procurement practices and made numerous recommendations on the organisation, management and development of public procurement; relationships with the private sector; and issues of integrity, transparency and tackling supplier collusion.

Acting on those recommendations, the ISSSTE took action to:

- tighten procurement co-ordination between central and decentralised units, and between central areas themselves, through increased outreach to decentralised units as well as institutional reorganisation, including a new organic statute (*Estatuto Orgánico*), which entered into force in June 2014
- consolidate its purchases with other Mexican healthcare suppliers and secure discounts through the use of e-auctions
- improve its stock and inventory management systems
- introduce barcodes for medicines
- provide training for procurement staff in co-operation with the Ministry of Public Administration (*Secretaría de la Función Pública*, SFP) and the Federal Competition Commission (*Comisión Federal de Competencia*, CFC).

Recent procurement-related successes include:

- Savings, in 2013 as compared to 2012, of approximately MXN 675 million, by consolidating purchases of generic and patented medicines and medical care materials with other Mexican healthcare providers, like the Mexican Institute of Social Security (*Instituto Mexicano del Seguro Social*, IMSS) and Mexican Petroleum (*Petróleos Mexicanos*, PEMEX; see Chapter 2).[5]
- The renegotiation and price reduction of important supply contracts, in particular those for comprehensive medical services (*servicios medicos integrales*; see Chapter 4). The renegotiation involved joint efforts from the General Secretariat, the Administration Directorate, the Medical Directorate, the Finance Directorate, the Legal Directorate and the Delegations Directorate.
- Total savings from the measures taken by the ISSSTE amounted to slightly more than MXN 1.7 billion, which went towards funding improvement works in medical centres. In 2013, more than 600 refurbishments took place in Mexico City and included work on primary-level healthcare units and the renovation of waiting rooms and bathrooms. According to the ISSSTE's Director of Administration speaking at an OECD workshop in Mexico City in 2014, more than 3 000 improvement works were planned nationwide in 2014 (Ahuactzin Ponce, 2014; Table 1.1).

Table 1.8. **ISSSTE's main programmes and works, 2013-15**

Programme/works	Investment (MXN millions)			
	2013	2014	2015	Total
Conservation programme	596.00	684.40	603.56	1 883.96
Maintenance programme	19.60	570.60	223.50	813.70
Infrastructure works	759.17	1 455.36	2 306.29	4 520.82
1. Completed works	163.53	337.79	0	501.32
2. Works in progress	595.64	1 117.57	2 130.49	3 843.70
3. Planned works	0	0	175.80	175.80
Public-private partnership projects	0	0	2 054.20	2 054.20
1. Construction of the new General Hospital Dr. Gonzalo Castañeda, DF	0	0	1 467.50	1 467.50
2. Construction of the new hospital clinic in Mérida, Yucatán	0	0	586.70	586.70
Total	1 355.17	2 139.76	4 964.05	8 458.98

Source: Information provided by the ISSSTE, Administration Directorate.

Improving procurement processes further to ensure good healthcare results

The ISSSTE is taking measures to better allocate resources – in accordance with its 2014 Organic Statute – and to improve healthcare results.

Against this background, the ISSSTE asked the OECD to undertake a second public procurement review to:

- assess the planning and co-ordination of its procurement processes and draw up an action plan for creating a Procurement Co-ordination Unit, thus following up on and further detailing the recommendations made in the first OECD peer review of the Institute (Chapter 2)
- recommend good practices in market intelligence and propose an action plan for the development of a Market Research Unit, also following the recommendations made in the first OECD peer review and taking into account the ISSSTE's achievements since that review (Chapter 3)
- review issues pertaining to the provision of comprehensive medical services by external suppliers (Chapter 4)
- analyse the proportion of contracts that the ISSSTE awards directly so as to allow the ISSSTE to take evidence-based measures to achieve competitive terms for its contracts (Chapter 5).

This review aims to support procurement effectiveness and efficiency at the ISSSTE and forms part of the long-term co-operation between the ISSSTE and the OECD. The review focuses on goods and services procured by the ISSSTE and therefore does not include public works. It examines procurement by central ISSSTE and delegations but does not review procurement carried out by other units and areas in the ISSSTE, such as medical centres and hospitals, the Housing Fund of the Mexican State's Employees' Social Security and Social Services Institute (*Fondo de la Vivienda del Instituto de Seguridad y Servicios Sociales de los Trabajadores del Estado*, FOVISSSTE), the National Pension Fund for State Workers (*Fondo Nacional de Pensiones de los Trabajadores al Servicio del Estado*, PensionISSSTE), the ISSSTE's supermarket and pharmacy branch (*Sistema de Tiendas y Farmacias de los Trabajadores al Servicio del Estado*, SuperISSSTE) and the ISSSTE's tourism branch (*Sistema de Agencias Turísticas del Instituto de Seguridad y Servicios Sociales de los Trabajadores del Estado*, TURISSSTE).

Notes

1. Article 45 of the Federal Public Administration Law (Ley Orgánica de la Administración Pública Federal) and Article 5 of the law establishing the ISSSTE.
2. State government employees are covered by the social security system of the state (federal region) for which they work. Each state determines the organisation of its system and the operation of its services in compliance with the Federal Health Law.
3. Not including employees of the Ministry of Defence (SEDENA), Ministry of the Navy (SEMAR) or Mexican Petroleum (PEMEX).
4. http://normateca.issste.gob.mx/view.asp?sesion=201502041031452225&infocard=201406181050098504&d=Y.
5. Savings refer to all entities that participated in the consolidated procurements.

References

Ahuactzin Ponce, J. (2014), Director of Administration at the ISSSTE, presentation at the OECD workshop on "Improving Public Procurement Practices in ISSSTE", Mexico City, 2-4 September.

Alejo, O. (2014), presentation at the OECD workshop on "Improving Public Procurement Practices in ISSSTE", Mexico City, 2-4 September.

ISSSTE (2014), "Acuerdo 57.1344.2014 de la Junta Directiva, relative a la aprobación del Estatuto Orgánico del Instituto de Seguridad y Servicios Sociales de los Trabajadores del Estado" (Organic Statute of the ISSSTE), *Diario Oficial de la Federación*, 18 June, available at: http://normateca.issste.gob.mx/view.asp?sesion=201502041031452225&infocard=201406181050098504&d=Y.

ISSSTE (2013a), *Anuario Estadístico del ISSSTE 2013* (*ISSSTE Statistics 2013*), www2.issste.gob.mx:8080/index.php/mdir-inst-finanzas-anuarios-anos/100-instituto/finanzas/2355-dir-finanzas-anuarios-capitulos2013 (accessed 17 February 2015).

ISSSTE (2013b), "Para la diabetes, Mide, el ISSSTE te apoya: Programa de Manejo Integral de Diabetes por Etapas (Mide) – Lineamientos 2014" ("For diabetes, Measure, the ISSSTE is supporting you: Programme for the Comprehensive Management of Diabetes in Stages (Mide) – Guidelines 2014"), ISSSTE, available at: http://sgm.issste.gob.mx/medica/diabetes/doctos/Lineamientos%202014.pdf (accessed 27 August 2014).

OECD (2015), *Recommendation of the Council on Public Procurement*, OECD, Paris, available at: http://acts.oecd.org/Instruments/ShowInstrumentView.aspx?InstrumentID=320&InstrumentPID=348&Lang=en&Book=False.

OECD (2013a), *Public Procurement Review of the State's Employees' Social Security and Social Services Institute in Mexico: Smart Procurement for Health Public Services*, OECD Public Governance Reviews, OECD Publishing, Paris, http://dx.doi.org/10.1787/9789264197305-en.

OECD (2013b), "Fighting bid rigging in public procurement in Mexico: A Secretariat analytical report on legislation, regulations and practices relating to procurement undertaken by ISSSTE", OECD, Paris, available at: www.oecd.org/daf/competition/mexicoissste2013.htm.

OECD (2013c), *Health at a Glance 2013: OECD Indicators*, OECD Publishing, Paris, http://dx.doi.org/10.1787/health_glance-2013-en.

OECD/IDB (2014), *Government at Glance 2014: Latin America and the Caribbean: Towards Innovative Public Financial Management*, OECD Publishing, Paris, http://dx.doi.org/10.1787/9789264209480-en.

Panapoulou, G., U. Giedion and E. González-Pier (2014), "The Universal List of Essential Health Services and the Catastrophic Health Expenditure Fund", in Giedion, U., R. Bitrán and I. Tristao (eds.) (2014), *Health Benefit Schemes in Latin America: A Regional Comparison*, Chapter 4, Inter-American Development Bank, http://publications.iadb.org/handle/11319/6484.

Further reading

OECD (2013), "Measuring health coverage", Directorate for Employment, Labour and Social Affairs, OECD, internal document.

Paris, V. and A. Belloni (2013), "Value in pharmaceutical pricing", *OECD Health Working Papers*, No. 63, OECD Publishing, Paris, http://dx.doi.org/10.1787/5k43jc9v6knx-en.

Chapter 2.

Strategic co-ordination of the ISSSTE's procurement

This chapter describes how procurement is organised and conducted at the State's Employees' Social Security and Social Services Institute (ISSSTE) in Mexico. The analysis focuses on centralised purchases carried out by the units of the ISSSTE's Administration Directorate. The chapter includes an overview of the regulatory environment; assesses planning, budgeting and co-ordination processes and challenges at the ISSSTE; and provides recommendations for improvements. An action plan for the establishment of a Procurement Co-ordination Unit at the ISSSTE is annexed at the end of this chapter.

The OECD's 2013 *Public Procurement Review of the State's Employees' Social Security and Social Services Institute* (ISSSTE) in Mexico found that, at the central level, the Institute has procurement co-ordination processes, gathers relevant information and takes strategic decisions. Nevertheless, its extensive geographical decentralisation, combined with the complexity and in some cases rigidity of Mexico's regulatory environment, prevented it from obtaining optimal results. The OECD also found that there was room for improving the regularity and effectiveness of the ISSSTE's procurement-related co-ordination.

This chapter includes an overview of the regulatory and operational environment, persistent weaknesses and recommendations for overcoming current challenges. The analysis focuses on centralised procurement, i.e. procurement carried out at central level by the Administration Directorate's units, covering centralised needs for goods, services and works across the ISSSTE. It accounts for 90% of the ISSSTE's procurements in terms of value and which requires strong, sustained two-way co-ordination between decentralised and central procurement units as well as within central units. Chapter 5, which looks at direct awards, will touch upon challenges related to non-centralised purchases carried out by these central and decentralised units, particularly regional delegations. Recommendations in this chapter are, however, applicable to the co-ordination of all procurement across the ISSSTE, which includes both centralised and non-centralised purchases.

During the fact-finding for this review, the OECD found that the ISSSTE experiences planning difficulties, as reflected in the significant number and cost of direct awards. Although shortcomings stem partly from delays in budgetary processes and approvals, better co-ordination of what needs to be bought (and when) can help secure high-quality supplies in good time and at a lower cost. Identifying and disseminating the ISSSTE's best planning practices – evidenced, for example, in instances of low numbers of direct awards – and results like higher patient satisfaction rates could prompt action to make successes into standard practice and overcome common challenges.

Procurement through decentralised units in a complex regulatory environment

Speaking at an OECD workshop, the ISSSTE's former Sub-Director of Material Supplies and Services explained that 92 units in the ISSSTE undertake procurement (Alejo, 2014). They comprise 4 central level sub-directorates of the Administration Directorate and 88 decentralised entities (Box 2.1).

All units need to comply with numerous primary and secondary rules ranging from the Mexican Constitution (*Constitución Política de los Estados Unidos Mexicanos*, CPEUM) to a series of laws, regulations, codes, decrees, institutional agreements and manuals.

Article 134 of the Constitution establishes that the procurement of goods and services by the federal public administration, states, municipalities and the Federal District is carried out through public tenders in order to achieve the best terms in price, quantity, financing arrangements and convenience. The principles set out in the Constitution are then detailed in a set of normative instruments, some of which apply to the federal public administration as a whole, while others are specific to the ISSSTE (OECD, 2013).

The Law on Acquisitions, Leasing and Services of the Public Sector (Ley de Adquisiciones, Arrendamientos y Servicios del Sector Público, LAASSP) regulates the procedure that all public institutions should follow when acquiring goods, commissioning services and making leasing arrangements. The LAASSP is complemented by regulations issued by the President of Mexico. In addition, every public sector institution is required to issue its own Policies, Ground Rules and Guidelines for Public Procurement, Leasing and Services (*Políticas, Bases y Lineamientos en Materia de Adquisiciones, Arrendamientos y Servicios*, POBALINES)[1] to ensure that institutional procurement processes are aligned with the LAASSP and other applicable laws.

Box 2.1. The ISSSTE's 92 centralised and decentralised procurement units

At the central level, four sub-directorates of the Administration Directorate carry out procurement procedures. They are the Material Resources and Services, Public Works, Conservation and Maintenance, and Medical Supplies Sub-Directorates. Two of the nine sub-directorates shown in Figure 2.1 – the Programing and Budgeting Sub-Directorate and the Management of Institutional Risks and Guarantees Sub-Directorate – do not play a part in the procurement processes as such, although the Programing and Budgeting Sub-Directorate is involved in the budgetary aspects.

Realising the strategic importance of co-ordinating and streamlining procurement activities, the ISSSTE has brought together sub-directorates with procurement responsibilities under the umbrella of the Administration Directorate. The move included the transfers in 2014 to the Administration Directorate of the Infrastructure Sub-Directorate from the Medical Directorate and of the Sub-Directorate of Programming and Budgeting from the Finance Directorate in accordance with the new organic statute (*Estatuto Orgánico*), which entered into force in June 2014. All healthcare activities are under the Medical Directorate.

Of the 88 decentralised entities that are active in procurement, there are 50 local units – the 35 delegations, the 14 regional hospitals and the National Medical Centre "20 de Noviembre". There are also procurement units within the Housing Fund of the State's Employees' Social Security and Social Services Institute (*Fondo de la Vivienda del Instituto de Seguridad y Servicios Sociales de los Trabajadores del Estado*, FOVISSSTE), SuperISSSTE (the ISSSTE's supermarket and pharmacy branch), the National Pension Fund for State Workers (*Fondo Nacional de Pensiones de los Trabajadores al Servicio del Estado*, PENSIONISSSTE) and TURISSSTE (the ISSSTE's travel agency branch).

Source: Information provided by the ISSSTE.

Figure 2.1. **Structure of the Administration Directorate, 2014**

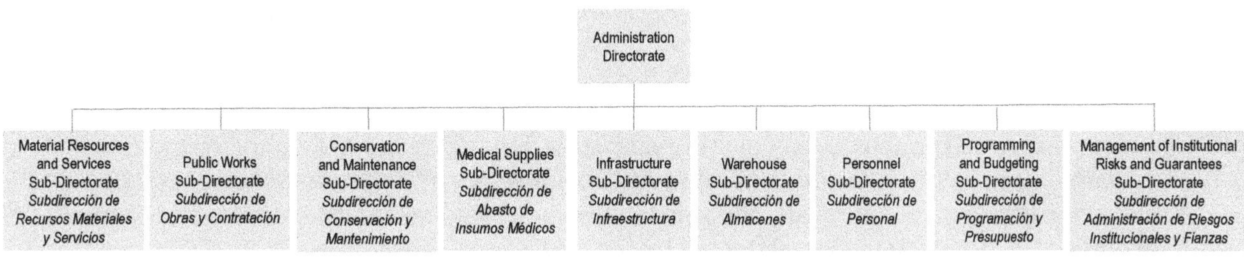

Source: ISSSTE (2014), "Acuerdo 57.1344.2014 de la Junta Directiva, relative a la aprobación del Estatuto Orgánico del Instituto de Seguridad y Servicios Sociales de los Trabajadores del Estado" (Organic Statute of the ISSSTE), *Diario Oficial de la Federación*, 18 June, available at: http://normateca.issste.gob.mx/view.asp?sesion=201502041031452225&infocard=201406181050098504&d=Y.

To further assist public procurement officials and describe the various procurement procedures, the Mexican government has released a general procurement manual – the

Administrative Manual for General Application concerning Acquisitions, Leasing and Services of the Public Sector (*Manual Administrativo de Application General en Materia de Adquisiciones, Arrendamientos y Servicios del Sector Público*, MAAGMAASSP), commonly known as the "General Procurement Manual".[2] It details procurement procedures step-by-step, supplies general guidelines and templates, and supersedes any internal procurement document that may duplicate its content.

Goods, services and public works are procured according to a classification system

The ISSSTE buys on the market a wide range of goods, services and works, both health-related and not.

All procured items and commissioned services are classified according to rules established by the Ministry of Public Administration (*Secretaría de la Función Pública*, SFP) through a standardised codification system used across the federal public administration – the Unique Classifier of Public Procurement (*Clasificador Único de Contrataciones Públicas*, CUCoP). The CUCoP builds on the codes created by the Ministry of Finance and Public Credit – item spending codes (*clasificadores por objeto de gasto*, COGs) to structure public expenditure in Mexico. The ISSSTE's goods and services COG codes are shown in Table 2.1.

Essentially, goods procured by the ISSSTE can be divided into the following categories:

- clinical: – medicines, medical materials and devices (2500), radiology equipment, laboratory materials and surgical instruments (2400 and 2500), and healthcare uniforms and clothes (2700)
- non-clinical: – office supplies and computer consumables (2100), food (2200) and tools (2300 and 2900)
- medical infrastructure: – medical and laboratory equipment (5300) and machinery (5600)
- administration: – office furniture and equipment (5100).

The ISSSTE plans the procurement of its clinical goods in accordance with its *Institutional Catalogue for Healthcare Supplies* (*Catálogo Institucional de Insumos de Salud*).[3] The catalogue is based on the *Basic Chart and Catalogue for Healthcare Supplies* (*Cuadro Básico y Catálogo de Insumos del Sector Salud*) developed, drafted, updated and disseminated by the General Health Council (*Consejo General de Salubridad*, CSG), a multidisciplinary organisation for which the Mexican Constitution contains a provision. The *Basic Chart and Catalogue for Healthcare Supplies* groups, characterises and codifies all the medicines, medical materials, instruments and diagnostic auxiliary equipment procured by the Mexican healthcare system. It also shows supplies for which safety and clinical efficiency and effectiveness have been tested and approved.

Table 2.1. **The ISSSTE's goods and services procurement classified by item spending codes**

Code	Subcode	Classification	Description
2000		Materials and supplies	Acquisitions related to the materials and supplies required for the provision of a public good or service
	2100	Office supplies	
	2200	Food and utensils	
	2300	Raw materials	
	2400	Materials and construction and maintenance supplies	
	2500	Chemical, pharmaceutical and laboratory products	
	2600	Fuels, lubricants and additives	
	2700	Clothing	
	2800	Supplies for public security	
	2900	Tools and spare parts	
3000		General services	Acquisitions for any type of service required by the public sector
	3100	Basic (e.g. water)	
	3200	Leasing	
	3300	Professional/technical	
	3400	Financial	
	3500	Maintenance	
	3600	Media	
	3700	Transportation and accommodation	
	3800	Official	
	3900	Other	
5000		Movable and immovable property	Acquisitions of movable (i.e. vehicles) and immovable property (i.e. buildings)
	5100	Office furniture and equipment	
	5200	Educational furniture	
	5300	Medical and laboratory equipment	
	5400	Vehicles	
	5500	Equipment for national defence	
	5600	Machinery and other equipment	
	5700	Biologically active substances	
	5800	Immovable property	
	5900	Intangible assets	
6000		Public investment	Acquisitions related to public investment projects (feasibility studies)
	6100	Public works (for public use)	
	6200	Public works (for own use)	
	6300	Investment projects	

Source: Summary of COG codes drawn up with information from the Spending Object Codes published in the Official Gazette on 28 December 2010, www.hacienda.gob.mx/EGRESOS/PEF/lyn_presupuestarias/clasificador_objeto_gasto/cog_dof281210.pdf (accessed 7 October 2014).

The ISSSTE's administration is putting in place strategies to ensure security of supply and generate savings in the procurement of medicines and medical supplies. In 2014, the Administration Directorate reviewed the *Catalogue of Medicines* (*Catálogo de Medicamentos*) to make sure that supplies met demands and those new medicines for medical units and laboratories are considered. About 80% of the total costs for medicines was reviewed, through the 152 medicine codes with better procurement potential and the evaluation of medicines with an equivalent therapeutic effect. The ISSSTE expects that the Programme of Therapeutic Equivalence will allow better planning of the consolidated and individual purchases that it carries out. In December 2014, the Medical Directorate and the Administration Directorate approved five therapeutically equivalent medicines and anticipate that this will generate savings of about MXN 250 million. In addition, the ISSSTE is reviewing the real consumption of medicines in its medical units and running a census of patients of high-specialty medicines, so that it improves the management of its inventories and rationalises the procurement of medicines.

The ISSSTE also commissions services like comprehensive medical services (see Chapter 4), the maintenance of buildings and of medical equipment, the leasing of vehicles and ambulances, cleaning, security, and insurance for premises and personnel (Table 2.1).

Some centralised procurement is consolidated with other healthcare providers

In order to increase competition, achieve savings through economies of scale and ensure uniform quality standards (OECD, 2013), the ISSSTE centralises the purchase of goods and services required throughout the organisation in large contracts awarded at the central level. Buying needs are identified by decentralised units (medical units in hospitals, for example, or delegations) and then aggregated at the central level. Central procurement units issue the tenders and award the contracts.

The POBALINES (see the next section) stipulates that the goods and services subject to centralised purchasing should be among the following:

- non-clinical goods:
  - uniforms and clothing
  - medical clothing
  - computer consumables
  - ambulances
  - disposable and non-disposable surgical clothing
  - clothing for medical residents
  - vehicles
  - medical gases for hospital use
- healthcare supplies:
  - medical goods
  - medical infrastructure
- services:
  - comprehensive medical services
  - medical equipment maintenance
  - photocopies services
  - food coupons
  - cleaning
  - security
  - collecting and washing surgical and medical clothing
  - insurance of premises and personnel.

According to 2012 OECD data (OECD, 2013) confirmed during the OECD mission in 2014, 90% of the ISSSTE's procurement budget is allocated to its central units, which spend it on centralised purchases of goods, services and works. Ten percent of the procurement budget goes to decentralised units.

The ISSSTE also consolidates purchases with other healthcare providers. For the purposes of this review, consolidated purchases mean joint purchases by more than one healthcare provider. In 2009, the Mexican Institute of Social Security (*Instituto Mexicano del Seguro Social*, IMSS), the country's largest public healthcare and social security agency, began buying medicines jointly with the Ministry of National Defence (*Secretaría de la Defensa Nacional*, SEDENA). The ISSSTE followed suit more recently. In 2012, it took part in nine consolidated public tenders (seven for medical products and two for medical equipment), earning estimated savings of about MXN 675 million on the prices it paid for medical products (OECD, 2013).

In 2013, the IMSS, ISSSTE, PEMEX, the Ministry of National Defence and the Ministry of the Navy (*Secretaría de Marina*, SEMAR), the Women's Hospital (*Hospital de la Mujer*), the Psychiatry Hospital (*Hospital de Psiquiatría*), the National Homeopathy Hospital, the Ministry of Health's Juarez Hospital (*Hospital Juarez del Centro de la Secretaría de Salud*), and the states of Baja California, Campeche, Colima, Tlaxcala and Veracruz, conducted the biggest procurement of medicines in the history of Mexico's public sector. It comprised 10 public tenders (5 contracts awarded through reverse auctions) for more than 1 800 generic and patented medicines and medical material worth almost MXN 43 billion.

The participation of suppliers was encouraged through meetings with the National Chamber of the Pharmaceutical Industry (Cámara Nacional de la Industria Farmacéutica, CANIFARMA), which brings together 95% of Mexico's medical manufacturers and suppliers, the National Chamber of Transformation Industries (Cámara Nacional de la Industria de Transformación, CANACINTRA) and the National Association of Health Supply Distributors (Asociación Nacional de Distribuidores de Insumos para la Salud, ANDIS). This inter-institutional consolidation effort resulted in overall savings of MXN 3.7 billion, of which MXN 3.1 billion came in the procurement of generic medicines and clinical materials, and MXN 600 million in patented medicines (ISSSTE et al., 2014).

The ISSSTE's total estimated savings through consolidated purchases in the years 2013, 2014 and 2015 are presented in Table 2.2.

Table 2.2. **Savings generated from consolidated healthcare purchasing, 2013-15**

	2013	2014	2015	Total
Number of codes	656	822	843	2 321
Total amount (MXN millions)	4 365.20	7 804.50	8 875.10	21 044.80
Savings (MXN millions)	674.40	1 040.00	959.00	2 673.40
Savings (%)	15.45	13.33	10.81	12.70

Source: ISSSTE, Administration Directorate.

Consolidated purchases of medical supplies, particularly medicines, is common practice across the OECD. In 2011, France, for example, launched its PHARE programme whereby hospitals group together to make purchases and savings through economies of scale (Box 2.2).

Box 2.2. **The PHARE programme in France**

In October 2011, the French Directorate General of Healthcare launched a nationwide programme to develop and structure procurement by public hospitals. The scheme, called "Hospital Performance for Responsible Procurement" (Performance hospitalière pour des achats responsables, PHARE), is designed to generate "smart savings", i.e. improved procurement practices that give hospitals fiscal space while maintaining the quality of healthcare.

The programme, which seeks EUR 910 million of savings over three years, specifically aims to:

- negotiate in order to obtain reasonable, justifiable product prices
- standardise purchased products so as to avoid the additional costs of over-specific products
- use lifecycle costing for products, a method that includes the cost of installation and maintenance requirements
- engage with the market to improve knowledge of the products and innovations available on the market so as to encourage competition between suppliers.

The PHARE scheme also aims to improve hospital performance through:

- Joint procurement. A recent joint procurement effort brought together 251 institutions with a large information technology group and generated savings of between 25% and 80% on purchased products.
- The appointment of a single procurement manager for each big hospital and for groupings of smaller ones.
- A genuine dialogue between these procurement managers and users in all categories of spending. The idea is that if procurers have better market knowledge, it will help users to routinely think of their needs in terms of offers that propose the best value for money.

PHARE brings together all stakeholders and decision makers. There is a pilot phase involving the procurement directors of large groups and hospital directors and doctors. There is also a national committee of hospital purchases, on which all of France's regional health authorities sit and which meets every month in order to share and promote good practices.

Source: Ministère des Affaires sociales, de la Santé et des Droits des femmes (French Ministry of Social Affairs, Health and Women Rights), "Les achats hospitaliers: Le programme Phare", www.sante.gouv.fr/les-achats-hospitaliers-le-programme-phare,9524.html (accessed 24 October 2014).

One specific form of consolidated procurement is the framework agreement. The SFP has put such agreements in place for particular goods or services procured by at least five different public institutions. The SFP aggregates the institutions' needs and negotiates with interested suppliers[4] to set quality standards for a certain volume of agreed sales. Entities which are parties to a framework agreement then purchase goods and services directly from the suppliers specified in the agreement either at a fixed price or, if it is not fixed, at a price calculated with a method stipulated in the framework agreement.

The SFP posts on its website its intention of putting in place a framework agreement so that potential suppliers may apprise themselves of the agreement's general characteristics and decide whether to bid.[5] In September 2013, 11 framework agreements were in place for the provision of: patented medicines; call centres; airline tickets (reservations, issuance and delivery); grocery vouchers; workwear, safety footwear and personal protection equipment; tree pruning; vaccines; organising events; preventive and corrective maintenance of vehicles.[6]

In the case of patented medicines, the Co-ordinating Commission for Negotiating the Price of Medicines and Other Health Supplies (Comisión Coordinadora para la Negociación de Precios de Medicamentos y otros Insumos para la Salud) negotiates a single price per medicine applicable nationwide for one year. That price is then used in related framework agreements and consolidated purchases for patented medicines. The ISSSTE participated in the framework agreement for vaccines in 2013.

Central and decentralised procurement co-ordination takes place on a yearly basis

The ISSSTE's Annual Procurement Programme (Programa Anual de Adquisiciones, Arrendamientos y Servicios, PAAAS) is the core document for planning yearly procurement activities (Table 2.3).

Table 2.3. **Guidance for the elaboration of the PAAAS by the Ministry of Public Administration ("General Procurement Manual")**

PAAAS procedure	Templates[1]
Identify needs in accordance with the item spending codes and the Unique Classifier of Public Procurement (CUCoP) classification	
Verify existing stock in order to avoid excess inventory caused by inadequate planning	
Prioritise needs according to how critical they are, strategic supply, recurrence, the likelihood of consolidation and budgetary forecast	
Estimate prices based on available information in Compranet or the institution's historical data	
Deliver the documents and information generated by the steps above to the aggregator unit	
Consolidate the institutional draft PAAAS	PAAAS format (FO-PPP-01)
Adjust the institutional draft PAAAS according to the authorised annual budget ceiling	
Approve the PAAAS	
Disseminate the PAAAS within the ISSSTE	
Update the PAAAS as needed through the fiscal year	

Note: 1. Format available at: www.funcionpublica.gob.mx/index.php/ua/sracp/uncp/General_Procurement Manual.html (accessed 14 September 2014).

The development of the PAAAS links to the elaboration and approval of the ISSSTE's annual budget. The budget preparation process begins in July and August when the Programming and Budgeting Sub-Directorate sends a table already filled in with historical spend data to decentralised and central units for them to confirm and amend. Depending on the feedback it receives, the sub-directorate prepares and sends an itemised budget request to the Ministry of Finance in September for approval and incorporation in the Federal Expenditures Budget (*Presupuesto de Egresos de la Federación*) which the ministry then submits to Congress. Once the budget has been adopted – in November – the Programming and Budgeting Sub-Directorate distributes the procurement budget to the ISSSTE's decentralised and central units.

The Congress-approved budget for the ISSSTE may be less than requested, which in practice means that not all needs will be covered. Prioritisation is required to meet primary needs and reduce the coverage of certain secondary needs. During the OECD fact-finding, certain delegations, however, reported that even primary medical supply needs may not be fully met, which jeopardises the delivery of effective healthcare.

The ISSSTE begins drawing up its PAAAS before the budget has been adopted and allocated. Every year between October and November, the Material Resources and Services Sub-Directorate (Subdirección de Recursos Materiales y Servicios)[7] sends the PAAAS template[8] – a detailed spreadsheet in practice – to the central and decentralised procurement units so that they can incorporate it into their annual procurement requirements. The units return the completed template during the first week of January.

The sub-directorate compiles the procurement units' feedback and draws up the final draft of the PAAAS which it submits to the Goods, Leasing and Services Committee (Comité de Adquisiciones, Arrendamientos y Servicios, CAAS) for review. The CAAS is an oversight body that reviews procurement programmes and budgets, supervises the drafting and implementation of the ISSSTE's PAAAS, and makes observations and recommendations. The Material Resources and Services Sub-Directorate considers and incorporates the CAAS's recommendations. The ISSSTE's Administration Directorate approves the finalised procurement budget, which may be updated during the fiscal year.

When the PAAAS has been approved, purchase requests may be submitted to procurement units.

Teams from decentralised areas reported to the OECD that they are not always aware how and why their requirements are adjusted in the PAAAS. They were particularly unsure why their requests had been modified or not taken into consideration. As the OECD recommended in 2013, the ISSSTE could take measures to ensure that decentralised units are systematically consulted in decision making, that positive and negative impacts of central decisions are assessed, and that corrective measures are taken if needed.

Central offices should consider and identify ways of communicating institutional choices that explain the rationale behind prioritising some requirements and modifying or not responding to others. Face-to-face meetings could be useful, as would internal blogs, given the geographical distances between some decentralised areas. Such blogs would, in addition, enable buyers to communicate with each other and understand how to cover their needs without overrunning budget limits. In that respect, an interesting example is the online platform introduced in the United States in the second quarter of 2014 to allow purchasers to engage with one another and exchange experiences and solutions (Box 2.3).

Box 2.3. "Welcome to the Open Dialogue" in the United States

The United States federal acquisition system is governed by numerous rules, both administrative and statutory, that are designed to help agencies maximise results from their contracts, make sure that contractors are qualified to do business with the federal government, and ensure consistency with key economic and social policies. Efforts to streamline, modernise and improve required procedures are designed to enable procurement agencies to carry out their tasks in a more efficient and effective manner.

To identify potential improvements, the Chief Acquisition Officers Council (CAOC) – in co-ordination with the Federal Acquisition Regulatory Council, the Chief Information Officers Council and the Office of Federal Procurement Policy (OFPP) in the Office of Management and Budget (OMB) – put up an online platform in the second quarter of 2014 to allow members of the acquisition community to engage with one another about burdens and barriers associated with the federal acquisition process and potential ways to address them.

Box 2.3. "Welcome to the Open Dialogue" in the United States (*Cont.*)

The United States federal acquisition system is governed by numerous rules, both administrative and statutory, that are designed to help agencies maximise results from their contracts, make sure that contractors are qualified to do business with the federal government, and ensure consistency with key economic and social policies. Efforts to streamline, modernise and improve required procedures are designed to enable procurement agencies to carry out their tasks in a more efficient and effective manner.

To identify potential improvements, the Chief Acquisition Officers Council (CAOC) – in co-ordination with the Federal Acquisition Regulatory Council, the Chief Information Officers Council and the Office of Federal Procurement Policy (OFPP) in the Office of Management and Budget (OMB) – put up an online platform in the second quarter of 2014 to allow members of the acquisition community to engage with one another about burdens and barriers associated with the federal acquisition process and potential ways to address them.

This dialogue was part of an effort to improve the federal acquisition system by identifying steps that could be taken to make it easier for agencies to do business with the best companies and enter into contracts that allow these companies to provide their best solutions for the taxpayer.

The dialogue sought to identify specific rules and requirements, tools, procedures and practices that impact the efficiency and effectiveness of federal procurement and ways to improve them by encouraging responses in the following areas:

- Reporting and compliance requirements – e.g. opportunities for re-engineering or automating collection processes and systems, eliminating duplicative reporting, reducing the frequency of reporting and changing outdated compliance thresholds.
- Procurement practices – e.g. opportunities where acquisition strategies can be modernised (to support more efficient and effective acquisition of IT, in particular), where the best commercial practices can be utilised, as well as efforts to promote greater consideration of innovative solutions and contracting practices.
- Participation by small and minority businesses, new entrants and non-traditional government contractors – e.g. opportunities for improving existing technical or strategic assistance programmes, making buying platforms for finding business opportunities and bidding more user friendly, and lowering the cost of doing business.

Using the online platform, interested parties submitted ideas, responded to questions posed by moderators and commented on other ideas – including those that they thought most promising and impactful.

Source: Chief Acquisition Officers Council (2014), "Open Dialogue on Improving How to Do Business with the Federal Government", http://cxo.dialogue.cao.gov.

Improving centralised procurement through stronger co-ordination

According to the ISSSTE's 2014 organic statute, the Administration Directorate is in charge of public procurement, including determining the requirements for medicines, medical goods and services. It develops cost-benefit and budget impact studies for procurements based on information on medical needs provided by the Medical Directorate, and plans, carries out and controls procurement, distribution and sufficiency of medicines and medical goods. It also carries out procurements for the maintenance of medical and electromechanical equipment.

The ISSSTE has honed a procedure for co-ordinating practices between the Administration Directorate, the Medical Directorate, the 35 delegations and the

15 hospitals (1 national and 14 regional) to annually group needs for clinical goods at all healthcare levels and plan procurement (ISSSTE, 2013). The practice, which the ISSSTE defines as a process for determining the national programmed demand for health supplies, is called CONCERTA (Box 2.4).

Box 2.4. How CONCERTA co-ordinated procurement in 2013

CONCERTA's goal was to co-ordinate and forecast health supplies so that they met the ISSSTE's needs.

To that end, it factored in:

- number of patients
- number of hospital beds
- mortality, demographic and epidemiologic profiles, and the seasonal nature of some illnesses
- number of prescriptions per speciality
- available budget per itemisation code
- cost-effectiveness of treatments.

Under the CONCERTA system, the ISSSTE co-ordinated and determined needs in two phases:

- Phase 1: Between 23 April and 31 May 2012, 48 working meetings were held. They brought together 31 state delegations, 4 Mexico City delegations, 14 regional hospitals, the "20 de Noviembre" National Medical Centre and the Medical Directorate.
- Phase 2: Between 5 September and 15 October 2012, another 48 working meetings were held in order to ratify the estimated quantities determined in Phase 1. In this phase, the *Institutional Catalogue for Healthcare Supplies* was updated and 27 codes were deleted as the goods they denoted were no longer sold. Economic constraints also led to a significant reduction in the value for items requested by the medical units.

CONCERTA procurement results in 2013 were as follows:

- The acquisition by the Administration Directorate of medicines classified under 623 codes (approximately MXN 2.9 billion) and medical materials under 215 codes (MXN 362 000) through inter-institutional consolidation with the IMSS and other institutions of the Mexican health sector.
- The local acquisition of 239 codes is categorised in Table 2.4 below.

Table 2.4. **Local requirements of medicines and healing materials, 2013**

Type	Purchase request	Code	MXN
Medicines	42	88	1 150 013 172
Patent medicines	43	77	3 302 529 887
Healing material	44	66	62 138 170
Radiologic material	45	4	3 886 656
STERRAD consumables	46	2	52 119 224
TAC consumables	47	2	43 335 310
Total	267	239	4 613 022 422

Source: Based on information provided by the Medical Directorate of the ISSSTE.

The procurement co-ordination process: CONCERTA

CONCERTA entails decentralised procurement units submitting their requirements for medical goods to the Administration Directorate. The units often determine their requirements at a prior stage in co-ordination with healthcare staff. They also rely on medical statistics extracted from the Supply Control Board (*Tablero de Control*)[9] forecasted demand, volumes of prescriptions, technical and medical rationale, and patient census reports that contain the most significant pathologies and epidemiological profiles of the population.

According to the ISSSTE's 2014 organic statute, the Administration Directorate validates requests according to factors such as historical data and the seasonal nature of illnesses. Each decentralised procurement unit also meets with the Medical Directorate in Mexico City to discuss any adjustments to their requirements. Periodic consultations take place, too, for the purpose of identifying changes in consumption behaviour and if they entail any changes to the agreed-upon requirements.

After requirements for clinical goods have been agreed through CONCERTA and the PAAAS has been approved, the Medical Supplies Sub-Directorate can start procuring. It reports that it procured centrally 427 coded medicines in 2013. As Box 2.4 shows, the CONCERTA process also yields information about the kind of therapeutic goods that can be procured through inter-institutional consolidation with other Mexican healthcare institutions.

CONCERTA outcomes are reviewed monthly and adjusted two to three times per year by the Administration Directorate in co-ordination with decentralised procurement units. In that way, it is possible to determine requirements in each healthcare service and product category and so plan quantities that cover the ISSSTE's medical goods throughout the year.

CONCERTA does not apply to medical infrastructure (which includes medical and laboratory equipment). In this case, decentralised procurement units submit their requirements to the Infrastructure Sub-Directorate. This sub-directorate determines the final requirements without further consultation with the decentralised units. Once the PAAAS has been approved, the Infrastructure Sub-Directorate carries out the market research and the Medical Supplies Sub-Directorate conducts the procurement procedure, handling the contract in collaboration with the Infrastructure Sub-Directorate.

Other non-clinical goods to which CONCERTA does not apply are clothing, computer consumables and vehicles. Decentralised procurement units send their requirements for such goods to the Material Resources and Services Sub-Directorate, the central unit that aggregates and procures non-therapeutic goods. Residual services – like leasing vehicles and ambulances, cleaning, security, laundry and insurance – also come under the responsibility of the Material Resources and Services Sub-Directorate, which purchases equipment requested by the ISSSTE's user areas.

Nor, finally, does the CONCERTA process apply to the purchase of medical gases, fumigation services, or the preventive and corrective maintenance of medical equipment and central administration immovables. They all come within the ambit of the Conservation and Maintenance Sub-Directorate, which makes acquisitions solely on the basis of requirements submitted by users.

The CONCERTA process is an institutional co-ordination effort that has streamlined planning for the acquisition of certain products and has yielded savings. The ISSSTE can therefore consider extending it to further categories – e.g. non-clinical goods, medical infrastructure and residual services – particularly if the ISSSTE can thereby secure savings that make co-ordination efforts worthwhile.

Data insufficiency can hinder procurement planning

During the fact-finding it was reported that CONCERTA is hindered by decentralised units' shortages of accurate data on which to base their requests. The ISSSTE runs different databases which may contain wrong or insufficient information, thus impeding the proper planning of procurement. Currently the ISSSTE is taking action to build a database with all procurement contracts by central units and plans to extend it, in the medium term, across all its units, including decentralised ones.

Mexico's Supreme Audit Institution (*Auditoría Superior de la Federación*, ASF) has also identified the ISSSTE's data weaknesses and, in particular, the lack of a single comprehensive information technology system giving an accurate central inventory of the medicines in stock. According to the ASF, the Supply Control Board used in the CONCERTA process is not always up to date or accurate. Furthermore, decentralised units that manage local warehouses may not have the information technology systems for calculating stock. Consequently, when they submit their requirements as part of the process, they send in the same request year after year without any real revision or update.

During the OECD's fact-finding and in the course of the workshop conducted by the OECD on 2-4 September 2014 in Mexico City, ISSSTE stakeholders highlighted the importance of full, accurate data, as did the OECD peer experts who have contributed to this review. The ISSSTE should develop a single comprehensive database that provides accurate procurement data. A comprehensive database would allow capturing consistent all-inclusive information on who buys what, when and on which terms (which is difficult to achieve when using multiple tools and databases) and, on this basis, support the efficiency of procurement processes and provide strategic insights into procurement trends and steps forward. The Australian e-procurement system, AusTender (Box 2.5), relies on a unified system of data collection, which makes it easy to generate reports on past spending and provides input for forecasting future purchases.

The ISSSTE could consider creating a task force of procurement officers from central and decentralised units with the job of developing such a comprehensive database and collecting information, led by the Procurement Co-ordination Unit (see Annex 2.A1). The task force could work under the co-ordination of the Administration Directorate which heads the ISSSTE central sub-directorates involved in procurement (see Annex of this chapter). In this respect, the ISSSTE could draw on the example of Denmark, where the regional authorities use a central pharmaceutical procurement service, called Amgros, to procure medicines for all public hospitals. Amgros keeps records of past sales in a single database and has a task force of officials in charge of gathering information. Speaking at an OECD workshop, the Head of the Procurement and Tendering Department at Amgros, Dorthe Bartels, explained that database's historical data are accurate and widely relied upon by hospitals (Bartels, 2014).

Additional information technology tools which can help assess quantities and levels of healthcare across the country and inform procurement decisions accordingly are databases on patients, patients' records and health profiles. As it happens, the United States Department of Defense is seeking to overhaul its health records database (Box 2.6) in recognition of the importance of comprehensive, accessible information.

Good planning needs sufficient lead time. The ISSSTE acknowledges that and started the process for centralising goods and services in early 2014. Accordingly, it sent out PAAAS spreadsheets to decentralised units earlier than usual so that they could enter their needs for 2015, which will be met through centralised contracts. Such an efficient practice can be formalised and used in the future with earlier fixed start and end times communicated to all units involved in the procurement process and in CONCERTA.

Box 2.5. Government spending statistics in Australia

The Australian e-procurement system, AusTender, provides centralised publication of Australian government business opportunities, annual procurement plans, multi-use lists and contracts awarded. Agencies are required by the Commonwealth Procurement Rules to publish on AusTender standing-offer arrangements and contracts with a value of AUD 10 000 or more. Since 2005, bodies governed by the Commonwealth Authorities and Companies Act are also required to publish details of certain contracts and standing offers.

On the AusTender website, it is possible to access reports on contract notices, standard offer notices and procurement plans.[1] As an example, the records on contract notices that are available online include information on the procuring entity, the procurement method, the contract value and period, a description of the contract and supplier details. The records are searchable by agency, date range, value range, category, confidentiality, supplier name, supplier's Australian Business Number (ABN) and report type. It is also possible to download summary records that include information on the total count and value.

Aggregated information extracted from AusTender is available on the website of the Department of Finance.[2] It includes statistics on:

- total procurement contracts reported, including a breakdown of total value and number of contracts per financial year
- procurement contracts by value threshold, including a breakdown of value, percentage of total value, number of contacts and percentage of total number of contracts
- participation of small and medium-sized enterprises (SMEs) in procurement
- overseas procurement contracts (contracts identified by agencies as primarily or entirely based outside Australia)
- individual business participation in procurement
- the ratio of goods to services contracts procured
- the top 20 categories for goods and services procurement contracts, including a breakdown of value, percentage of total value and percentage of SME participation
- the top 10 procuring Financial Management and Accountability Act 1997 agencies, including a breakdown of value, percentage of total value and rank in previous years compared to the most recent ranking.

In addition, the Department of Finance – together with the consulting and internal audit firm Protiviti – has conducted an analysis of AusTender data for 2010-11 and 2011-12 on: 1) the split (by value) between the procurement of goods and services by the Australian government; 2) the total value of Australian government procurement for each United Nations Standard Products and Services Code (UNSPSC) in relation to total expenditure in Australia; 3) the total value of goods procured that are likely to be "Australian made" and services procured that are delivered from within Australia; and 4) the total value of goods or services procured by the Australian government that are likely to be imported in order to determine the impact the Australian government procurement market has on the Australian economy. The report is available on the Department of Finance's' website.[3]

Notes: 1. Available at: www.tenders.gov.au/?event=public.reports.list. 2. www.finance.gov.au/publications/statistics-on-commonwealth-purchasing-contracts/index.html. 3. www.finance.gov.au/procurement/analysis-of-australian-overseas-purchasing-contracts.html.

Source: Australian government, Department of Finance, Canberra, www.finance.gov.au.

Box 2.6. Pentagon to bid out the modernisation of its healthcare records

The United States' Department of Defense plans to award an up to ten-year healthcare management system modernisation contract, valued at an estimated USD 11 billion. The aim of the project is to revamp the department's health IT system – covering more than 6 million war veterans and 9 million active-duty service members – so that patient records may be easily transferable between military treatment locations, the Department of Veterans Affairs and outside health systems.

The contract was to be awarded in June 2015. The system would include initial operating capabilities by 2017 and full functionality by 2023. Once the interoperability of the electronic health records system has been improved, an analytics system will help gather data on patient treatment, so that the Department of Defense can plan ahead and improve the way in which treatment is delivered.

Source: Konkel, F. (2014), "Coming soon: Pentagon's multi-billion dollar health records contract", NexGov website, 25 April, available at: www.nextgov.com/defense/2014/04/coming-soon-pentagons-multi-billion-dollar-health-records-contract/83230.

Centralised procurement requires effective communication

Regular and prompt co-ordination is also required to manage supplier performance. The ISSSTE's centralised purchases are centrally managed and supervised, while deliveries are local. If there is no direct line of communication between delegations and suppliers, problems can surface. For example, when equipment is purchased at the central level with maintenance included in the contract as part of the warranty, delegations' and hospitals' user groups cannot access suppliers directly to request an intervention when there is a defect. Delegations have reported delays – sometimes long – in getting problems attended to.

Similar issues have arisen with uniforms, also centrally purchased. To purchase uniforms, each delegation creates a mixed ad hoc sub-commission, made up of members of the delegation and the ISSSTE's employees union.[10] The sub-commissions are responsible for determining the delegations' needs with respect to types of uniforms, their number and sizes. Those needs are then conveyed to the Material Resources and Services Sub-Directorate for centralisation.

During the fact-finding mission in March 2014, delegations reported that they did not always receive the number, size or kind of uniforms they had requested. However, because delegations are not the official contract managers, they could not reject the unsuitable uniforms or contact the supplier for new ones – they had to ask the central sub-directorate to do so, on their behalf. Delegations cited several instances of the centralisation process affecting levels of inventory – because not all the products and services requested had been received – or the quality of goods and services, i.e. when purchases failed to live up to the required quality.

In procurement arrangements where only central entities communicate with suppliers, co-ordination between central and local areas must be reinforced. Delegations should report problems immediately, via a web-based tool, to the central areas which should be under the obligation to contact suppliers immediately. In this respect, service-level agreements with suppliers specifying the agreed quality of service – including response time in case of defects and contractual penalties for non-performance, such as withholding payment – can be helpful. For example, in the framework agreement for cleaning services awarded by the French central purchasing body UGAP, public buyers must notify the UGAP as soon as they notice a defect in supplier performance and the UGAP is under an obligation to forward this to the supplier. The agreement also provides for specific quality performance levels, response time for defects and contractual penalties for non-performance (Box 2.7).

Box 2.7. Quality assurance plan: An example of cleaning services in France

The Union des groupements d'achats publics (UGAP, Union of Public Purchasing Groups) is a French central purchasing body which buys products and services and sells them to the government and government agencies, regional authorities and hospitals. Its purchasing categories include vehicles, IT, furniture and equipment, medical supplies, maintenance and technical services and facility management services.

In 2014, the UGAP concluded a framework agreement for cleaning services. The agreement has a duration of 4 years and is divided into 26 regional lots. For each lot, seven to ten suppliers are selected. When buyers wish to place a purchase order, they conduct a mini-tender in which suppliers submit bids to win the order, in accordance with the mini-tender award criteria defined in the framework agreement.

This agreement includes a quality assurance plan to evaluate the quality of the services rendered by the supplier and assess whether it is within the specific thresholds established by the UGAP. The quality assurance plan formed part of the tender documents, so bidders were aware that they would be bound to it if they were awarded the contract.

In order to evaluate the quality of services, the quality assurance plan foresees three different kinds of inspections of the services, to take place at agreed intervals (once a month or per trimester):

1. self-inspections carried out by the supplier
2. planned inspections carried out by the supplier and the public buyer
3. unplanned inspections carried out by the supplier and the public buyer.

For the self-inspection, the supplier has to monitor the quality of its own services, carrying out verification operations and taking immediate corrective measures where needed. At the end of the inspection, the supplier has to evaluate the level of services according to a predefined index and is responsible for the accuracy of the information.

For the planned inspections, the buyer has to inform the supplier at least 48 hours before the inspection. At the end of the inspection, the supplier has to evaluate the level of services according to the predefined index. If the rating is below a certain threshold, the supplier has 48 hours to solve the problem and is liable for a penalty. The amount of the penalty depends on the extent of the defect in performance, i.e. the amount increases as the level of quality decreases.

The unplanned inspections are carried out after an obvious worsening of the quality of the services which does not correspond to the agreed quality levels. The supplier and buyer carry out the inspection 24 hours following a demand. At the end of the inspection, the supplier has to evaluate the level of services according to the predefined index. If the rating is below a certain threshold, the supplier has 48 hours to solve the problem and is liable for a penalty.

In addition, any buyer who notices defective performance of services has to inform the UGAP through a webpage. The UGAP monitors the webpage and forwards the information to the supplier. The supplier has 48 hours to solve the problem, otherwise he can be excluded from the next phase of the framework agreement.

Source: Information provided by the UGAP.

Purchase needs arise within user areas, particularly among healthcare practitioners. The co-ordination process should include, first, checking which medical areas buy what and then discussing with them what they really need and whether any products can be substituted by similar ones. It may even be possible to replace several products by fewer or just one, so standardising purchases.

A parallel process would be to check non-standard purchases and find why they have been bought – i.e. discuss whether they reflect real needs, ignorance of alternatives, or negligence, or whether they point to corruption. Products and services whose use cannot be justified may thus be ruled out and non-standard ones may be acquired only when medically required. It is important to invest time and effort in overcoming the resistance of healthcare practitioners and patients when products or services are changed – through communication and by enforcing decisions which specify which products should be bought and which should not.[11]

Co-ordination can be strengthened through an explicit procurement strategic document

The ISSSTE's Board of Directors decides its strategic priorities. With regard to procurement, the Director General, the Secretary General and the Administration Directorate set the strategic directions, which the central and decentralised units then implement.

The strategic importance of procurement is thus acknowledged at the central level. What appears to be missing at the ISSSTE is a single, explicit, non-legal procurement strategy that defines priorities and targets and the main ways to achieve them. In 2013, the OECD recommended the development and dissemination of a comprehensive procurement strategy covering all phases of the procurement process, from needs assessment to contract close-out (OECD, 2013a, 2013b). This strategy would need to establish the overarching long-term vision for procurement at the ISSSTE and identify priorities, timelines and targets. Of all of the actions to be considered by the ISSSTE, this one is a priority, as such a strategy, designed specifically to the needs of the ISSSTE, would allow the ISSSTE to progress over time.

An example of the way to go could be the procurement document drafted by the National Health Service (NHS) of the United Kingdom. It sets out action intended to deliver productivity and efficiency savings in its procurement system over a three-year period (Box 2.8).

Evaluating performance and beneficiaries' satisfaction can help focus co-ordination where it is most needed

Evaluations of the performance of the ISSSTE's procurement activities are currently based on indicators for controlling stock levels and quality issues, particularly in relation to medicines and medical services. Those indicators are included in the Internal System for Institutional Performance Evaluation (*Sistema Interno de Evaluación de Desempeño Institucional*, SIEDI). The purpose of SIEDI is to process information that allows programmes to be monitored, help measure the performance of the ISSSTE's services and support the decision-making process.

Box 2.8. United Kingdom's Procurement Development Programme for the National Health Service

The United Kingdom operates a National Health Service (NHS) that is provided free at the point of need to all citizens. The NHS was founded in 1948 and is primarily funded from public taxation. Each UK country (England, Scotland, Wales and Northern Ireland) manages its own healthcare arrangements. In the 2014-15 financial year, the NHS in England had a budget of GBP 110 billion that served a population of 53.5 million people.

The NHS's purchasing power is greater than any other UK organisation, but it has for a long time been unable to harness that power. There is a perception that anyone in any NHS organisation can buy anything at any time at any price. There is too much variation across the NHS – too many examples of different solutions to the same problem and different prices being paid for the same product. The NHS has acknowledged that such an approach is not good business sense and that it needs to change so as to improve the quality of care while maximising value for money.

Therefore, to radically improve its procurement capability the NHS issued in 2013 its "Better procurement, better value, better care: A procurement development programme for the NHS", a public strategy to build a modern, effective and efficient procurement capability – among the best in the world – that truly delivers taxpayer value, supports innovation, stimulates growth, and most importantly, delivers the highest quality patient care. The strategy focuses on four key initiatives:

1. a series of interventions to deliver immediate efficiency and productivity gains
2. actions to improve data, information and transparency
3. an initiative to fundamentally rethink clinical engagement in the procurement of high-value medical devices and the subsequent relationship with the device industry, initially focusing on orthopaedic implants by improving outcomes at reduced cost through clinical procurement review partnerships
4. the creation of a new national "enabling function" to support leadership and build better capability throughout the system, but primarily focused on trusts capability and how they work with procurement partners.

Implementing this strategy the NHS has identified a potential for GBP 500 million savings by embracing better procurement.

Source: National Health Service (2013a), "Better procurement, better value, better care: A procurement development programme for the NHS", National Health Service, Department of Health, Crown copyright, London, available at: www.gov.uk/government/uploads/system/uploads/attachment_data/file/226835/procurement_development_programme_for_NHS.pdf (accessed 17 October 2014).

Most SIEDI indicators focus on medical services. Some relate to procurement and include the number of contracts, the percentage of contracts registered, the proportion of audited projects that comply with applicable regulations, the share of qualified suppliers and the average number of days it takes to sanction suppliers. These indicators are either quantitative or focus on compliance with regulations. Yet, there is limited evaluation of the efficiency and outcomes of procurement as such. Many procurement units reported to the OECD that their way of measuring success indicators of good performance is few or no remarks from the Internal Control Office or formal complaints (*inconformidades*) from suppliers on their procurement procedures.

The OECD *Recommendation of the Council on Public Procurement* encourages countries to "develop indicators to measure performance, effectiveness and savings of the public procurement system for benchmarking and to support strategic policy making on public procurement" (OECD, 2015). For example, the United Kingdom's NHS has developed a Procurement Dashboard with performance metrics and indicators that help understand and benchmark the procurement performances of NHS healthcare provider organisations (Box 2.9). The ISSSTE could develop a similar system, tailored and adapted to its needs, to measure the performance of its procurement activity, with supporting monitoring arrangements. It is part of the ISSSTE's current plans to assess the feasibility of proposing uniform performance indicators which allow measuring efficiency and savings and enabling comparisons.

SIEDI also measures users' perception of the services provided by the ISSSTE against the metric, "*satisfacción de usuarios/derechohabientes con recetas surtidas completamente*" (user/beneficiary satisfaction with the delivery of prescribed medicines). It indicates the availability of prescription medicines in the ISSSTE's medical units and, in general, whether the Institute beneficiaries' needs for medicines are met.

Box 2.9. **The National Health Service's Procurement Dashboard**

The NHS Procurement Dashboard is a tool developed to improve transparency and help understand the procurement performance of NHS healthcare provider organisations. It provides a balanced scorecard of core metrics focused on three areas of procurement performance:

- enabling business continuity
- procurement efficiency
- mitigating risk.

It supports internal governance and the continual improvement of procurement performance, external reporting, transparency, and the identification and exchange of good practices.

The NHS Procurement Dashboard model follows a balanced scorecard approach. To enable comparison, the model provides a set of core metrics against which all organisations are encouraged to measure their practice and performance. Those core metrics include:

- supply failure impacting on patient care
- expenditure captured electronically
- savings
- cost to procure
- proportion of spend via national or regional contracts
- progress against national procurement standards
- proportion of staff with procurement qualifications.

The core metric data are produced on an annual basis to guide NHS organisations towards achieving certain standards as a minimum. The data support the regular communication of performance data to key stakeholders and can be aligned with financial reporting processes.

Source: National Health Service (2013b), "NHS Procurement Dashboard: Specification: Version 1", National Health Service, Department of Health, Crown copyright, London, October, available at: www.gov.uk/government/uploads/system/uploads/attachment_data/file/255875/nhs_procurement_dashboard_specification.pdf.

Satisfaction is gauged through standardised quantitative surveys in the pharmacies of medical units. The surveys are carried out randomly one day a month on samples of 30 patients who have visited an ISSSTE medical unit pharmacy to receive prescribed medicines. The results of each survey are placed in a standard Excel spreadsheet and aggregated – first at decentralised and then at central level by the Medical Directorate. The satisfaction level is calculated from the aggregated results. This satisfaction metric makes it possible to monitor levels of supply and assess the percentage of beneficiaries satisfied with the availability of medicines.[12]

The results obtained using the satisfaction metric between May 2013 and May 2014 are shown in Figure 2.2.

Figure 2.2. **Evaluations using the metric "user/beneficiary satisfaction with the availability of prescribed medicines", 2013-14**

A. Aggregate results, May-December 2013 and January-May 2014
Percentage of fully supplied prescribed medicines and satisfied beneficiaries

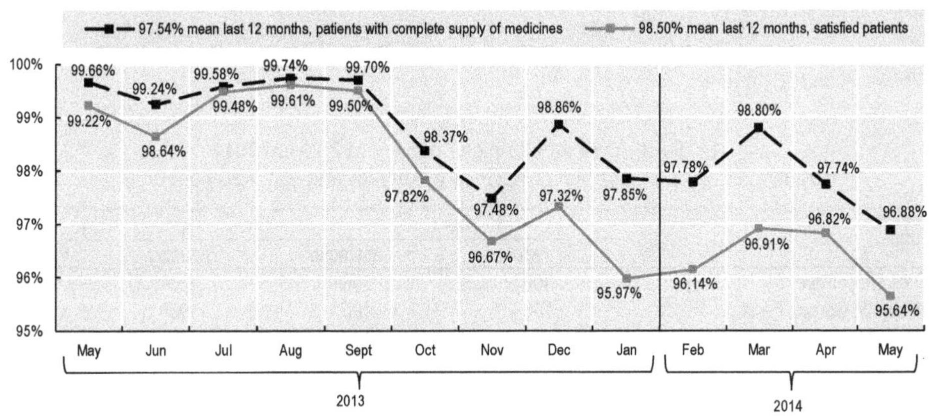

Source: Survey carried out in 199 medical units of the ISSSTE's medical units staff (May): 120 first level and 79 second level.

B. Delegations' results, survey of 23 May 2014
Percentages of fully supplied prescribed medicines

Greater than 97%		
	April	May
Tlaxcala	100	100
Puebla	100	100
Morelos	100	100
Campeche	100	100
Zona Sur	99.68	100
Tabasco	98.89	100
Veracruz	98.81	100
Michoacán	96.35	100
Baja California	100	99.83
San Luis Potosí	100	99.72
Zona Oriente	99.18	99.52
Aguascalientes	100	99.05
Quintana Roo	100	98.89
Durango	98.94	98.37
Hidalgo	95.74	98.16
Guerrero	100	97.95

Less than 97%					
	April	May		April	May
Colima	98.46	96.86	Yucatán	96.48	93.15
México	91.53	96.78	Zona Norte	96.12	92.51
Guanajuato	99.89	96.77	Sinaloa	96.53	91.29
Nayarit	93.55	95.40	Querétaro	94.95	90.96
Nuevo León	99.50	95.36	Zona Poniente	91.02	90.78
Sonora	97.60	94.70	Chihuahua	88.69	90.19
Jalisco	95.13	93.82	Oaxaca	91.53	88.11
Tamaulipas	96.11	93.77	Zacatecas	98.80	86.83
Chiapas	95.23	93.74	Coahuila	94.99	81.60
Baja California Sur	92.88	93.49			

Note: Supply: 95.64%.

Source: Survey carried out in 199 of the ISSSTE's medical units in 35 delegations, (60.30%) first-level units and (39.70%) second-level units.

C. Delegations results, survey of 23 May 2014
Percentages of satisfied beneficiaries

Greater than 97%					
	April	May		April	May
Zona Oriente	100	100	Michoacán	96.35	100
Veracruz	100	100	San Luis Potosí	100	99.72
Tlaxcala	100	100	Nayarit	95.70	99.70
Quintana Roo	100	100	Sonora	98.89	99.15
Morelos	100	100	Guerrero	100	99.08
Durango	100	100	Aguascalientes	100	99.05
Campeche	100	100	Hidalgo	96.20	98.92
Baja California	100	100	Puebla	99.61	98.73
Zona Sur	99.68	100	Colima	98.46	98.56
Tabasco	98.89	100	Nuevo León	99.83	98.29
Yucatán	97.77	100	Guanajuato	99.89	97.88

Less than 97%		
	April	May
México	97.89	96.78
Oaxaca	98.40	96.22
Querétaro	97.98	96.02
Tamaulipas	97.08	95.85
Zona Norte	97.50	95.84
Sinaloa	96.28	95.51
Chihuahua	93.11	93.14
Chiapas	100	92.62
Jalisco	95.73	92.19
Zona Poniente	92.91	91.44
Zacatecas	97.60	88.02
Baja California Sur	93.78	85.70
Coahuila	97.66	81.60

Note: Satisfaction: 96.88%.

Source: Survey carried out in 199 of the ISSSTE's medical units in 35 delegations, (60.30%) first-level units and (39.70%) second-level units.

D. Third-level units' results, survey of 23 May 2014
Percentages of fully supplied prescribed medicines and satisfied beneficiaries

Medical unit	April		May	
	% supply	% satisfaction	% supply	% satisfaction
CMN "20 de Noviembre"	100	100	100	100
HR "Dr. Valentín Gómez Farías"	100	100	100	100
HR "Dr. Manuel Cárdenas de la Vega"	100	100	100	100
HR Puebla	100	100	100	100
HR "Lic. Adolfo López Mateos"	99	100	100	100
HR "1° de Octubre"	98	100	100	100
HR León	97	100	100	100
HR "Pdte. Juárez"	92	96	100	100
HR Mérida	100	100	99	99
HR "Bicentenario de la Independencia"	100	100	98	98
HR "Gral. Ignacio Zaragoza"	100	100	98	98
HR "Centenario de la Revolución"	98	98	99	98
HR Monterrey	91	100	86	100

Note: Third-level mean: 99.22% supply; 99.64% satisfaction.

Source: Information provided by the ISSSTE based on the survey applied in its third-level medical units.

During the fact-finding mission two-thirds of the delegations and some central areas reported that they were not aware of the existence of the SIEDI user/beneficiary satisfaction survey. It was also mentioned that the results shown in Figure 2.2 may be inaccurate because units and delegations may interfere with the randomness of the sample – by, for example, choosing to carry out the survey with beneficiaries who had received all the medicines that they had requested and would therefore express satisfaction.

One indication of the survey's lack of representativeness is that while the satisfaction levels were very high, some patients complained that prescribed medicines are not available – which contradicts the results of the survey. The ISSSTE has acknowledged this shortcoming and is considering using an external organisation to run surveys to prevent any bias.

As in other instances of data collected by the ISSSTE, complaints are registered by the medical units that receive them but are not consolidated across the ISSSTE to paint a full picture. While survey findings may yield input on the availability of medicines and beneficiary satisfaction, they do not measure general levels of satisfaction with the standard of the healthcare services provided by the ISSSTE. Some delegations, like Zona Poniente, have taken concrete steps to measure the satisfaction of medical staff and beneficiaries on specific issues through surveys (Box 2.10). Managers in the Zona Poniente Delegation also talk directly with beneficiaries to find out how satisfied they are and hear any remarks about the medical attention they receive.

Box 2.10. Example of a survey conducted by the Zona Poniente Delegation

The Zona Poniente Delegation surveys staff in medical units in order to assess the quality and condition of medical equipment and maintenance requirements. Through its surveys, the delegation collects information on:

- medical staff's awareness of the delegation's equipment maintenance programme
- the quality of maintenance services provided by suppliers
- common causes of equipment failure
- the service provided by the Sub-Directorate of Conservation and Maintenance
- the obsolescence of medical equipment.

The Zona Poniente Delegation also conducts monthly surveys of patients hospitalised for surgery, emergency treatment and specialised medical care. Medical staff give the surveys to patients, who answer if they wish. In any given month, the delegation tries to run the following surveys:

- 44 surveys of hospitalised surgery patients (at least four surveys a day – two in the morning and two in the evening)
- 48 surveys of patients undergoing specialised treatment (at least eight surveys a day: four in the morning and four in the evening)
- 72 surveys of emergency patients (at least 10 surveys a day).

The surveys seek information on:

- how patients are treated when they ask for a medical appointment
- the attention provided by the medical staff
- the quality and condition of medical equipment and facilities
- timelines of appointments with a doctor and for laboratory tests and X-rays
- attitudes of doctors (i.e. whether they clearly explain to patients their condition and the details of any medical procedures they are to undergo)
- whether medical services are provided without discrimination
- whether any illegal fees were requested
- the availability of medicines.

The overriding purpose of collecting the information spelled out above is to enable the Zona Poniente Delegation to improve the quality of its services, better plan its supplies and, accordingly, to adapt its requests to the ISSSTE's central units for centralised purchases.

Source: Information provided by the Zona Poniente Delegation.

In the first public procurement review of the ISSSTE, the OECD recommended that the ISSSTE strengthen existing communication channels and implement new ones, where appropriate, between procurement units to facilitate knowledge development and transfer as well as the adoption of good practices. For example, the Zona Poniente good practice could be communicated, institutionalised and, as appropriate, made mandatory across the ISSSTE to measure levels of performance across the organisation, which should include satisfaction with products and services provided by suppliers.

Currently, doctors in the ISSSTE are consulted as to their satisfaction with suppliers – e.g. in order to support demands for remedial action by suppliers, apply penalties in case of sub-standard performance, and to store such information as input for future contract decisions. Staff from central sub-directorates are also sometimes asked to fill in questionnaires about how satisfied they are with suppliers. However, the points of view of the ISSSTE's beneficiaries are taken into consideration only when they lodge complaints.

Surveys or information technology tools for gathering data on supplier performance can help inform future contracting decisions. The United States, for example, requires its contracting officers to determine that a supplier is a "responsible source" before going ahead and awarding a contract. It has introduced electronic systems to help officers in this respect (Box 2.11). To be deemed a responsible source, a prospective contractor must, for example, show a satisfactory performance record and a history of integrity and sound business ethics. Contracting officers are allowed considerable discretion deciding whether a supplier is, or is not, a "responsible source".

Using clinical guidelines and protocols procurement goals

The ISSSTE has therapy guidelines and treatment protocols for Mexico's most common illnesses and most expensive treatments. The Institute could consider regularly updating them to help focus procurement on achieving its set goals. An instructive example in that regard is the Danish experience in building common clinical guidelines through a specialised council for the national procurement of expensive hospital medicines (Box 2.12).

Setting up a Procurement Co-ordination Unit

OECD experience shows that the benefits of better co-ordination are many. The following are just an indication:[13]

- efficient procurement planning that meets demands
- standardised procurement processes that save time and human and material resources
- standardised healthcare-related product and service quality
- economies of scale
- uniform standards of healthcare.

Box 2.11. Vendor performance information in the United States

In working to build the right supplier relationships, the United States focuses on doing business with contractors who place a premium on integrity, performance and quality. To that end, agencies have been directed to improve the quantity, quality and utilisation of vendor performance information. Vendors' past performance information – which includes identification and description of relevant contracts, ratings across six dimensions (quality, schedule, cost, utilisation of small businesses, etc.) and a narrative for each rating – is contained within the Past Performance Information Retrieval System (PPIRS).

Additional information regarding certain business integrity issues – e.g. contracts terminated for default or for cause; information on criminal, civil or administrative procedures related to a federal contract; and prior findings that a contractor is not responsible – is captured in the Federal Awardee Performance and Integrity Information System (FAPIIS). Agencies are taking steps to improve the value of both systems by providing information that is both more complete and more useful.

Agencies are required to report past performance information, which will then be available to other contracting officers within the PPIRS, on all contracts and orders of a value above USD 150 000 (with some exceptions). However, an initial analysis has shown that compliance varies widely among agencies. As a result, in March 2013, the United States established a tiered model of annual performance targets to bring all agencies up to 100% compliance by 2015. To improve reporting compliance in FAPIIS, the United States uses information contained in the Federal Procurement Data System, Next Generation (FPDS-NG), to identify contracts that should have entries in FAPIIS (e.g. those where the contract was terminated for default or for cause on the part of the vendor). By cross-checking with existing data sources, agencies are provided with a cost-effective mechanism to improve compliance.

Finally, recognising that both systems are only as useful as the quality of the data that is entered into them, agencies were directed to ensure that their acquisition professionals were familiar with past performance regulations and procedures and trained to use the reporting tools appropriately.

These are all important steps as the United States continues to explore ways to ensure that the most relevant and recent past performance information is accessible, useful, readily available and transparent to acquisition officials before award decisions are taken.

Source: United States Office of Federal Procurement Policy (OFPP) (2013), "Improving the collection and use of information about contractor performance and integrity", Executive Office of the President, Office of Management and Budget, Washington DC, 6 March, available at: www.whitehouse.gov/sites/default/files/omb/procurement/memo/improving-the-collection-and-use-of-information-about-contractor-performance-and-integrity.pdf.

However, as this chapter has argued, co-ordination requires internal action such as:

- a procurement strategy and guidelines
- human resources devoted only to procurement
- capacity-building and purpose-designed training modules
- IT solutions and tools (e.g. databases, online forums with questions and answers, online guidance).

Box 2.12. **Danish Council for the Use of Expensive Hospital Medicines (RADS)**

The background to RADS

In October 2009, the Board of the Danish Regions (the interest organisation for Denmark's five regions) decided to set up the Council for the Use of Expensive Hospital medicines (RADS).

RADS brings together representatives from the five regions, the Danish Health and Medicines Agency, the Danish Society of Clinical Pharmacology, and Amgros, the central pharmaceutical procurement service for public hospitals. The chairman of RADS is appointed by the regions.

RADS ensures that all patients nationwide have equal access to treatment that requires expensive hospital medicines. That goal is accomplished through compulsory national clinical treatment guidelines for the use of each medicine. The guidelines are prepared, on an on-going basis, by RADS-appointed committees of leading national experts in different clinical fields. The treatment guidelines are revised when necessary.

The reason for developing common clinical treatment guidelines is, on the one hand, to ensure equal healthcare for all and, on the other hand, to standardise purchases, thus generating opportunities for regions to consolidate their procurement and lower prices through economies of scale.

RADS addresses:

- medicines that are a major hospital expense
- medicines characterised by a fast-growing rise in costs
- new medication with a high-cost potential
- areas in which common regional consensus is needed.

Openness and involvement in RADS

In order to ensure as much openness and transparency as possible, each guideline is published on the Danish regions' website immediately after it has been approved by RADS. When a new clinical committee is established, all relevant patient associations have the opportunity to send it any information that they believe should be taken into consideration. The industry may also take the opportunity to present new medicines to the clinical committees.

Guideline implementation

Amgros conducts each tender on the basis of RADS guidelines. After it has awarded a contract, RADS receives feedback on the results of the tender, medicine-related recommendations and compliance goals for medicines. This information is then sent to the regions, which are responsible for implementing the guidelines.

Monitoring and follow-up

Amgros has introduced a method of monitoring the quantity of medicines the regions use. This management information is based on consumption data and affords an indication of medicines consumption in each region as well as any deviation from the stipulated compliance goals.

This system monitors the regions' drug consumption down to hospital medical level. Such monitoring can be an aid when discussing actual use from a clinical point of view in individual hospitals.

Source: Presentations made at the OECD workshop on "Improving Public Procurement Practices in ISSSTE", Mexico City, 2-4 September 2014, by Dorthe Bartels, Head of Procurement and Tendering Department at Amgros, the pharmaceutical procurement service for regional authorities in Denmark.

Following up from OECD recommendations in 2013 (OECD, 2013a, 2013b), the ISSSTE has considered creating a Procurement Co-ordination Unit responsible for leading action and improving its procurement planning and management. A detailed action plan for creating such a unit can be found in Annex 2.A1. It is based on priorities drawn from ISSSTE and OECD good practices and has been discussed with OECD peer experts.

The action plan may be implemented partly or by stages. Implementation is predicated upon the availability of sufficient human and financial resources and internal (ISSSTE) and external (e.g. Ministry of Finance) approval.

Proposals for action

- Develop an explicit, performance-focused procurement strategy. This strategy would contain a long-term vision for procurement, priorities, sequencing of actions and timelines, monitoring mechanisms and adjustment strategies (immediate action – priority).
- Examine ISSSTE good practices in procurement planning and outcomes (immediate action).
- Institutionalise good practices beyond specific persons or units in the ISSSTE. Good practices include surveys to measure levels of satisfaction of medical staff and beneficiaries with products and services provided by suppliers (immediate action).
- Continue the good practice of starting co-ordination for the elaboration of the PAAAS earlier in the year (immediate action).
- Put in place a comprehensive, consistent database able to capture inclusive information on who buys what, when and on which terms, building on current initiatives to ensure a reliable patients' census for high-specialty medicines and put together a data set for procurement contracts in central units. The database should allow reports to be generated on past spending and information to be extracted for forecasting future purchases (medium-term action).
- Reinforce communication between central and decentralised ISSSTE areas through web-based tools, including internal blogs, as well through face-to-face meetings (immediate/medium-term action).
- Create and apply indicators measuring the efficiency and outcomes of procurement (immediate/medium-term action).
- Create model service-level agreements with suppliers and apply them (immediate/medium-term action).
- Create a Procurement Co-ordination Unit if there are available human and financial resources and approvals, in accordance with the annexed action plan (medium-term action).
- Measure and record the past performance of suppliers with web-based tools and use it to inform future contracting decisions (medium-term action).

- Extend CONCERTA to more supply categories, such as non-clinical goods, medical infrastructure and residual services, if the volume and value of such procurements make it worthwhile (medium-term action).
- Consider an interoperable electronic health records system for gathering medical input for future supply needs, taking into consideration the need to respect the privacy and confidentiality of health data (medium-/long-term action).
- Regularly update treatment guidelines and protocols (medium-/long-term action).

Notes

1. Agreement 34.1330.2012 of the ISSSTE's Board of Directors, on the approval of policies, bases and guidelines for public procurement, leasing and services (*Acuerdo 34.1330.2012 de la Junta Directiva, relativo a la aprobación de las políticas, bases y lineamientos en materia de adquisiciones, arrendamientos y servicios del ISSSTE*).
2. The Minister of Public Administration (*Secretaría de la Función Pública*) published the "General Procurement Manual" in 2010, to guide public bodies in complying with the LAASSP. The manual standardises administrative procurement practices and aims to strengthen transparency and accountability. It is available at: www.funcionpublica.gob.mx/index.php/ua/sracp/uncp/maagmaassp.html (accessed 11 September 2014).
3. Acuerdo 34.1330.2012 de la Junta Directiva, relativo a la aprobación de las políticas, bases y lineamientos en materia de adquisiciones, arrendamientos y servicios del ISSSTE. Available at: http://normateca.issste.gob.mx/webdocs/X7/201203020727062781.pdf?id=062004 (accessed 29 August 2014).
4. Article 41, Section XX of the Law on Acquisitions, Leasing and Services of the Public Sector (*Ley de Adquisiciones, Arrendamientos y Servicios del Sector Público, LAASSP*). Available at: www.diputados.gob.mx/LeyesBiblio/pdf/14_101114.pdf (accessed 7 October 2014).
5. Article 14 of the LAASSP bylaws, available at: www.diputados.gob.mx/LeyesBiblio/regley/Reg_LAASSP.pdf (accessed 7 October 2014).
6. Ministry of Public Service's website: www.funcionpublica.gob.mx/index.php/ua/sracp/upcp/contratos-marco.html (accessed 13 September 2014).
7. POBALINES provide that the PAAAS manager is the Material Resources and Services Sub-Directorate (*Subdirección de Recursos Materiales y Servicios*) of the Administration Directorate (*Dirección de Administración*).
8. Format F0-PPP-01 of the "General Procurement Manual". Available at: www.funcionpublica.gob.mx/index.php/ua/sracp/uncp/maagmaassp.html (accessed 14 September 2014).

9. The Supply Control Board was developed by the ISSSTE in February 2012. It covers more than 900 codes of medicines and medical products in the National Distribution Centre (*Centro Nacional de Distribución*). For each product, the Supply Control Board provides visibility of a large range of information such as: stock available in each medical unit and in the central warehouse; supplier name, unit cost, expected coverage with existing stock in central warehouse (based on calculated average consumption), contractual quantity already delivered and remaining; and the status of products for which stock is insufficient in a medical unit, such as their availability from the central warehouse, status of delivery from suppliers, status of contracting procedures, etc. The information is also consolidated at the medical unit and organisational levels to provide rapid visibility on the percentage of products under each status – for example: sufficient stock; to be provided by the central warehouse; imminent delivery by the supplier to the central warehouse; late delivery by the supplier; product without contractual agreement, but with a procurement process underway; and without contractual agreement and without any process underway. The Supply Control Board website can be accessed at: http://isssteapache.issste.gob.mx/transparenciaproactiva.

10. In accordance with Article 16 of the Rules for ISSSTE's Work Uniforms.

11. Based on conclusions of OECD workshop on "Improving Public Procurement Practices in ISSSTE" (2-4 September 2014, Mexico City). It was also suggested by OECD peer experts that one way to start the standardisation process would be bottom-up rather than top-down: standardise first at the level of a major hospital and thereafter gradually standardise across the ISSSTE.

12. Methodology criteria: Design of survey for measurement of the indicator, Ministry of Health. (Criterios metodológicos: Diseño de encuesta para la medición del indicador: "Surtimiento Completo de Recetas", Ministerio de Salud). Document provided by the ISSSTE. Also: Operational Guidelines for the Monitoring System for Quality Management: First Level Healthcare (*Lineamientos Operativos del Sistema de Monitoreo Para la Gestión de la Calidad -Primer Nivel*) IMSS, ISSSTE, Ministry of Health.

13. Based on the conclusions of the OECD workshop on "Improving Public Procurement Practices in ISSSTE", Mexico City, 2-4 September 2014.

Bibliography

Alejo, O. (2014), presentation at the OECD workshop on Improving Public Procurement Practices in ISSSTE", Mexico City, 2-4 September.

Australian government, Department of Finance website, www.finance.gov.au.

Bartels, D. (2014), Head of Procurement and Tendering Department at Amgros, the pharmaceutical procurement service for regional authorities in Denmark, presentation at the OECD workshop on "Improving Public Procurement Practices in ISSSTE", Mexico City, 2-4 September.

Chief Acquisition Officers Council (2014), "Open Dialogue on Improving How to Do Business with the Federal Government", http://cxo.dialogue.cao.gov.

ISSSTE (2014), "Acuerdo 57.1344.2014 de la Junta Directiva, relative a la aprobación del Estatuto Orgánico del Instituto de Seguridad y Servicios Sociales de los Trabajadores del Estado" (Organic Statute of the ISSSTE), *Diario Oficial de la Federación*, 18 June, available at: http://normateca.issste.gob.mx/view.asp?sesion=201502041031452225&infocard=201406181050098504&d=Y.

ISSSTE (2013), "Guidelines for the determination of needs for health supplies for medical sub-delegates and director of third-level hospitals" ("Lineamientos para la determinación de necesidades de insumos para la salud por subdelegados médicos y directores de hospitales del tercel nivel de atención"), internal document.

ISSSTE et al. (2014), "Ahorro superior a los 3 mil 700 millones de pesos en la compra consolidada de medicamentos" ("Savings of more than 3 million 700 pesos with the consolidated purchase of medicines"), joint press release, Mexico City, 13 January, available at: www.imss.gob.mx/sites/all/statics/i2f_news/003_PDF_0.pdf.

Konkel, F. (2014), "Coming soon: Pentagon's multi-billion dollar health records contract", NexGov website, 25 April, available at: www.nextgov.com/defense/2014/04/coming-soon-pentagons-multi-billion-dollar-health-records-contract/83230.

Ministère des Affaires sociales, de la Santé et des Droits des femmes (French Ministry of Social Affairs, Health and Women Rights), "Les achats hospitaliers: Le programme Phare", www.sante.gouv.fr/les-achats-hospitaliers-le-programme-phare,9524.html (accessed 24 October 2014).

National Health Service (2013a), "Better procurement, better value, better care: A procurement development programme for the NHS", National Health Service, Department of Health, Crown copyright, London, available at: www.gov.uk/government/uploads/system/uploads/attachment_data/file/226835/procurement_development_programme_for_NHS.pdf (accessed 17 October 2014).

National Health Service (2013b), "NHS Procurement Dashboard: Specification: Version 1", National Health Service, Department of Health, Crown copyright, London, October, available at: www.gov.uk/government/uploads/system/uploads/attachment_data/file/255875/nhs_procurement_dashboard_specification.pdf.

OECD (2015), *Recommendation of the Council on Public Procurement*, OECD, Paris, available at: http://acts.oecd.org/Instruments/ShowInstrumentView.aspx?InstrumentID=320&InstrumentPID=348&Lang=en&Book=False.

OECD (2013a), *Public Procurement Review of the State's Employees' Social Security and Social Services Institute in Mexico: Smart Procurement for Health Public Services*, OECD Public Governance Reviews, OECD Publishing, Paris, http://dx.doi.org/10.1787/9789264197305-en.

OECD (2013b), "Fighting bid rigging in public procurement in Mexico: A Secretariat analytical report on legislation, regulations and practices relating to procurement undertaken by ISSSTE", OECD, Paris, available at: www.oecd.org/daf/competition/mexicoissste2013.htm.

United States Office of Federal Procurement Policy (OFPP) (2013), "Improving the collection and use of information about contractor performance and integrity", Executive Office of the President, Office of Management and Budget, Washington DC, 6 March, available at: www.whitehouse.gov/sites/default/files/omb/procurement/memo/improving-the-collection-and-use-of-information-about-contractor-performance-and-integrity.pdf.

Further reading

A.T. Kearney (2004), "Improving the medicine supply chain", A.T. Kearney, Inc., Chicago, Illinois, available at: www.atkearneypas.com/knowledge/publications/2004/Medicines_Monograph_S.pdf (accessed 24 February 2015).

National Health Service (2014), "NHS eProcurement Strategy", Procurement, Investment & Commercial Division, National Health Service, Department of Health, Crown copyright, London, April, available at: www.gov.uk/government/publications/nhs-e-procurement-strategy (accessed 24 February 2015).

National Health Service (2013), "NHS standards of procurement", National Health Service, Procurement, Investment & Commercial Division, Version 2 – updated June 2013, Department of Health, Crown copyright, London, available at: www.gov.uk/government/uploads/system/uploads/attachment_data/file/210335/nhs_standards_procurement_2nd_ed.pdf (accessed 24 October 2014).

Moïse, P. and E. Docteur (2007), "Pharmaceutical pricing and reimbursement policies in Mexico", *OECD Health Working Papers*, No. 25, OECD Publishing, Paris, http://dx.doi.org/10.1787/302355455158.

Annex 2.A1
Action Plan for a Procurement Co-ordination Unit

The role of procurement

To grasp how a procurement co-ordination unit can support the wider procurement function, it needs to be commonly understood what procurement is and does. Figure 2.A1.1 illustrates the key activities that constitute it.

Figure 2.A1.1. **The component activities of procurement**

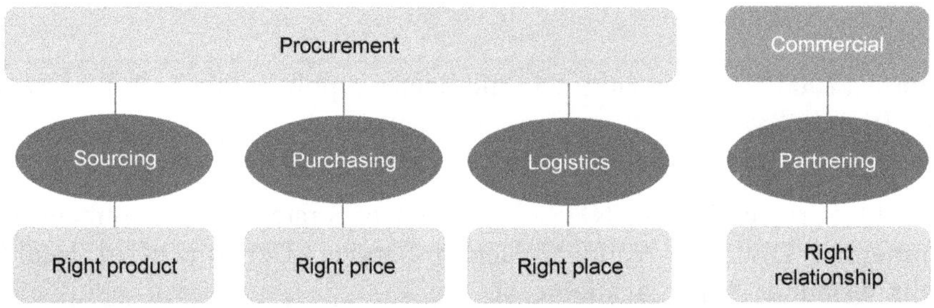

- Sourcing encompasses the selection of goods and services, working with end users to define their requirements and agree specifications that meet their needs and the available budget.
- Purchasing denotes the agreement of supply contracts with the supplier base. It includes outsourcing as well as financing arrangements such as leasing.
- Logistics refers to the physical flow of goods and services, together with the supporting information flow for the full purchase-to-pay process.
- Commercial denotes partnering arrangements with suppliers. They may include public-private partnerships and joint ventures.

Procurement acts as both a service and control function, ensuring that internal customers have the goods and services they need and that they comply with procurement processes and controls. Figure 2.A1.2 illustrates how procurement's constituent activities act as a bridge between internal customers within the ISSSTE and its outside supplier base. It shows the key outputs of each activity and their relation to both internal customers and external suppliers.

Figure 2.A1.2. **The procurement model and its key outputs**

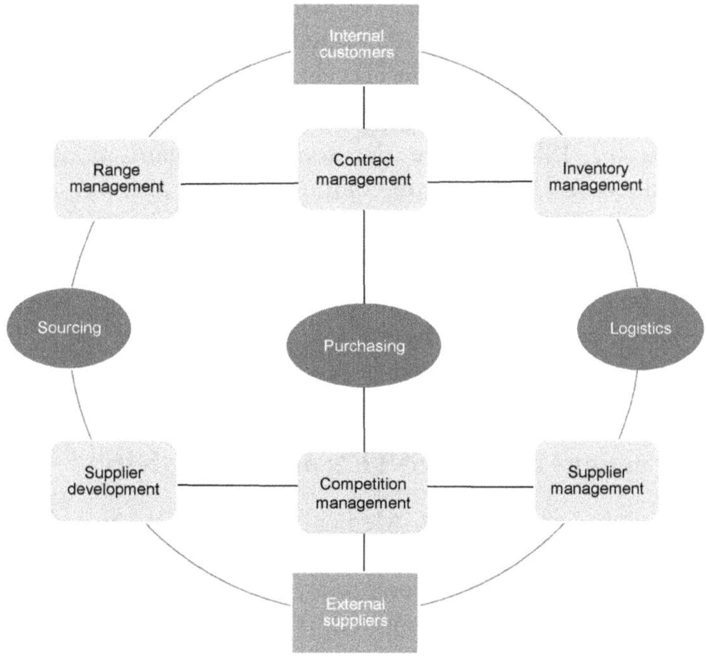

- Range management: covers the agreement of requirements with the internal customer and controls to prevent non-compliance with the agreed range.
- Supplier development: involves working with the supplier base to identify and reach out to new or existing suppliers and goods and services so as to improve organisational outcomes and/or lower operating costs.
- Contract management: means working with internal customers to ensure that maximum value for money is derived from the supply contracts put in place through procurement.
- Competition management: is the process of ensuring a full, open competitive tendering process for all contracts to ensure optimum value for money.
- Inventory management: covers ordering, receipt, distribution, stock management and payment of goods and services.
- Supplier management: refers to the on-going process of working with suppliers to ensure that their goods and services arrive when expected and conform to the agreed quality, addressing issues of supply resilience and risk management.

This action plan is based on recommendations made by the OECD in the first public procurement review of the ISSSTE (OECD, 2013) and on a draft proposal by the ISSSTE's Sub-Directorate of Medical Supplies dated March 2014 and reproduced in Annex 2.A2. It also draws on OECD fact-finding and communications between the ISSSTE and the OECD in the course of the year 2014.

The role of the Procurement Co-ordination Unit (PCU) as proposed by the ISSSTE is to define standard processes and procedures and monitor procurement performance across the ISSSTE. A prerequisite for ensuring optimal results is that the ISSSTE's procurement function should work in a cohesive manner towards clear priorities. Effective standards (see "1. Establish standards") and the dissemination of good practices (see "9. Best practices") can drive on-going improvements in procurement activities. The PCU would be a central delivery initiative in support of standardised processes (see "2. Document management") and procedures (see "3. Standardisation") and the monitoring of procurement performance across the ISSSTE (see "4. Monitoring").

The action plan proposal envisages a small core central team supported by collaborators across the ISSSTE (see the section, "Organisational structure of the Procurement Co-ordination Unit"). If sub-committees were also put in place, they would engage with the directorates and provide ownership to support the development and embedding of standard processes and procedures across the Institute.

The PCU could be placed under the Administration Directorate, which is in charge of all procurement activities following the entry into force of the ISSSTE's new organic statute in June 2014, and provide inputs and proposals directly to the Director of Administration, so as to guide high-level procurement-related decisions.

Clearly prioritising key actions in the ISSSTE's areas of activity

The ISSSTE's Sub-directorate of Medical Supplies suggested what the PCU's functions should be in its draft proposal of March 2014. The following section proposes key areas of activity for the PCU. An overarching plan that prioritises each area and sets a broad timetable for delivery will be required. To help with this, it may be helpful to assess and score each area according to its impact across the ISSSTE, set against the effort required to achieve the impact. The following scoring methodology could be used.

Table 2.A1.1. **Priorities scoring methodology**

Criteria	Low	Medium	High
Impact	1	2	3
Complexity	3	2	1
Time to deliver	3	2	1
Resources required	3	2	1

One simple way to establish priorities would be to take the score of each of these four metrics and multiply the scores with each other, with the highest score equating to the highest priority. Under such an approach, the lowest score would be 1 and the highest 81. Once the areas of activity have been prioritised, it should be possible to put together a delivery plan for the PCU such that it focuses its efforts on those areas that blend the highest impact with the least delivery effort.

Areas of activity

1. Establish standards: Assist in putting in place standards, policies and guidelines for the efficient co-ordination of procurement actions across the ISSSTE

Procurement has a key role to play in supporting the delivery of high-quality patient care whilst ensuring value for money. Senior management teams in each medical area should have an understanding of the applicable policies and standards so that they can ensure their area is meeting the procurement requirements of the Institute. Consideration can be given to making an executive director in each area responsible for delivering the required procurement actions. He or she would then be accountable for ensuring that the local procurement team understands and achieves the standards.

To establish standards, policies and guidelines, an inclusive approach will be needed for ensuring that all the players involved across the ISSSTE are able to comply with the agreed requirements. A lead manager for the job should be appointed – preferably someone with experience of working at all levels of the Institute and, if possible, with a procurement background. To ensure that the lead manager takes a rounded view, a representative working group should be put in place to contribute to the process of developing standards, policies and guidelines. Once a draft proposal has been produced, it should be shared across the ISSSTE procurement community with feedback encouraged. The working group should sign off on the final version.

An implementation plan will be required and is likely to involve the development of a training programme. Training should involve the relevant procurement staff and any relevant medical executive directors to ensure that the local teams comply with the agreed standards. Records of training delivered should be maintained, and new staff should receive training if their role requires compliance with the standards. In effect, an on-going training capacity will be required.

An off-the-shelf collaborative software solution could support action. Such software provides an online portal, enables documentation to be shared and evolved, and any issues to be discussed. Performance could also be shared, so encouraging all of the ISSSTE's procurement units to match the performance of the best. The portal could also be used to submit, collect and collate responses to central calls for information, as well as act as a repository for best practice guidance and online training materials. The National Health Service in the United Kingdom uses an online collaborative portal to support its procurement function (Box 2.A1.1).

The PCU will need to develop a structured action plan to address the requirement for an online collaborative portal. Consideration should be given to developing it as one of a wider set of procurement standards, with a supporting performance management process.

Box 2.A1.1. The National Health Service's collaborative portal for procurement efficiency

The Department of Health in the United Kingdom has put in place an online collaborative portal for use by the procurement community across the NHS in England. The site uses the Kahootz commercial software solution. The NHS site requires log-in credentials, but the front page can be viewed at: https://nhscpe.kahootz.com/connect.ti/cpeteam/view?objectId=4598704.

The following link is for the Kahootz product, although this is one of a number of commercially available solutions: www.kahootz.com.

Source: NHS Centre for Procurement Efficiency, National Health Service, Department of Health, United Kingdom.

2. Document management: Propose action to simplify requirements awarding contracts and to help improve document management and standardisation

An inclusive consultative process will be required to agree document management standards. An online portal will facilitate the process, and can be used as a central repository for standard documents. In this way, any updates or amendments to the standard documents can be centrally managed using a version control methodology. All staff registered on the portal can then have access to the full set of standard procurement documentation.

The supplier community should also have a say in the development of the standard procurement documents which they receive. One key goal of the procurement documents is that they will support procurement performance by providing a consistent approach to both procurement staff and suppliers. However, care must be taken to get the balance right when standardising documents. If standardisation is too rigidly applied it can stifle creativity and interfere with procurement results. An inclusive development process will help to understand which parts of which document can be standardised and those that require a degree of flexibility.

The PCU will need to develop a structured action plan to address the document management and standardisation requirement.

3. Standardisation: Lead the standardisation of procedures

Consideration should be given to the adoption of a procurement methodology that best suits the needs of the ISSSTE, chosen from one of several procurement methodologies that exist. One frequently used by the procurement community worldwide is the A.T. Kearney seven-step procurement methodology (Box 2.A1.2). A single category management methodology with some flexibility to cover specific procedures that may be required by the ISSSTE would be preferable for standardisation purposes. An extensive training programme would be required to drive adoption of the standardisation process, and monitoring would be needed to ensure compliance.

Box 2.A1.2. **Example of a procurement methodology: A.T. Kearney**

The A.T. Kearney seven-step sourcing process is an internationally established procurement methodology. An example of its use can be found at: www.atkearneypas.com/knowledge/articles/2005/7steps.pdf.

Although the cost in time and money of putting in place an organisation-wide procurement methodology may be significant, the benefits will be substantial over time. They will be reaped from greater, more effective competition that leads to lower purchase prices and goods and services that optimise value for money.

A summary of agreed standard procedures could be produced and each healthcare area could then be required to adopt them as part of their local arrangements for repeat orders. The summary and supporting details can be kept posted on the portal, so that the ISSSTE's procurement professionals can access it at any time.

4. Monitoring: Establish the monitoring of decentralised units' procurement performance and identify opportunities for aggregation

The monitoring of the decentralised units' procurement performance hinges on the availability of data and information. Monitoring may address two distinct areas: the procurement process and procurement results.

A procurement audit regime on a managed cycle can be built into the financial auditing process of each healthcare area with audit reports provided to each area's management team for any remedial action with copies to the PCU. The PCU can then aggregate all the procurement audit reports and identify trends and recurring themes. Significant common issues can then be addressed by revisiting the agreed procurement methodology and standard procedures (and making any required amendments), followed up with revision to training and education materials, and supported by further mandatory training for those units which perform the poorest.

The PCU will need to work with the procurement, finance and audit communities to agree an appropriate procurement audit regime and ensure its implementation.

There is likely to be a high degree of correlation between the quality of the procurement processes followed by the decentralised units and the results that they achieve. It will be important to understand the procurement results. In essence, they can be gleaned from the products and services that the units buy, and the quantities thereof in relation to the activity of the healthcare area and the prices paid.

To be able to make performance comparisons between healthcare areas, the Market Intelligence Unit (see Annex 3.A1) will need to provide the PCU with the necessary internal intelligence. It should include spend analysis to show the quantities purchased and price paid of any given item.

Analysis of the data will reveal poor performances, in which event the PCU will be able to recommend appropriate intervention to resolve issues. Recommended action may be to investigate how the highest performing units achieve their results and sharing that knowledge with the lowest performing units so that they can take action accordingly. The PCU will need to establish formal processes for any intervention to ensure that remedial action is taken and sustained.

Analysis of the data will also reveal opportunities for aggregation. The data should be shared with the category management teams who will have the right category knowledge to interpret the data. For example, it may be tempting to target product groups with high levels of expenditure. However, if there is adequate and effective competition in the market, aggregation may not yield any additional benefit. A category expert could make such an assessment – it would more meaningful than simply relying on a set of numbers. Conversely, there may be areas with lower levels of expenditure that could derive significant benefits from aggregation.

The key is to have access to timely, accurate data that can be readily analysed and interpreted. It may take time to produce such data, however.

The PCU will also need to compile a contracts database to include the procurement agreements of central and decentralised units. This database will show contract title, contract period, supplier name and contract line data, including prices. The PCU will need to consider introducing a standard set of contract titles so that contracts awarded by different decentralised units can be readily compared.

Another option would be to feed the raw data back to the decentralised units so that they can make their own analysis and undertake remedial action without the intervention of the PCU.

5. Communicate policies: Report and disseminate the policies established in the ISSSTE's procurement

The process of establishing and implementing policies within the ISSSTE should be well understood by the procurement community. The portal can be used to disseminate policies, with the software being able to track all document views by each registered individual. However, viewing a document does not mean it has been understood or even read.

A short test could be integrated into the portal so that a user would have to answer questions after viewing a new or revised policy. The PCU could then check the answers to ensure that policies have been read and understood. The tests could be supported by video-based learning materials for more complex development areas.

6. E-procurement: Lead efforts related to electronic procurement systems implemented by the Ministry of Public Service

The PCU will need to respond to the e-procurement requirements of the Ministry of Public Service (*Secretaría de la Función Pública,* SFP). To do so, the PCU will have to have an understanding of the electronic systems already in place and their gaps. It will need to conduct a survey that assesses the use of such systems within the ISSSTE and how they may be improved. Close co-ordination with the SFP at all times will be very useful.

7. Compliance: Issue reports on the monitoring of compliance by the ISSSTE's suppliers

Based on a database of contracts, the PCU will be able to compare actual prices paid against contract prices so that any significant discrepancies can be reported and investigated. This will reveal accurate details of cases where suppliers have accepted a contract but not fulfilled their requirement at all, or in part, or at prices different to those contracted.

8. Report management: Submit reports on contracts to the internal control areas of the ISSSTE and other agencies and institutions, like audit institutions, upon request

The PCU will need to assess the volume and complexity of the demands that will be placed upon it and ensure that it has the resources to address them. It should anticipate the requests it receives and, where appropriate, draw up and publish standardised reports that address most of them.

9. Best practices: Drive action for continuous improvement by incorporating best practices

The challenge here is to be able to recognise good practices by, for example, asking other organisations for examples and case studies and making them available to a wider audience.

It is important to actively seek good practices based on empirical performance data. This requires the PCU taking a proactive approach to assessing performance data and identifying pockets of high achievement. Once it has identified them, it should follow up with corresponding procurement officials to produce case studies. It should examine how to drive improvement. It can be done simply – by sharing and/or mandating examples of good practice – or by reviewing and updating policies and procedures to accommodate improvements.

To develop a culture of continuous improvement and acknowledge and celebrate the best examples of high achievement, an annual conference with an awards ceremony could be introduced. Where there are pockets of expertise, consideration should be given to establishing lead units. For example, a particular decentralised unit could take the lead on a particular area of activity or category of spend in which it has achieved good results.

Relying on its expertise, the decentralised unit could take a wider or national lead role to maximise the benefits of its specific capability.

Enabling activities

The above areas of activity cannot be considered in isolation from other initiatives required across the procurement landscape. A procurement strategy will be required that addresses a wider spectrum of actions related to procurement as well as the specific areas of market intelligence and procurement co-ordination.

The wider procurement strategy will need to be supported by a programme of procurement activities, which will need to be subject to formal governance, performance reporting, and programme and project management processes.

A procurement plan that sets out the contracting timetable for the coming years (three, for example) should be shared publically so that suppliers are aware of planned contracting business that is likely to happen if sufficient budget is secured.

Organisational structure of the Procurement Co-ordination Unit

The size of the PCU and the scale of its role will depend to some degree on the available budget. An example of what its organisational structure would look like is shown in Figure 2.A1.3. The staff mix and size will depend on a number of factors – e.g. the value of spend and volume of contracting activities undertaken across the ISSSTE; the types of products and services procured; and the amount of support that the sub-directorates will require to drive engagement, improvement and the sharing of information.

Figure 2.A1.3. **Possible organisational structure of the Procurement Co-ordination Unit**

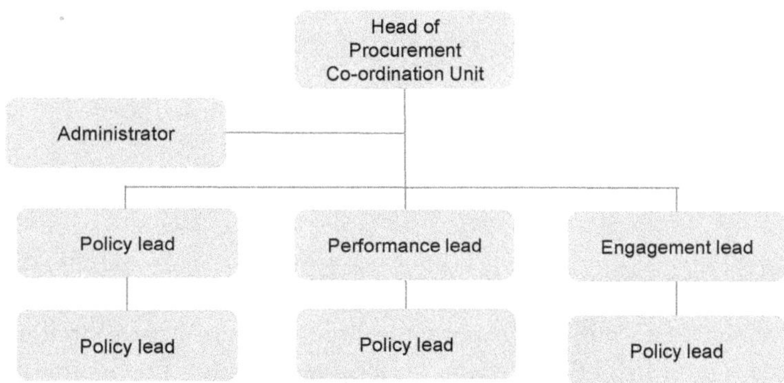

To support such structure, a number of committees and working groups would be required to facilitate co-ordination and ensure that maximum value is being achieved. Groups that could be considered include:

- The sub-directors: This group would ensure that procurement meets the needs of each sub-directorate and is aligned with the wider organisation strategy. Although it would not need to meet frequently, this group would have an essential role in supporting and managing change.
- The sub-directorates' procurement leads: To support behavioural change, the sub-directorate procurement leads will need to commit to and support the PCU. This group will provide oversight and ensure the implementation of the PCU's

policies and procedures. It will also provide feedback to ensure that the PCU is supporting needs. The group will need to meet frequently.

- Category management groups: They will comprise key contacts from the sub-directorates in order to provide strategic direction and develop category plans. Regular meetings will be required to draw up plans and monitor progress, addressing any issues that may arise.
- Standardisation groups: When the PCU develops and standardises policies, procedures and documentation it will need to draw on input from the wider procurement community across the ISSSTE. Whilst the PCU will have responsibility for development, stakeholder engagement and consultation will be critical to ensuring that local requirements are supported and implemented.

Within each sub-directorate, it may be advisable to create working groups drawn from expenditure categories to address the implementation of central policies, central procedures and central contracts, and to manage procurement business.

Key deliverables

Table 2.A1.2. **List of tasks and projected completion date**

Deliverable	Projected completion date
Engage with teams across the ISSSTE to develop requirements	2-3 months
Appoint a programme lead	2-3 months
Determine the PCU's requirements	2-3 months
Develop any business cases required	2-3 months
Recruit for the programme	2-3 months
Undertake research and engage with sub-directorates	6-9 months
Produce outputs, form working groups and consult	2-3 months
Embed the PCU into routine business	9-12 months

High-level professionals

High-demand, highly skilled professionals would be needed to create the PCU. Indicative profiles follow.

Head of the Procurement Co-ordination Unit

The Head of the PCU will be responsible for the overall development of policy and engagement across the ISSSTE. He or she will be responsible for raising the profile of the PCU, including the benefits that it can deliver across the organisation.

- Responsibilities:
  - developing and implementing a senior stakeholder management strategy
  - establishing key networks and forums
  - recruiting a dedicated team within the PCU
  - managing, developing and supporting the team
  - developing and managing work plans and budgets.

- Requirements:
  - excellent organisational skills
  - ability to influence
  - articulate and confident with good presentation skills
  - outstanding listening and communication skills, both written and oral
  - ability to set and meet schedules
  - expertise with Word, Excel and the Internet.

Policy lead

The policy lead will be responsible for identifying and developing policy. He or she will take a lead in ensuring that policy meets the government's and regulatory requirements and will develop the strategic policy agenda for the ISSSTE's procurement.

- Responsibilities:
  - drawing up and establishing the strategic policy framework
  - developing and supporting the implementation of key policies
  - providing expert advice and guidance
  - supporting strategic planning within a performance management framework
  - communicating and developing relationships with clients (sub-directorates)
  - developing and managing work plans and budgets
  - formulating analysis plans
  - scheduling and co-ordinating internal and external resources
  - overseeing projects and reviewing data quality and written recommendation reports.
- Requirements:
  - excellent organisational skills with an eye for detail
  - outstanding listening and communication skills, both written and oral
  - ability to influence
  - articulate and confident with good presentation skills
  - desire to learn and work with others
  - ability to develop and meet schedules
  - ability to handle complex issues and communicate them clearly to a variety of audiences
  - expertise with Word, Excel and the Internet
  - experience as a public policy professional
  - good time- and project- management skills and the ability to set priorities.

Engagement lead

The engagement lead will be responsible for building strong stakeholder relationships both at practitioner level and at senior level, influencing people with different agendas to adopt new concepts and different ways of working. As a senior member of the team, he or she will frequently need good advocacy skills to "sell" the benefits of the PCU to stakeholders, and be able to influence and persuade to bring about changes in views and practices.

- Responsibilities:
  - communicating and developing relationships with clients (sub-directorates)
  - developing and managing work plans and budgets
  - working with the engagement managers to support work plans
  - scheduling and co-ordinating internal and external resources
  - developing and implementing the engagement strategy
  - reviewing the performance of sub-directorates working with the PCU.
- Requirements:
  - excellent engagement skills – ability to work with all levels of staff across the ISSSTE
  - organisational skills, with a particular focus on managing multiple stakeholders
  - outstanding listening and communication skills, both written and oral
  - desire to learn and work with others
  - ability to develop and meet schedules
  - expertise with Word, Excel and the Internet
  - extensive stakeholder management/engagement experience
  - influencing skills
  - articulate and confident with good presentation skills.

Rolling out the Procurement Co-ordination Unit

The PCU could be rolled out in phases. In this way, it would be possible to judge from results that requirements are met and whether there is evidence to support the need for a PCU. One approach could be to take a single policy area as a pilot.

This action plan may be implemented partly or by stages. Implementation is conditional upon the availability of human and financial resources, and on endorsement internally (ISSSTE) and externally (by other competent bodies, like the Ministry of Finance) of its formal incorporation into the ISSSTE's organisational structure.

Reference

OECD (2013), *Public Procurement Review of the State's Employees' Social Security and Social Services Institute in Mexico: Smart Procurement for Health Public Services*, OECD Public Governance Reviews, OECD Publishing, Paris, http://dx.doi.org/10.1787/9789264197305-en.

Annex 2.A2

Executive proposal: ISSSTE Medical Supplies Sub-Directorate "Creation of a Public Procurement Co-ordination Unit"

Objective

This annex seeks to propose an organisational structure for addressing the recommendations made by the OECD in the context of the agreement signed in June 2012 between the OECD, the Mexican State's Employees' Social Security and Social Services Institute (*Instituto de Seguridad y Servicios Sociales de los Trabajadores del Estado, ISSSTE*) and the Mexican Federal Competition Commission (*Comisión Federal de Competencia, CFC*), the aim of which was to fight bid rigging in the ISSSTE's public procurement processes. The outcome was set out in November 2013 in the report entitled "Fighting bid rigging in public procurement in Mexico: A Secretariat analytical report on legislation, regulations and practices relating to public procurement undertaken by ISSSTE" (OECD, 2013).

Justification

This annex was drafted on the basis of the public procurement recommendations made to the ISSSTE in connection with fighting collusion in bidding processes, and bearing in mind the importance of eliminating these practices, which prevent fair competition amongst suppliers and limit opportunities for the administration to make greater savings, allowing a better use of resources and an effective procedure for procuring and using goods, services and works for the benefit of beneficiaries.

The proposed structure is based on the areas for possible improvement identified in the 66 recommendations made to the ISSSTE by the OECD. Those recommendations propose better co-ordination within the ISSSTE in order to standardise the various bidding processes undertaken by the procurement areas of central and decentralised agencies. Such co-ordination would allow an overall picture of those processes to be obtained and to generate effective strategies and instruments to prevent collusion, through better co-ordination of those areas using standardised, specific processes, allowing the behaviour of interested bidders to be monitored and potential collusion to be detected in good time.

In order to act upon and comply with the recommendations made by the OECD and, in particular, the creation of Public Procurement and Market Research Units, it is necessary to build on the experience and expertise of the ISSSTE's human resources, and also to develop an area which, at central level and in terms of procurement, has been the subject of an ongoing process of institutional reshuffling and redesign in recent years, thereby permitting a saving of resources through joint procurement processes with other agencies (consolidated purchases).

These measures go hand in hand with the incorporation of information and communications technologies (ICTs), to provide an overall picture of the goods and services of the procurement process and the performance of public works.

However, the use of different types of procurement procedures hampers co-ordination between the various procurement areas with a view to detecting instances of collusion, which make it impossible to obtain the best price, quality or financing of purchases.

Achieving better co-ordination between these areas in order to standardise procurement processes, strengthen the ability to negotiate with bidders so as to obtain the best price for products and services, extend this to infrastructure and public works, and implement these measures at public administration level, as has been done with medicines and medical supplies, means applying this experience to other areas of procurement and investment; for this reason, this annex proposes bringing to the Public Procurement Co-ordination Unit human resources which, with their experience, expertise and knowledge of the mechanisms, procedures and instruments used for making consolidated purchases, have achieved the relevant inter-institutional co-ordination for maximising the benefits of that work.

With this in mind, the proposed organisational chart in Figure 2.A2.1 incorporates the Public Procurement and Market Research Units recommended by the OECD for linking product and service purchasing and public works procurement processes.

Figure 2.A2.1. **Proposed organisational chart**

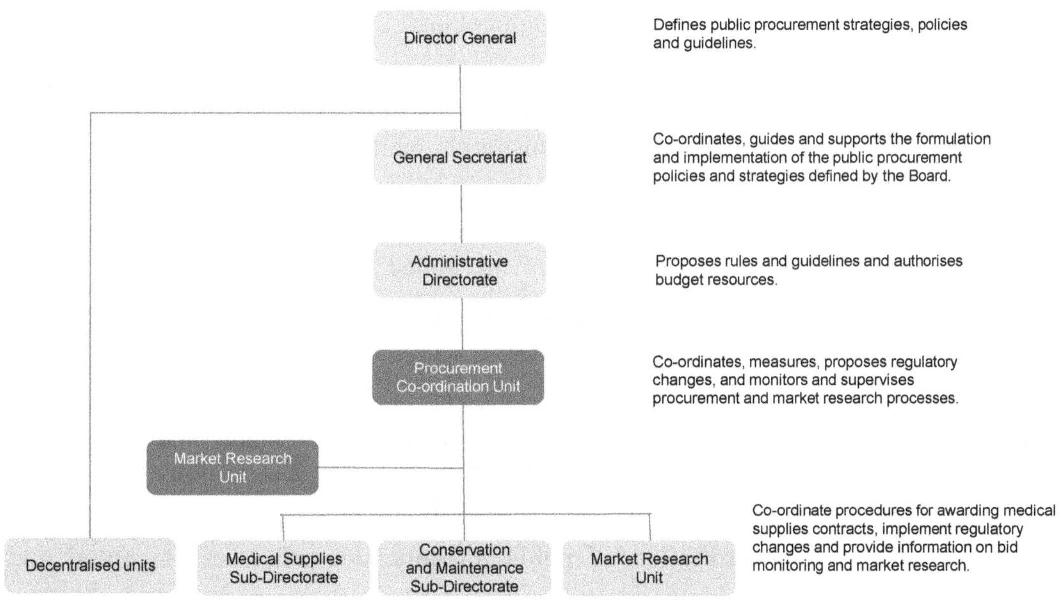

This organisational chart takes into account the provisions of the third indent of Article 5 of the Budgeting and Fiscal Responsibility Law concerning the budgetary autonomy of the decentralised administrative units when establishing their direct relationship with the Head of the ISSSTE.

Similarly, it aims to build on experience acquired in the co-ordination of inter-institutional procurement processes by continuing the supervisory and co-ordination measures in that field undertaken by the Administration Directorate which, additionally, ties those measures in with planning, programming, implementation and budget control activities. These powers are intended to facilitate co-ordination with decentralised units so that the standardisation of procurement procedures can lead to harmonisation of budget allocation criteria in the public procurement and financial co-ordination procedures of other agencies and institutes in the federal and local public administration.

Legal basis

- Political Constitution of the United Mexican States, Articles 26 and 134
- National Development Plan, objective 2.3, strategies 2.3.4 and 2.4.3
- Planning Law, Article 14, indent VII
- Basic Law on Public Administration, Article 39
- Federal Law on Budgeting and Fiscal Responsibility, Article 5, indent III
- Law on Acquisitions, Leasing and Services and its implementing regulation
- ISSSTE Law, Article 207
- Organic Statute of ISSSTE, Article 59
- Technical Guide for drafting a proposal to alter the basic structure of ISSSTE.

Proposed Co-ordination Unit

Based on the OECD's recommendations, it is proposed that the Public Procurement Co-ordination Unit should have the following functions:

- To assist the Administration Directorate in establishing regulations, policies and guidelines for the effective co-ordination of the ISSSTE's procurement activities with a view to improving the administrative management of the acquisition of medical supplies.
- To propose ways of simplifying requirements for the award of contracts in order to improve the processing of the documents aimed at formalising those contracts.
- To head the co-ordination of procurement activities undertaken by the ISSSTE's central and decentralised units, in order to standardise the procedures carried out in each of those units.
- To establish a system for monitoring and assessing procurement activities on the part of the areas responsible for purchasing medical supplies, in order to reinforce the ability to address any opportunities identified.
- To head the standardisation of public procurement processes at central and decentralised levels.
- To inform and disseminate the ISSSTE's procurement policies.
- To head activities regarding the electronic procurement systems implemented by the Ministry of Public Administration.
- To issue a compliance monitoring report in relation to successful suppliers contracted by the ISSSTE.
- To produce the procurement reports requested from the ISSSTE by fiscal areas and other requesting agencies and institutions.
- To carry out measures to implement a continuous improvement process through the incorporation of best practices.

Reference

OECD (2013), "Fighting bid rigging in public procurement in Mexico: A Secretariat analytical report on legislation, regulations and practices relating to procurement undertaken by ISSSTE", OECD, Paris, available at: www.oecd.org/daf/competition/mexicoissste2013.htm.

Chapter 3.

Achieving value for money: Market intelligence in the ISSSTE

This chapter looks at market research in procurement at the State's Employees' Social Security and Social Services Institute (ISSSTE) in Mexico. The chapter provides recommendations for improving market intelligence to identify cost-effective opportunities and develop strategies that meet buying needs, based on OECD good practices. An action plan for the formalisation and reinforcement of the ISSSTE's Market Intelligence Unit is annexed at the end of this chapter.

Market intelligence is information on the characteristics and behaviours of specific goods or services or sectors of economic activity. In procurement, that information helps identify cost-effective purchasing opportunities and develop strategies that meet buying needs. Market intelligence has two aspects:

1. an internal one – understanding buying needs
2. an external one – understanding supply solutions and capacity and identifying market trends, which is also referred to as market research and/or analysis.

Although this chapter deals mainly with external/supply market intelligence (Box 3.1), it also makes recommendations, which apply to both internal and external aspects.

The ISSSTE's market research is process-oriented and implemented in compliance with complex, detailed rules

The definition and compulsory nature of supply market research prior to tendering can be found in Article 2 of the Law on Acquisitions, Leases and Services in the Public Sector (*Ley de Adquisiciones, Arrendamientos y Servicios del Sector Público*, LAASSP). Market research matters are also regulated in the LAASSP's implementing regulation, the "General Procurement Manual" (*Administrative Manual for General Application concerning Acquisitions, Leasing and Services of the Public Sector – Manual Administrativo de Aplicación General en Materia de Adquisiciones, Arrendamientos y Servicios del Sector Público*, MAAGMAASSP), and the Policies and Guidelines Concerning the ISSSTE's Acquisitions, Leasing and Services (*Políticas, Bases y Lineamientos en Materia de Adquisiciones, Arrendamientos y Servicios*, POBALINES).

The LAASSP defines supply market research as gathering information on the availability of goods and services, the existence of national or international suppliers, and estimated price. Its purpose is to help public officials choose the best contract strategy and pricing scheme, as well as, in certain cases, substantiate a decision not to use public tendering. The ISSSTE's POBALINES provide that every purchase request must be accompanied by market research.

The ISSSTE has shaped its market research activities to meet the requirements of the regulations that govern them – particularly the LAASSP, its implementing regulation and the POBALINES. The requirements are that the market research should validate: 1) the existence of the requested good or service in the market; 2) the existence of providers at national and/or international level; 3) the estimated contract price. The good or service is specified before any market research which, therefore, serves to validate or adjust specifications, but not to shape them.

Steps in the market research procedure at the ISSSTE are:

- Receive request to conduct market research.
- Verify that the request includes the necessary minimum information (technical description, required quantity, delivery requirements).
- Identify potential suppliers:
  - in the e-procurement system, Compranet, by searching for suppliers of similar goods or services to another Mexican entity

- in the ISSSTE's historical data, particularly in the registered suppliers list (*padrón de proveedores*), which includes suppliers who have previously worked with the ISSSTE
- in lists of suppliers registered in relevant chambers and associations
- on the Internet.

Box 3.1. Common aims, outputs and benefits of supply market research and analysis

Supply market analysis provides a strategic understanding of:

- how a market works
- the direction in which a market is heading, including technological developments
- the competitiveness of a market
- the capability, capacity and performance of a market
- information on key suppliers, market shares and risks of collusion
- how markets can be developed to better meet customer requirements
- how pricing on the market works – i.e. its cost structures and recent price trends
- what the market's risks are and how to prepare to mitigate them
- the probability, or not, of market failure.

The outputs of market analysis as regards tender procedures include:

- planning and budgeting the procurement activity
- designing tender documents which match the ISSSTE's needs with the suppliers' available solutions, including the right specifications and evaluation and award criteria
- choosing the right procurement procedure and strategy – both in terms of how the market currently operates as well as how it may operate in the future in relation to new entrants or innovative technology
- structuring public tenders so as to obtain healthy competitive bids
- procuring without negatively affecting the supply base and, in particular, providing contract opportunities for small and medium-sized enterprises (SMEs).

Key outcomes are:

- improved value for money
- identification and management of supply-related risks
- more and fairer opportunities for suppliers.

The benefits of supply market analysis increase in proportion to the degree of business risk and/or expenditure on the goods or services.

Source: Based on presentations by Steve Graham, Hadley Graham Ltd, advisors to United Kingdom's Department of Health and Marjorie Ramírez, former Head of Division of Framework Agreements at ChileCompra, the Chilean central purchasing body, at the OECD workshop on "Improving Public Procurement Practices in ISSSTE", Mexico City, 2-4 September 2014.

- Address, through electronic and paper means, an invitation for indicative price quotes (FOCON 04, described in the "General Procurement Manual") to at least three suppliers – five in the case of purchases grouping different goods and services.
- Receive and analyse information by suppliers, to verify that it complies with the requirements of the ISSSTE.
- Use an Excel spreadsheet (FOCON 05, described in the "General Procurement Manual") [1] to calculate the estimated price of each good or service as a statistical median of quotes provided by those suppliers who fulfil requirements and respond to the request for price quotes. When the criterion for awarding the contract is the lowest price, called "*sistema binario*" (binary system), supplier price quotes determine the contract reference price which is stated in the tender documents, as well as the lowest and highest price that may be accepted from bidders. During the fact-finding mission, stakeholders – who included ISSSTE staff and suppliers – mentioned that the binary system is the one the most used by the ISSSTE as it is easier and provides simple grounds for justifying the award decision.
- Deliver the market research file to the unit which requested it.
- The relevant unit uses information included in the market research, like the estimated price and the origin of goods, in order to determine the procurement procedure to be followed.

The market research procedure followed by the ISSSTE ensures that the institution complies with the minimum requirements of the law, but, usually, does not play any part in designing the procurement strategy (what to buy, how, under what terms, etc.). The ensuing procurement process is routine, using the technical specifications defined before market research and evaluating offers on the basis of the lowest price (binary system) falling within the limits of the estimated price. The market research price quotes and the estimated prices derived from them are therefore major factors for determining the outcome of the procurement procedures. The Mexican legal framework does, however, allow technical (i.e. not only price-related) evaluations of offers using a system of points or percentages (*puntos o porcentajes*), i.e. a point-based weighted evaluation of each different component of a bid. The weights must be specified in the tender documents (SFP, 2010).

Many suppliers also reported that they did not want to provide a real price quote during the market research phase because they were afraid that the information would leak and that their competitors would undercut their bid and win the contract. By the same token, suppliers sometimes quote inflated prices to gain a margin for discounts during tenders or increase profit if they are awarded the contract.

In general, the quotes system has often led to inaccurate input that does not truly reflect the market situation. Prices that are too high or too low during market research can also have the effect of encouraging the ISSSTE not to use competitive bidding and award contracts directly under the terms of Article 41 of the LAASSP (see Chapter 5 on direct awards).

Insufficient knowledge and support for marked research

The ISSSTE's central and decentralised units both conduct market research into the goods and services they procure, with different entities in charge of different categories of goods and services (Table 3.1).

Table 3.1. **How market research in the ISSSTE is structured**

Procurement strategy	Good/service	Level	Institution/unit
Inter-institutional consolidation	Medicines and healing materials	Central	IMSS based on information provided by the ISSSTE Medical Supplies Sub-Directorate
Internal centralisation	Medicines and healing materials	Central	Medical Supplies Sub-Directorate
	Comprehensive medical services	Central	Medical Supplies Sub-Directorate
	Medical equipment	Central	Medical Supplies Sub-Directorate
	Residual services	Central	Conservation and Maintenance and Materials Resources and Services Sub-Directorates
Local	Goods/services	Decentralised	Procurement Unit (sometimes "user areas")

Note: IMSS: Mexican Institute of Social Security (*Instituto Mexicano del Seguro Social*).

Source: Based on information provided by the Administration Directorate of the ISSSTE.

As Table 3.1 shows, it is not always clear who carries out market research in local non-centralised procurement. It is sometimes a user area (healthcare units in most cases), sometimes a procurement unit, sometimes both.

It emerged from fact-finding that, in approximately 50% of all delegations, user areas determine (before market research) the technical specifications of goods or services (Figure 3.1).

Figure 3.1. **Who draws up technical requirements in Type A and Type B delegations?**

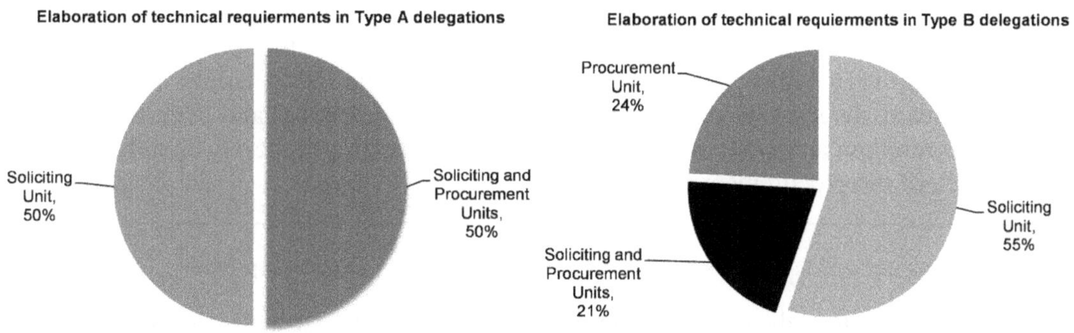

Note: Type A delegations have a higher volume of procurement activity and two procurement units: one for goods (Departamento de Adquisiciones) and one for public works and general services (Departamento de Obras y Servicios Generales). Type B delegations have a lower volume of procurement activities and only one procurement unit (Departamento de Recursos Materials y Obras) that purchases a wide range of goods and services.

Source: Information provided by the ISSSTE.

However, responses to questions from the OECD review team reveal that, in Type A delegations, procurement units conduct market research more frequently than user areas (Figure 3.2). Some of the delegations interviewed said that user areas do not want to carry out the market research because they consider that they do not know how to do it.

Figure 3.2. **Market research in Type A and Type B delegations**

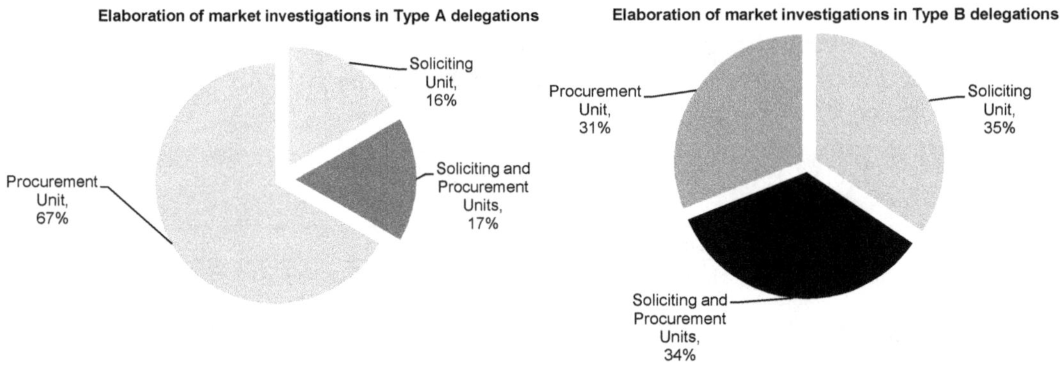

Note: Type A delegations have a higher volume of procurement activity and two procurement units: one for goods (*Departamento de Adquisiciones*) and one for public works and general services (*Departamento de Obras y Servicios Generales*). Type B delegations have a lower volume of procurement activities and only one procurement unit (*Departamento de Recursos Materials y Obras*) that purchases a wide range of goods and services.

Source: Information provided by the ISSSTE.

The growing trend in OECD countries is to entrust market research to category managers who are familiar with specific product or service categories and certain sectors of economic activity. Procurement specialists, which includes legal staff, usually intervene after market research, working together with category managers in strategy design and procedure oversight. The Italian central purchasing body, Consip SpA, appoints one category manager per procurement. This person also participates in all market research activities and meetings with suppliers (Box 3.2).

ISSSTE staff reported to the OECD that the number and complexity of rules and procedures governing market research – combined with lack of knowledge, training or (in the case of delegations) clearly defined responsibility for conducting market research – had led them to view market research as a burdensome administrative task and not as a strategic intelligence activity. Officials focus on following the procedure and not breaching the regulations rather than on identifying the best supply solutions. In particular, many delegations stated that they lacked time, resources and expertise to carry out market research and were unsure of its benefits, perceiving it merely as only a formal prerequisite of the procurement procedure.

Box 3.2. **Market analysis process at the Italian central purchasing body, Consip SpA**

Consip SpA is the Italian central purchasing body, wholly owned by the Italian Ministry of Economy and Finance. Consip awards contracts (usually framework agreements) for goods and services for the Italian public sector.

To improve its procurements, Consip has developed a standard internal process on how to run market analysis and how to interact with suppliers (economic operators, EOs) during the market analysis.

The process, shown in Figure 3.3, identifies the activities to be carried out during the market analysis in order to complete a "feasibility study" as a preliminary step to tender design and tender notice publication.

The entire process is supported by: 1) internal market analysis guidelines; 2) market consultation questionnaires; 3) the Sourcing Activities yearly Plan (SAP).

Box 3.2. Market analysis process at the Italian central purchasing body, Consip SpA *(cont.)*

Figure 3.3. **Market analysis process at the Italian central purchasing body, Consip SpA**

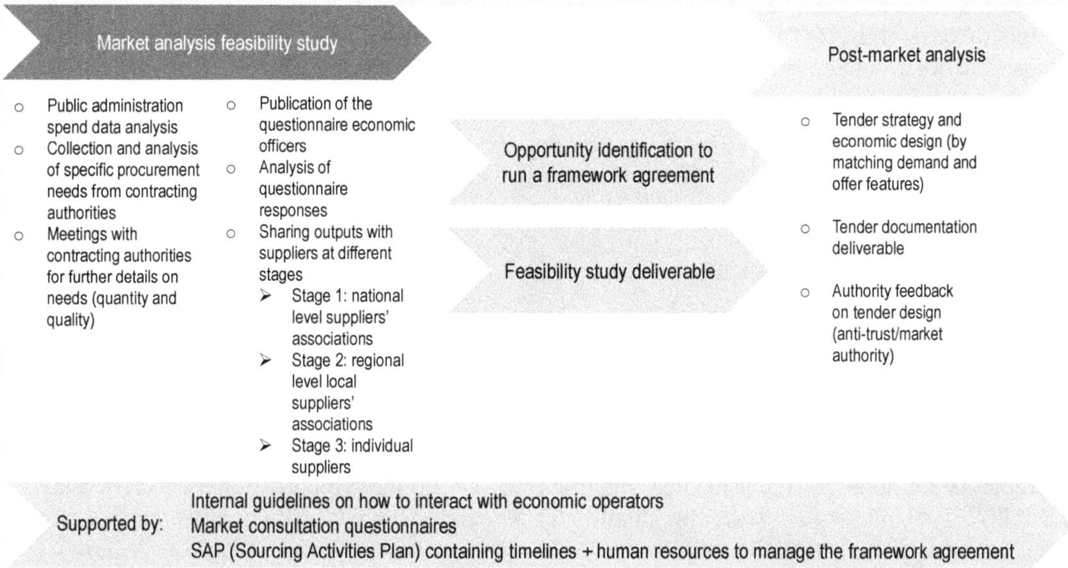

Internal market analysis guidelines

Internal market analysis guidelines aim to guide the interaction with businesses during market research. The goal of the market analysis is to collect the following data and characteristics on the goods and services to be procured:

- market size and the state's procurement volume in relation to market size
- market structure: percentage of small and medium-sized enterprises on this market segment or domination by bigger companies
- the most important suppliers in the market
- maturity of the products/services, pricing models and different conditions offered by suppliers, potential standardisation of the products/services and their commercial capacity
- market development outlook for the coming years.

This information is useful to define the procurement characteristics, the tender strategy, potential splitting into lots and the reference price.

Information may be collected by means of interviews with the suppliers' national associations and, if necessary, with individual suppliers, following the market analysis guidelines.

Market consultation questionnaires and meetings with economic operators

The market consultation activity starts by publishing project-customised questionnaires on the national e-procurement portal and on Consip's website. The aim of the questionnaires is to gain insight on market features, ensure business participation and information spreading. The questionnaires are valid up until the publication of the tender notice.

Box 3.2. **Market analysis process at the Italian central purchasing body, Consip SpA** (*cont.*)

There may be meetings with the economic operators, which must be requested by email and attended by at least two Consip employees (head of project and category manager). During the meeting, Consip presents the customised market questionnaire and distributes a copy of its code of ethics. The questionnaire is then completed by all of the meeting participants.

Questions are asked and answered during the meeting but no additional information to that already published is provided, so that suppliers that are not participating in the meeting are not at a disadvantage. The tender strategy (if existant) is not discussed and no comparison among the potential bidders takes place.

Sourcing Activities Plan (SAP)

The SAP is the general plan that Consip's Sourcing Division uses in order to plan and monitor its yearly activity. It matches procurement phases with resources and timelines. It indicates the complexity of the procurement, the category manager in charge of it, the starting and final month of each main phase, and the forecasted contract availability date.

According to the complexity of procurement (low, medium or high), different phase implementation durations are estimated, ranging from two to three months for the market analysis feasibility study phase and six to nine months for the tender strategy and complete documentation drafting phase (post-market analysis).

The SAP is for internal use, but the estimated month of the contract availability is published on the national e-procurement portal to prepare buyers and suppliers.

Source: Consip SpA.

A more strategic approach to supply market research at the ISSSTE is recommended so as to keep up to date with market developments and seek out solutions that provide high-quality services. Market intelligence should lead, not follow, the procurement cycle from the early stage of needs assessment, on the condition of complying with legal requirements. It should also have dedicated human and material resources and be backed by sufficient IT support and training.

Market intelligence requires preparation, planning and building capacity over time

OECD experience shows that a number of preliminary steps should be taken before commencing market intelligence actions and supply-side analysis.[2]

First, the internal requirements for a product or service should be clearly understood to ensure that the market analysis focuses on the right industries and markets. To that end, ISSSTE procurement officers should engage with users – who include medical staff and beneficiaries.

Second, the ISSSTE should check whether a similar market analysis has already been conducted – either by the ISSSTE or another organisation with which the ISSSTE collaborates. Using existing information may avoid wasting time and speed up the market analysis process. For example, the Mexican Institute of Social Security (*Instituto Mexicano del Seguro Social*, IMSS) and the ISSSTE, who often buy the same products and services, could pool their market intelligence results to avoid duplication of efforts.

Before gathering market intelligence, a plan should be developed to determine:

- the key activities and timelines
- goals, objectives and scope
- the key resource requirements (e.g. staffing, finances, office space, etc.).

ChileCompra follows a seven-step methodology to set up framework agreements for goods and services which includes market research (Figure 3.4). The steps are: 1) analyse demand and identify product or service category; 2) analyse supply market; 3) define the buying strategy; 4) validate the strategy with stakeholders (including suppliers); 5) carry out the tender procedure; 6) implement the purchase action plan; 7) manage the suppliers.

Step 2 (supply market analysis) is undertaken on the basis of a plan and includes looking for suppliers, alternatives, other buyers, critical risks. The results of this analysis define the entire buying strategy, tender documents and process, and the terms of the ensuing contract.

Figure 3.4. **ChileCompra's seven-step procurement method**

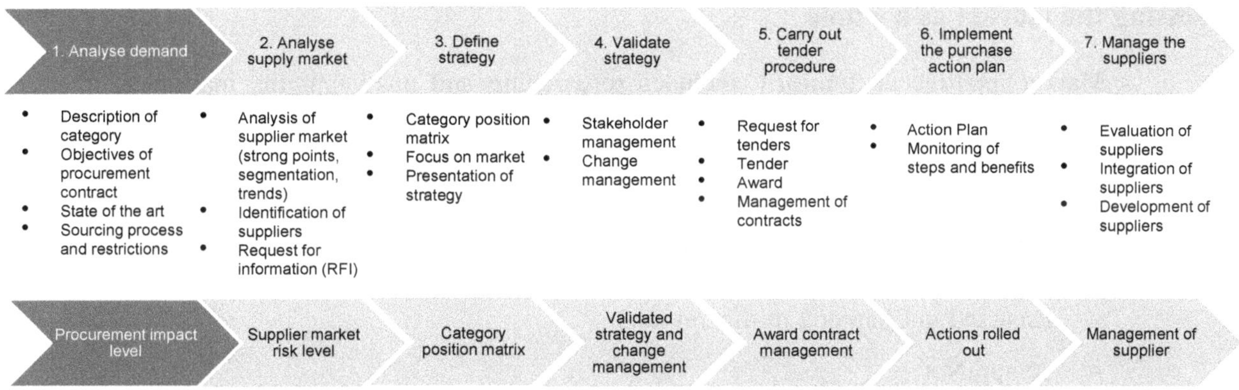

Source: Presentation at the OECD workshop on "Improving Public Procurement Practices in ISSSTE", Mexico City, 2-4 September 2014, by Marjorie Ramírez, former Head of Division of Framework Agreements at the Chilean central purchasing body, ChileCompra.

The component of the market intelligence plan which identifies resource requirements should also help assess whether assistance from external advisors is needed. It emerged from fact-finding that the IMSS has, for example, transferred part of its market intelligence activity to external advisors. The Portuguese National Public Procurement Agency (*Agência Nacional de Compras Públicas*, ANCP) followed a similar course at its inception (Box 3.3).

The diagram in Figure 3.5 is a summary flowchart of the procurement of medicines and healing materials at the ISSSTE. Market research feeds the whole process. The flowchart shows key activities and milestones, but does not provide specific timelines or detail required human and material resources. Nor does it provide variations according to the degree of critical importance or complexity of a procurement.

Box 3.3. **Building capacity for market research in Portugal**

Established in 2007, the National Public Procurement Agency of Portugal (Agência Nacional de Compras Públicas, ANCP),[1] conducted market research to develop strategies for the consolidated procurement of commonly used goods and services through framework agreements. Initially, the ANCP outsourced its market research to external advisors when it lacked in-house capacity, e.g. for projects with specialised technical features. The proviso was that the cost of the market research study against the value of the procurement made it worthwhile. The ANCP outsourced the market research study for its first framework agreement in 2009, which was for IT supplies and software. Over time, it has built considerable procurement and market expertise and relied to a large extent on its own market intelligence capacity.

Note: 1. The ANCP was merged with the Shared Services Entity for the Public Administration (ESPAP) in September 2012.

Source: OECD (2013a), *Colombia: Implementing Good Governance*, OECD Public Governance Reviews, OECD Publishing, Paris, http://dx.doi.org/10.1787/9789264202177-en.

Assessing the market as a whole

Market intelligence typically includes researching and analysing the market as a whole. It is a stage-by-stage procedure of identifying suppliers and gathering information on them and the market.

A number of written information sources are available for the ISSSTE. They include:

- end users of goods and services, e.g. medical staff and the beneficiaries of ISSSTE healthcare services (the value of satisfaction surveys in this respect is discussed in Chapter 2 of this review)
- CompraNet
- suppliers and industry associations, like the National Chamber of the Pharmaceutical Industry (*Cámara Nacional de la Industria Farmacéutica, CANIFARMA*), the National Chamber of Transformation Industries (*Cámara Nacional de la Industria de Transformación*, CANACINTRA), the National Association of Health Supply Distributors (*Asociación Nacional de Distribuidores de Insumos para la Salud*, ANDIS)
- trade journals and sector-related specialised publications
- online databases and media sources (information from the Internet should be checked against other sources for accuracy)
- research organisations and institutes.

The ISSSTE could also draw on the expertise of outside entities, like the Ministry of Health, that specialise in matters of public health. The ISSSTE is co-operating with the Co-ordinating Commission for Negotiating the Price of Medicines and other Health Supplies (*Comisión Coordinadora para la Negociación de Precios de Medicamentos y otros Insumos para la Salud*) to improve the procurement of medicines. The Chilean central purchasing body, ChileCompra, for example, relies on healthcare experts designated by the Ministry of Health to support the procurement of healthcare supplies and services.

Figure 3.5. **Summary flowchart for the procurement of medicines and healing materials at the ISSSTE**

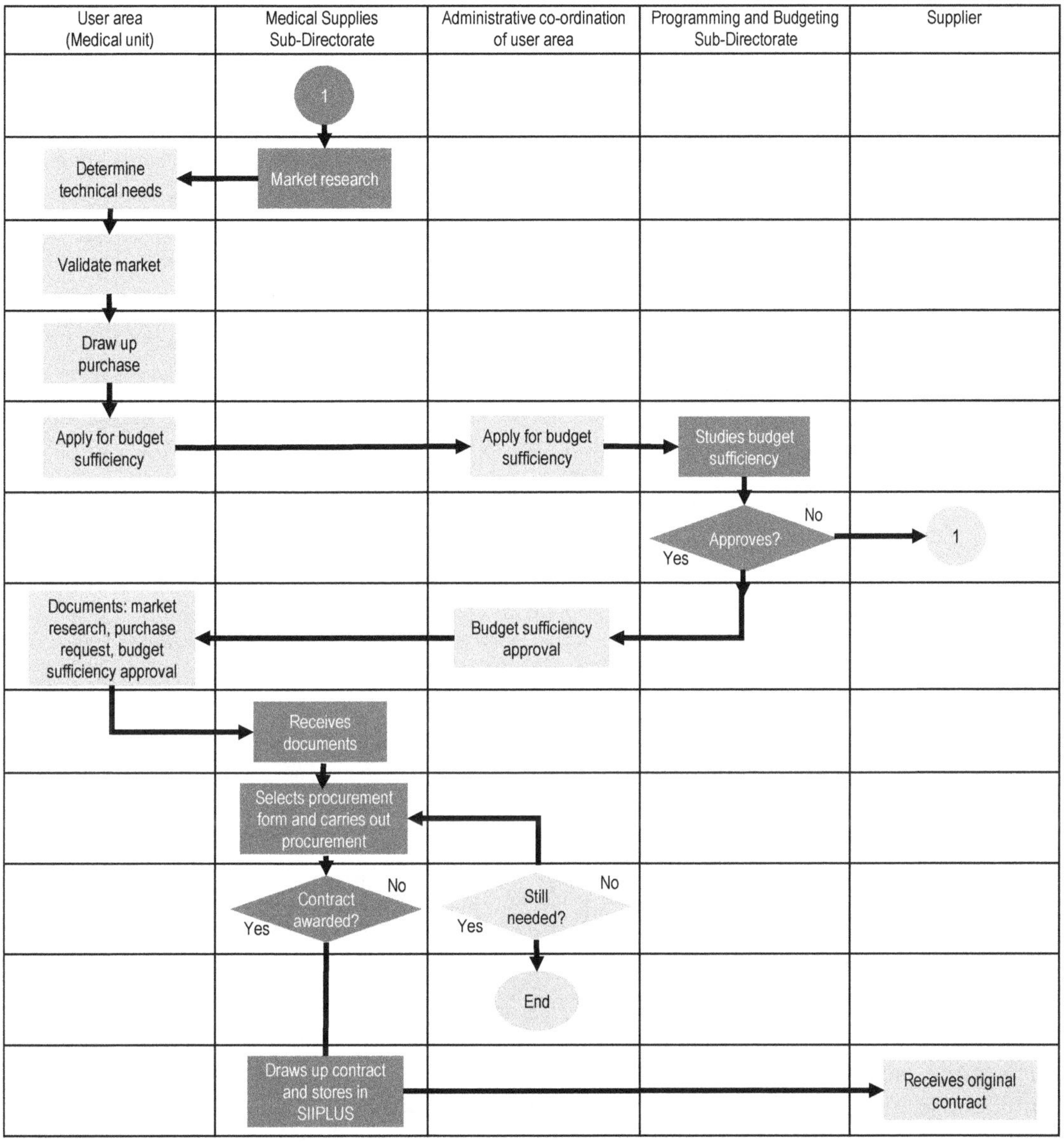

Source: Information provided by the ISSSTE.

Good relationships with suppliers is critical to procurement success

Early engagement with potential suppliers is vital to understanding the key issues before the procurement process begins and can be critical to its success. The OECD *Recommendation of the Council on Public Procurement* provides that countries should:

> …engage in transparent and regular dialogues with suppliers and business associations to present public procurement objectives and to assure a correct understanding of markets. Effective communication should be conducted to provide potential vendors with a better understanding of the country's needs, and government buyers with information to develop more realistic and effective tender specifications by better understanding market capabilities. Such interactions should be subject to

due fairness, transparency and integrity safeguards, which vary depending on whether an active procurement process is ongoing. (OECD, 2015)

Box 3.4. Reliance on healthcare experts by ChileCompra

The Chilean central purchasing body ChileCompra manages the country's electronic procurement system and runs procurement procedures (up to the awarding and signing of contracts) for agreements, particularly framework agreements, for commonly used goods and services.

ChileCompra's remit is to:

- increase competition for public contracts
- generate savings through economies of scale
- achieve advantageous commercial conditions
- standardise quality
- save time spent on procurement.

Although under no legal obligation to do so, ChileCompra conducts market research to improve its purchases. Despite its great buying expertise, however, it does not have specialists – doctors to inform medical suppliers, for example – in all market categories. It has therefore struck co-operation agreements with public bodies which can provide relevant sector knowledge – the Ministry of Health, for example, which assigns healthcare experts.

Healthcare professionals thus provide the technical know-how for purchasing at the stages of defining requirements and preparing tender documents as well as at the bid evaluation and contract award stages. Standardisation is a joint effort between the healthcare experts and ChileCompra, which ensures that non-necessary items are not bought. ChileCompra teams also pay actual visits to medical facilities – like haemodialysis centres – to understand their needs and objectives.

Source: Based on presentations at the OECD workshop on "Improving Public Procurement Practices in ISSSTE", Mexico City, 2-4 September 2014, by Marjorie Ramírez, former Head of Division of Framework Agreements at ChileCompra, the Chilean central purchasing body.

Obtaining information from suppliers could be done through written questions and answers or face-to-face meetings. Structuring interactions between public officials and suppliers is a priority in Mexico, in accordance with the "eight executive actions to prevent corruption and avoid conflicts of interest" announced by Mexico's Presidency in February 2015 (Presidency of Mexico, 2015). Executive action 4 provides that "protocols for contracts between individuals and public officials in charge of defining public procurement, licensing, concessions and permits procedures will be established".

Meetings should be structured and organised so as to yield maximum results (Box 3.5).

Procurement units should tread carefully when consulting suppliers so as not to distort competition. Operating transparently and creating an audit trail are important in this respect. It is useful, therefore, to design a template for recording and filing the results from meetings with a supplier. It might also prove valuable when procuring similar goods, services or works from similar markets in the future.

Box 3.5. Suggestions for structuring information meetings with suppliers

Some questions that should be borne in mind when meeting suppliers are:

- Are you interested in this opportunity? If not, why not?
- Is the business model realistic?
- Are the business aims realistic? Is the business attractive?
- What do you see as the risks?
- Can you give an early indication of cost, the chief cost drivers and how they can be minimised?
- Can you give a broad indication of the likely timescales for set-up and implementation?
- Are there other, better, approaches?
- What added value could the supplier provide?
- Are there examples of good or bad practice in the ways in which other organisations have tried to secure the same products or services and what can be done to ensure clarity and improve the outcome?

It is useful to meet different types of suppliers to inform strategic options, e.g. the views of small and medium-sized enterprises (SMEs) may be different from those of big companies.

Procurement officers should be present at meetings with suppliers. On the supplier side, someone with a grasp of requirements who can offer innovative solutions and constructive advice should be present. The right attitudes must be adopted: confidentiality, flexibility and openness.

The objective is to identify the desired procurement outcomes and risks. Communicating and meeting with suppliers also enables them to provide feedback on how the outcomes might be achieved, on issues as they see them, and on timescale, feasibility and affordability.

Output from supplier meetings helps shape requirements so that they match what the market is able to provide. The market can also be encouraged to evolve in directions that meet requirements in the future.

Source: Based on presentations by Steve Graham, Hadley Graham Ltd, advisors to United Kingdom's Department of Health at the OECD workshop on "Improving Public Procurement Practices in ISSSTE", Mexico City, 2-4 September 2014.

ChileCompra has adopted specific transparency measures to support its consultation process, level the playing field for suppliers, and mitigate the risk of improper dealings between officials and suppliers. Box 3.6 offers an example of how ChileCompra consults with suppliers.

Fact-finding missions revealed that individual suppliers and CANIFARMA would like to be contacted before tenders are issued and that they harboured concerns about the transparency and effectiveness of market research. CANIFARMA, for example, reported that some of the suppliers who submitted price quotes were possibly short on the requisite capacity or quality. Low quotes from suppliers unable to actually deliver the goods may lead to a false estimated price that no reliable supplier is willing or commercially able to compete for. The result may be that bidding fails and has to be restarted, or that a contract is awarded directly without competition.

Box 3.6. Suppliers' consultation initiatives by the Chilean central purchasing body ChileCompra: The way to transparency and effectiveness

Prior to issuing a tender, ChileCompra carries out an open consultation process with suppliers, which it announces on line at: www.mercadopublico.cl. The consultation aims to obtain information about prices, the characteristics of the required goods or services, the timeline needed to prepare bids and any other information that might contribute to a successful tendering process.

Also, following the online publication of a procurement notice (request for proposals), ChileCompra conducts roundtable meetings with suppliers, which are also announced on the website. The purpose of these meetings is to inform suppliers about the main goals of the procurement and guide them in how to place a bid. For purposes of transparency, ChileCompra records the meetings and uploads them to the same website, as a folder attached to the request for proposals, so that suppliers who were not at the meetings may be informed as well.

ChileCompra has, in addition, an online forum with questions and answers for each tender in advance of deadlines for submitting bids. The forum is particularly practical for providers who are geographically distant from the capital, Santiago (where ChileCompra's offices are located), and need remote access to questions and answers. Such an arrangement ensures transparency, equitable treatment and fair competition.

With such practices, ChileCompra has achieved a high level of transparency and effectiveness in its tenders.

Source: Based on presentations at the OECD workshop on "Improving Public Procurement Practices in ISSSTE", Mexico City, 2-4 September 2014, by Marjorie Ramírez, former Head of Division of Framework Agreements at ChileCompra, the Chilean central purchasing body.

CANIFARMA has also pointed out that some companies which quote prices may be foreign-based and lacking the capacity to deliver in Mexico. They may also be ineligible to bid under Mexico's rules on national preference in public procurement. Public bidding – the most widely used process in Mexico (the other two being invitations to at least three suppliers and direct awards, which are analysed in Chapter 5) – is open only to Mexican firms and for products that comprise more than 50% of local content. Local content is determined by considering manpower and components manufactured in Mexico, in accordance with Article 28 FR. I of the LAASSP. International bidding is allowed under certain conditions – e.g. when no domestic supplier exists or the procurement procedure has failed, or when it is compulsory under the terms of any international treaty to which Mexico is party, like the North-American Free Trade Agreement (NAFTA).

The ISSSTE meets regularly with industry groups and supplier associations, but such meetings focus chiefly on the difficulties encountered in the procurement process. It would be useful if their scope was widened and structured, as proposed above, to gain a better understanding of the market for specific products and services. Some decentralised units, like the Zona Poniente Delegation (Mexico City West), mentioned that they are in regular communication with suppliers to get to know the market better and improve their procurement planning. Indeed, the Zona Poniente Delegation is among those that have made the fewest direct awards, although it is not clear whether that is directly related to the practice of regularly consulting suppliers.

There is some resistance from procurement units to holding supplier consultations for fear of allegations of wrongdoing and breaching the LAASSP. However, according to the Ministry of Public Administration (*Secretaría de la Función Pública*, SFP; Ramos, 2014), such fears stem from a misinterpretation of the LAASSP which, in fact, encourages action to promote value for money in public purchases – such as meetings with suppliers and trade and professional associations. In this respect, clear, written guidelines and on-going managerial support would be beneficial. OECD countries like Norway have moved in this direction (Box 3.7).

Box 3.7. Ethical purchasing guidelines for public procurement officials in Norway

To help public procurement officers to carry out their tasks efficiently and in line with public goals as well as to increase citizens' trust in the integrity of procurement practices, the South-Eastern Norway Regional Health Authority has issued ethical guidelines for the procurement of goods and services and contacts with suppliers. Guideline 7 refers specifically to "relationships with suppliers and other business contacts" and contains guidance and examples of behaviour which may be considered to be inappropriate.

The guidelines apply to all employees of the South-Eastern Norway Regional Health Authority, including all subsidiaries, subdivisions and Board members or elected representatives. Managers have the responsibility to ensure that their employees are familiar with and act in compliance with the guidelines. The guidelines lay down minimum requirements. Laws, regulations, internal rules and industry-specific ethical guidelines also apply.

Source: South-Eastern Norway Regional Health Authority (2012), "Ethical guidelines", available at: www.helse-sorost.no/omoss_/english_/Sider/ethical-guidelines.aspx (accessed 27 January 2015).

Market outreach can help to drive innovation

Market outreach – developing good market knowledge and consulting with suppliers and suppliers' associations openly and honestly – offers the ISSSTE opportunities for shaping the market and encouraging innovation. Yet ISSSTE staff told the OECD that they were uncertain of the added value of innovation. Likewise, most of the ISSSTE's suppliers stated that they did not invest in research and innovation or in the development of new products as they believed that the investment would be a waste of money, since the ISSSTE neither specifies innovative products nor grants them preference in its procurement procedures. As mentioned above, most contracts are awarded on the basis of price, not through weighted points-and-percentages technical assessments. The market thus has little incentive for investing in innovation which, although it may add value, also increases the cost of the final product. Yet CANIFARMA stressed during the fact-finding mission that innovative products and services can improve the quality and efficiency of health services and, ultimately, bring savings.

When suppliers bring to market a new product, they sometimes contact the ISSSTE's medical units to present it, so affording valuable insights into how the market is evolving. These contacts are not, however, conducted in a regular structured manner, recorded or made public. Also, suppliers often approach medical units in a random way as they are not sure whom to contact.

The concept of fostering innovation through procurement is not new and some countries have been pursuing policies to that end for decades. A number of OECD governments have recently given renewed impetus to using procurement as a way of encouraging innovation. The United Kingdom, for instance, has actively sought to integrate procurement for innovation across government since 2003. Germany, too, has introduced the Agreement on Public Procurement of Innovation. Under the terms of the agreement, six federal ministries (Interior, Economics, Defence, Transport, Environment, and Research) publish long-term demand forecasts, engage in continuous market analysis to identify potential new solutions, offer professional training on legal options for promoting innovation, and foster a strategic dialogue and the sharing of experience between procuring agencies, end users and industry. Finland, the Netherlands and Spain all operate programmes for innovation through procurement, and it is reported that Austria might spend up to EUR 2 billion a year to that end. Legislation to support the procurement of innovation is also in place in France, while the United States was estimated to be spending approximately USD 50 billion a year on the procurement of R&D services (OECD, 2014).

A 2012 survey by the OECD suggests that while most OECD countries seek to use procurement for innovation in some way, only a few had set aside a separate budget for that purpose (Figure 3.6). Nevertheless, many had at some point used performance-based tender specifications to encourage innovation, given guidance to procurement officers, or involved suppliers at an early stage in the tender process to foster innovation.

Figure 3.6. **Use of procurement to promote innovation**

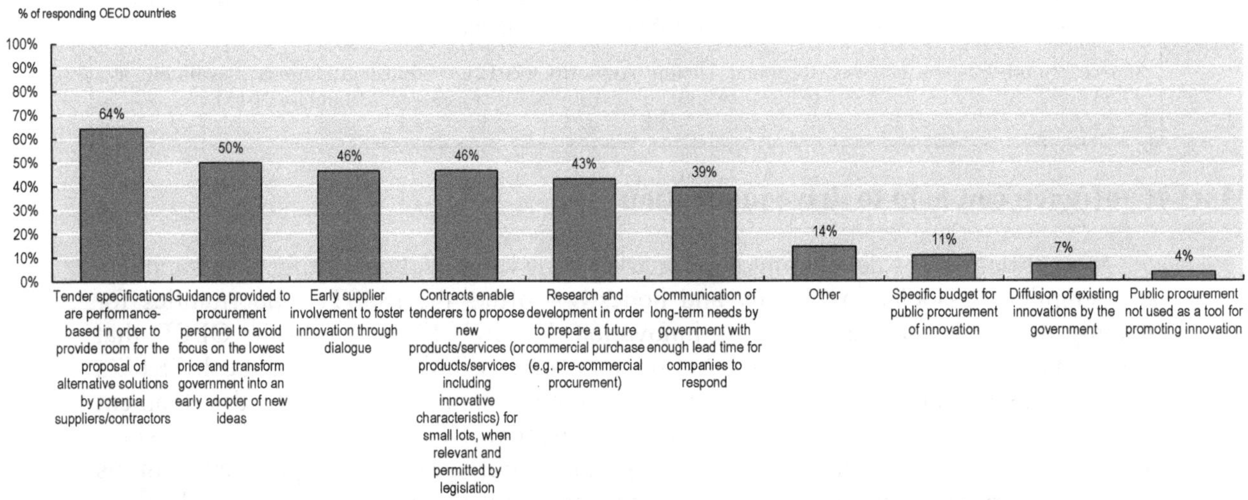

Source: OECD (2014), "Intelligent demand: Policy rationale, design and potential benefits", *OECD Science, Technology and Industry Policy Papers*, No. 13, OECD Publishing, Paris, http://dx.doi.org/10.1787/5jz8p4rk3944-en.

The European Union also supports the use of public procurement to buy innovative products, works and services. Innovation is formally acknowledged as playing a key role in improving the efficiency and quality of public services, achieving value for public money, and producing wider economic, environmental and societal benefits. The new EU Directive on Public Procurement recommends that public authorities make the best of strategic use of public procurement to spur innovation (Box 3.8).

Procurement provides the ISSSTE with the opportunity to nudge the market towards meeting its requirements in new ways and to provide services that are at the forefront of developments.

Box 3.8. Innovation in public procurement in the European Union

EU Directive 2014/24/EU of 26 February 2014 on Public Procurement sets forth principles and procedures which should be followed by suppliers and by the public authorities in the member states of the European Union in the course of the procurement of works, goods or services.

The directive is part of a wider European Union legislative package on public procurement and concessions. It seeks to:

- create a modern public procurement legislative framework
- ensure public procurement efficiency and value for money
- simplify rules and make them more flexible
- reduce the administrative burden on public authorities and contractors
- facilitate the participation of small and medium-sized enterprises
- stimulate greater competition across the European single market
- switch to electronic procurement
- promote innovation and contribute to a better use of resources.

The directive defines innovation as the implementation of a new or significantly improved product, service or process, including but not limited to production, building or construction processes; a new marketing method; or a new organisational method in business practices, workplace organisation or external relations. In short, innovation is the process of generating new ideas and translating them into innovative output.

To promote the use of public procurement to support innovation, the directive establishes a new procedure, called the "Innovation Partnership". It allows a public authority to enter into a structured partnership with a supplier with the objective of developing an innovative product, service or works not available on the market and thereafter purchasing the outcome.

The aim of the scheme is to enable public and private organisations to work in partnership towards a shared goal without foreclosing the market and to reward successful solutions by allowing public authorities to buy them. Innovation partnerships should be structured to provide the necessary "market pull" and incentivise the development of an innovative solution.

The directive also recommends that innovation should be promoted by technical specifications that express, as far as possible, functional and performance-related requirements. The requirements should be sufficiently precisely specified to allow bidding suppliers to determine what the contract is for and to allow contracting authorities to compare bids and award the contract.

Lastly, to promote suppliers' creativity and make procurement more flexible, the directive states that public authorities should, as often as possible, encourage variant bids. To that end, they should specify that they welcome variants, but must first spell out in their procurement documents the minimum requirement that suppliers' bids should meet. The criteria on which contracts are awarded should be applicable to fully compliant bids and to variants which meet minimum requirements.

Source: European Commission (2014), "Directive 2014/24/EU of the European Parliament and of the Council of 26 February 2014 on Public Procurement and repealing Directive 2004/18/EC", *Journal of the European Union*, http://eur-lex.europa.eu/legal-content/EN/TXT/?uri=celex:32014L0024

Market intelligence brings savings, consolidation and long-term contracts

Market intelligence not only fosters innovation, it can be used to improve business in other ways, too. A decentralised procurement unit in the ISSSTE used market analysis to shape requirements in a way that generated savings (Box 3.9).

Box 3.9. Exploring supply solutions to generate savings: Photocopy services in the Delegation of Oaxaca

In 2014, the Delegation of Oaxaca carried out an assessment of its photocopy, printing and scanning requirements against the number of computers and printers available. The Procurement Unit, in co-ordination with the IT Department, used this information to determine the number of multifunctional stations required per area within the delegation. The outcome of the analysis was that 708 network nodes were needed to connect the delegation's computers. Once it had established its needs, the Procurement Unit carried out market research for solutions that met its needs. Drawing on the information that it had collected and analysed, the delegation initiated a procurement process that led to it leasing 53 multifunctional stations. As a result, the Oaxaca Delegation cut the overall cost of its photocopy expenditure, as shown in Table 3.2.

Table 3.2. Monthly expenditure on photocopies and savings

Monthly expenditure on photocopies in 2013	Monthly expenditure on photocopies in 2014	Monthly savings	Annual savings
MXN 53 682	MXN 44 967	MXN 8 715	MXN 104 582
Monthly expenditure in toner, 2013	Monthly expenditure in toner, 2014	Monthly savings	Annual savings
MXN 123 421	MXN 80 713	MXN 42 707	MXN 512 494
There were no more preventive and corrective maintenance expenses. The annual unit cost of the service is approximately MXN 2 000 per printer. The delegation has 346 printers			Annual savings of MXN 692 000

Thanks to its market research, the Oaxaca Delegation leases multifunctional stations. They have enabled it to:

- Control its use of paper and consumables.
- Reduce its electricity bill (the stations are in standby mode when not in use).
- Cut the use of printing and photocopy services since staff now have to walk to the printing station. (It is estimated that the distance deterrent has led to annual savings of MXN 1 309 076).

Source: Information provided by the Delegation of Oaxaca.

Market analysis has also helped OECD member countries to identify categories of procurement expenditure that are conducive to consolidation and joint procurement or where, inversely, aggregation would be detrimental to competition. Ireland, for example, analysed purchase demands and supply conditions, which enabled it to target 50 categories of procurement expenditure where it can make savings (Box 3.10).

On the basis of supply and demand analysis, the ISSSTE, too, could identify opportunities for procurement through multi-annual contracts or framework agreements, like the ones put in place by the Chilean central purchasing body ChileCompra (Box 3.11). ChileCompra uses its market knowledge to break down agreements into smaller jobs that can be undertaken by small and medium-sized enterprises (SMEs).

Box 3.10. Market analysis helps identify categories for action in Ireland

Ireland established its National Procurement Service (NPS) in 2009 as part of an effort to secure value for money in the procurement of goods and services. The NPS takes a strategic approach to public procurement – particularly through the aggregation of purchases across government departments, agencies and the non-commercial state sector in order to reduce prices paid for goods and services. Drawing on supply and demand analysis, the NPS has identified 50 categories of procurement expenditure where it can intervene most effectively to get more for its money. Intervention may involve aggregating demand to leverage public sector buying power, designating and supporting lead procurement organisations for particular categories (e.g. pharmaceuticals, catering or security) and facilitating collaboration among public purchasers. In 2012, the NPS had 40 national frameworks in place for high-spend requirements with a total value of over EUR 400 million.

The NPS is governed by a board of senior procurement stakeholders chaired by a minister of state with responsibility for public sector reform. An advisory panel of three procurement experts (two of whom are from the private sector) ensures access to leading-edge procurement practices and market developments.

Savings across all focus areas of the NPS have been achieved with a combination of price reductions, administrative efficiencies and demand management.

Source: OECD (2013b), *Implementing the OECD Principles for Integrity in Public Procurement: Progress since 2008*, OECD Public Governance Reviews, OECD Publishing, Paris, http://dx.doi.org/10.1787/9789264201385-en.

Box 3.11. ChileCompra experience in framework agreements

ChileCompra awards framework agreements for common products and services needed by the Chilean public sector. Each framework agreement typically covers a range of products and/or services within the same category (e.g. office supplies broken down by item) which can be offered by several suppliers throughout the country. The framework agreements set the terms (technical characteristics, quantities, price, delivery, guarantees, payment deadlines, etc.) for the purchases. The supplier handles warehousing and distribution.

Agreements are divided into smaller regional lots so as to ensure delivery in all regions through suppliers who have the capacity to deliver regionally and to support SMEs who may only be able to supply small quantities. ChileCompra is able to divide contracts into smaller lots because its market research has yielded the knowledge it needs to do so.

ChileCompra has currently 35 such contracts for more than 95 000 products and services in which more than 1 500 suppliers participate. Seven of the contracts cover the following health products and services:

- healing materials
- haemodialysis, peritoneal dialysis for adults and children
- medicines (ended in December 2014)
- medicines II
- orthotics, prosthetics and endo-prosthetics
- additional life insurance with health and dental insurance
- compulsory personal accident insurance.

Box 3.11. **ChileCompra experience in framework agreements** (*cont.*)

All agreements are placed in an electronic marketplace created by ChileCompra. Any public entity that needs a product or service places a purchase order on the marketplace, receives the supplies and pays the suppliers directly. In the case of framework agreements with many suppliers, the buyer selects the final supplier, following the terms and conditions of the agreement. Clauses in agreements provide for discounts for large volumes of purchases, or bulk buying. Since purchase orders are placed online, the discount is calculated automatically through filters in the system.

All agreements are published online at: www.mercadopublico.cl.

Source: Presentations at the OECD workshop on "Improving Public Procurement Practices in ISSSTE", Mexico City, 2-4 September 2014, by Marjorie Ramírez, former Head of Division of Framework Agreements at ChileCompra, the Chilean central purchasing body.

Setting up a market intelligence service

The ISSSTE is aware of the challenges addressed in this chapter and there is a general consensus at all levels of the institute – as well as among external stakeholders – that shortcomings in market intelligence are one of the biggest challenges that it encounters in procurement (OECD, 2013b).

As a result, market intelligence is an area which, in recent years, has been the subject of an on-going process of organisational redesign at the central level. Acting on recommendations in the first OECD public procurement review as well as the OECD report on fighting bid rigging in the ISSSTE (OECD, 2013b; 2013c), the ISSSTE moved in 2012 to put in place a market intelligence team within the Medical Supplies Sub-Directorate. In 2014, it consisted of four officials, three of whom carry out market intelligence activities and one who deals with administration (Horta, 2014). Although it is not formally defined or incorporated in the ISSSTE's organisational structure, its creation was an important step in the right direction.

The Market Intelligence Unit has drafted a questionnaire on items that should be evaluated in a market research process and which it sent to suppliers. It is also grouping data on the origins of goods, the size of companies, their supply and delivery capacity, and their financial solvency. For the time being, the focus is on medicines only.

The unit, although successful, cannot provide full support to the ISSSTE, even at central level. The reasons are:

- The lack of sufficient human, material and IT resources.
- The sheer volume of requests for support which it needs to prioritise and sequence and which prevent it from responding to all of the requests.
- A budget that does not currently allow it to hire additional, experienced staff.
- There is no central institutional database from which the Market Research Unit can draw information. It is therefore compelled to base its analyses on the historical data that it started to collect when it was created in 2012.

Strengthening the Market Research Unit should be a priority for the ISSSTE. It should take steps to formalise the unit, sequence its roll-out, select staff with the right job profiles to support it and determine its priority tasks.

The ISSSTE should also build on the experience and expertise of its human resources and create a network of procurement officials specialised in market research. Central and decentralised areas could designate people from their own staff, who would then be trained by the officials in the Medical Supplies Sub-Directorate's Market Intelligence Unit. This network could meet at regular intervals either in person or remotely to share experiences, practices and tasks with a view to improving their effectiveness.

Currently the ISSSTE is reviewing the real consumption of medicines in its medical units. It should develop a robust database that brings together expenditure and needs information from all medical areas to inform and guide the work of market intelligence. It is one of the key demands of the staff currently working in market intelligence at the ISSSTE. The database could be made available to all procurement units within the ISSSTE and develop into a valuable source of market intelligence across the organisation.

Annex 3.A1 sets out an action plan with recommendations for strengthening the ISSSTE's market intelligence capability and formalising the Market Intelligence Unit by building on the team already in place in the Medical Supplies Sub-Directorate. The recommendations highlight the importance of internal and external market intelligence, the need to build a stronger organisational structure for the market intelligence team, the key role played by the market intelligence activity and the value of its output.

The action plan – like the one for creating a Procurement Co-ordination Unit – may be implemented in stages. Implementing the plan is predicated on the availability of human and financial resources, as well as internal and external approval.

Proposals for action

- Develop a market intelligence methodology and plan, assessing human and material resources required for market intelligence across the ISSSTE and including method variations according to the degree of critical importance or complexity of procurement (priority).
- Formalise the Market Intelligence Unit in the Medical Supplies Sub-Directorate insofar as the available human and financial resources and approvals make it feasible (medium term action).
- Work with other healthcare providers and healthcare expects to pool knowledge (immediate action).
- Consult on line and in person with suppliers on an established, structured footing, and record such contacts (immediate action).
- Increase the use of the weighted point-and-percentage evaluation system for purchases that are not commodities (immediate action).
- Consider using external market research consultants for limited high-cost expenditure items while gradually developing in-house capacity (immediate action).
- Strengthen data collection (immediate/medium-term action).
- Select people with the appropriate skills to create an informal network procurement officials, and ask staff in the Medical Supplies Sub-Directorate's Market Intelligence Unit to train the network of procurement officials (medium-term action).

- Use procurement to promote innovation and develop new solutions (long-term action).
- Allow alternative solutions and variants – as far as is possible under the applicable framework – to promote suppliers' creativity and seek the assistance of the Ministry of Public Administration (SFP) in interpreting the law (long-term action).

Notes

1. FO-CON-05, included in the General Procurement Manual.

2. Presentations made at the OECD workshop on "Improving Public Procurement Practices in ISSSTE", 2-4 September 2014, Mexico City, by experts from Chile, Denmark, Portugal and the United Kingdom.

References

European Commission (2014), "Directive 2014/24/EU of the European Parliament and of the Council of 26 February 2014 on public procurement and repealing Directive 2004/18/EC", *Journal of the European Union*, http://eur-lex.europa.eu/legal-content/EN/TXT/PDF/?uri=CELEX:32014L0024&from=EN.

Graham, S. (2014), Hadley Graham Ltd, advisors to United Kingdom's Department of Health, presentation at the OECD workshop on "Improving Public Procurement Practices in ISSSTE", Mexico City, 2-4 September.

Horta, M. (2014), Sub-Director of Medical Supplies, presentation at the OECD workshop on "Improving Public Procurement Practices in ISSSTE", Mexico City, 2-4 September.

OECD (2015), *Recommendation of the Council on Public Procurement*, OECD, Paris, available at: http://acts.oecd.org/Instruments/ShowInstrumentView.aspx?InstrumentID=320&InstrumentPID=348&Lang=en&Book=False.

OECD (2014), "Intelligent demand: Policy rationale, design and potential benefits", *OECD Science, Technology and Industry Policy Papers*, No. 13, OECD Publishing, Paris, http://dx.doi.org/10.1787/5jz8p4rk3944-en.

OECD (2013a), *Colombia: Implementing Good Governance*, OECD Public Governance Reviews, OECD Publishing, Paris, http://dx.doi.org/10.1787/9789264202177-en.

OECD (2013b), *Implementing the OECD Principles for Integrity in Public Procurement: Progress since 2008*, OECD Public Governance Reviews, OECD Publishing, Paris, http://dx.doi.org/10.1787/9789264201385-en.

OECD (2013c), "Fighting bid rigging in public procurement in Mexico: A Secretariat analytical report on legislation, regulations and practices relating to procurement undertaken by ISSSTE", OECD, Paris, available at: www.oecd.org/daf/competition/mexicoissste2013.htm.

Presidency of Mexico (2015), "8 acciones ejecutivas para prevenir la corrupción ("Eight executive actions to prevent corruption"), 3 February, available at: www.presidencia.gob.mx/8-acciones-ejecutiivas-para-prevenir-la-corrupcion/?ref=relacionadas.

Ramírez, M. (2014), former Head of Division of Framework Agreements at ChileCompra, presentation at the OECD workshop on "Improving Public Procurement Practices in ISSSTE", Mexico City, 2-4 September.

Ramos, A.L. (2014), Head of the Public Procurement Policy Unit, Mexican Ministry of Public Administration (SFP), presentation at the OECD workshop on "Improving Public Procurement Practices in ISSSTE", Mexico City, 2-4 September.

SFP (2010), "Lineamientos para la aplicación del criterio de evaluación de proposiciones a través del mecanismo de puntos o porcentajes en los procedimientos de contratación" ("Guidelines for the application of evaluation criteria through the points and percentages system in tender procedures"), *Diario Oficial de la federación*, 9 September, Secretaría de la Función Pública, available at: www.funcionpublica.gob.mx/unaopspf/doctos/comunes/dof09-09-2010_C2.pdf (accessed 14 September 2014).

South-Eastern Norway Regional Health Authority (2012), "Ethical guidelines", available at: www.helse-sorost.no/omoss_/english_/Sider/ethical-guidelines.aspx (accessed 27 January 2015).

Further reading

National Health System Leadership Academy (2013), "Healthcare leadership model: The nine dimensions of leadership behaviour", version 1.0, NHS Leadership Academy, Leeds, West Yorkshire, England, available at: www.leadershipacademy.nhs.uk/wp-content/uploads/dlm_uploads/2014/10/NHSLeadership-LeadershipModel-colour.pdf (accessed 24 February 2015).

Annex 3.A1
Action Plan for a Market Intelligence Unit

The action plan for a Market Intelligence Unit is based on recommendations from the first OECD public procurement review of the ISSSTE (OECD, 2013) and on fact-finding and communications between the ISSSTE and the OECD in the course of 2014.

A Market Intelligence Unit is crucial to supporting the inward- and outward-facing key roles and outputs of the procurement function. The unit will draw on information from activity data generated within the ISSSTE as well as from markets' and suppliers' data and will rely upon the quality of such data. Accordingly, consideration should be given to the use of interoperable standards that improve data quality over time.

When the ISSSTE creates its Market Intelligence Unit, it should give thought to whether all market intelligence actions should be undertaken by the in-house team, an external service provider or a combination of the two. Like many procurement activities, market intelligence can benefit from scale. As the ISSSTE is establishing its internal Market Intelligence Unit, it is worth considering whether it could be supplemented by specialist external market intelligence support so that additional capacity and capability can be harnessed to meet peaks in demand or address skills shortages.

This proposed action plan envisages a small core central team that could draw on the experience and expertise of the four-strong Market Research Unit currently working within the ISSSTE's Sub-Directorate of Medical Supplies. The current unit could thus remain and be formalised and reinforced, in terms of capacities and skills as well as financial and technical resources, in accordance with the detailed proposals contained in this action plan.

Internal intelligence

An essential source of information is the transaction data generated by each of the ISSSTE's healthcare areas (central medical units, delegations' medical units and hospitals). It can be gathered by frequently and routinely extracting procurement transaction data from accounts-payable and purchase order systems, then transferring the data electronically to the Market Intelligence Unit for analysis. Where a healthcare unit does not have electronic systems to record transactions, it should be required to implement software to avoid any need to manually gather transaction information.

Transaction data will enable the analysis of procurement activity at the healthcare unit level and, by merging the data through a suitable software application, prices can then be compared across all healthcare areas in the ISSSTE and with those of other healthcare providers, like the Mexican Institute of Social Security (*Instituto Mexicano del Seguro Social*, IMSS).

Without data standards in place, identical goods and services will be described and coded differently by different healthcare units and the Market Intelligence Unit will initially have to spend time extracting, cleansing and mapping data. With suitable software, data extracts can be automated and mapping tables, once created, can be applied to the data extracts, enabling them to be aggregated. Mapping tables are used to take a description or code from an extract and map it to the correct description or code. Mapping is a requirement for both supplier and product information: it enables expenditure by supplier and by product to be consistently and repeatedly identified and aggregated.

Data extraction and cleansing can be done in-house, outsourced or both. Outside commercial operators could supplement an internal team, shortening the time needed to produce useful information. The cleansing work will taper out over time. Eventually it will be required only as part of maintenance and for previously unmapped goods and services, so minimising and even eliminating dependency upon external support.

Clean and consistent data then need to be turned into information and then into "actionable intelligence". Here, the value-adding contribution of the Market Intelligence Unit will come into its own. It will analyse data and provide specific, tailored information outputs to the relevant procurement teams, together with insights into that information. These insights produce the actionable intelligence that supports each procurement activity.

To meet the burgeoning demand for transparency in public procurement, all or part of the internal intelligence gathered by the Market Intelligence Unit can be made publicly available through a suitable web-enabled medium – like that used by the National Health Service (NHS) in the United Kingdom.

Box 3.A1.1. Transparency in the National Health Service in the United Kingdom

As part of its transparency agenda, the NHS makes compulsory the publication of line-level procurement expenditure data by healthcare providers. A copy of its Procurement Transparency guidance can be found at: www.gov.uk/government/uploads/system/uploads/attachment_data/file/299137/Transparency_Guidance_Effective_1_April_2014.pdf.

Source: Procurement, Investment & Commercial Division (2014a), "Procurement transparency", National Health Service, Department of Health, London, March.

Examples of how internal intelligence can be used

Sourcing

In sourcing, actionable intelligence will identify where healthcare areas use multiple competing products and services. The sourcing team will thus be able to commence standardisation and rationalisation activity across all of the ISSSTE's procurement units. Once a mandatory range of products and services has been defined, the Market Intelligence Unit will be able to identify any non-compliance, enabling corrective action to be taken with the non-compliant ISSSTE purchases.

Market intelligence insights will reveal trends in the consumption of certain goods and services and in volumes bought from specific suppliers. It might transpire that there is a need to find new suppliers or groom existing suppliers to boost competition.

Purchasing

In purchasing, spotting consumption trends will improve contract management and enable a course of action. If, for example, intelligence reveals that a healthcare area's volume of activity is growing and its use of clinical devices is increasing accordingly, the purchasing team can use the intelligence to renegotiate prices.

Logistics

As for logistics, insights into consumption trends will enable inventory managers to identify new goods and services that need to be brought under the control of inventory management, and to inform delivery and distribution scheduling arrangements.

External intelligence

Internal intelligence takes data from the healthcare units for analysis within a single unit or comparison with other units. Conversely, external intelligence takes data and information gathered from outside the ISSSTE.

External market analysis includes supplier analysis and horizon scanning to identify future trends, developments and innovations against which the Market Intelligence Unit can produce briefing reports for the procurement teams, particularly in relation to goods and service that are new to the market or will shortly be coming to market.

As with internal intelligence, outsourcing has a part to play. External providers can provide useful additional capacity and capability and international providers can undertake overnight work when intelligence is urgently needed. Outside consultants may also be able to employ market and product category experts, so enriching market intelligence and complementing the ISSSTE's internal input.

Examples of how external intelligence can be used

Sourcing

External comparisons can show how different organisations use alternative goods and services for the greater benefit of patients and taxpayers. Such intelligence will provide sourcing teams with powerful information for standardising and rationalising the product ranges that the ISSSTE uses. Knowledge of innovative technologies can, for example, inform internal discussions on introducing new products that yield better healthcare outcomes.

Purchasing

Market intelligence is critical to the development of procurement and competition strategies. Internal intelligence will help assess demand and external intelligence supply market capacity and capability. An understanding of prices paid will inform the development of pricing strategies within the competitive bidding process, while the ability to interpret financial data is valuable for identifying supplier risk.

Logistics

External benchmarking reveals trends in cost-cutting methodologies, such as vendor-managed inventory or radio-frequency identification technologies.

The role of standards

Data quality is critical to the ability of a market intelligence unit to provide insight and analysis. The adoption of standards by healthcare units will improve the quality of data from within the ISSSTE and provide the basis for comparison with prices paid by other organisations. Systems with globally unique goods and services codes enable organisations to consistently identify them. Using standards within purchase order and inventory management systems increases supply chain efficiency and patient safety, and lays the foundations for accurate expenditure analysis. The NHS in the United Kingdom has made the use of uniformly applied standards mandatory.

Box 3.A1.2. **The use of standards by the National Health Service**

As part of its national e-procurement strategy, the NHS requires healthcare providers to use GS1 standards. The strategy also includes the development of a national spend analysis service, which acts as a source of data for market intelligence activity. The *NHS eProcurement Strategy* can be found at: www.gov.uk/government/publications/nhs-e-procurement-strategy.

Source: Procurement, Investment & Commercial Division (2014b), *NHS eProcurement Strategy*, National Health Service, Department of Health, London, April.

How the Market Intelligence Unit would be organised

The size of the Market Intelligence Unit's staff and its level of skill will depend to some degree on the available budget. As suggested, the Market Intelligence Unit could be an extension of the Market Research Unit currently working under the Sub-Directorate of Medical Supplies, formalised and reinforced in accordance with the detailed proposals contained in this action plan.

For an organisation of the size of the ISSSTE, the Market Intelligence Unit may need a team organised in line with Figure 3.A1.1.

Figure 3.A1.1. **How the Market Intelligence Unit might be structured**

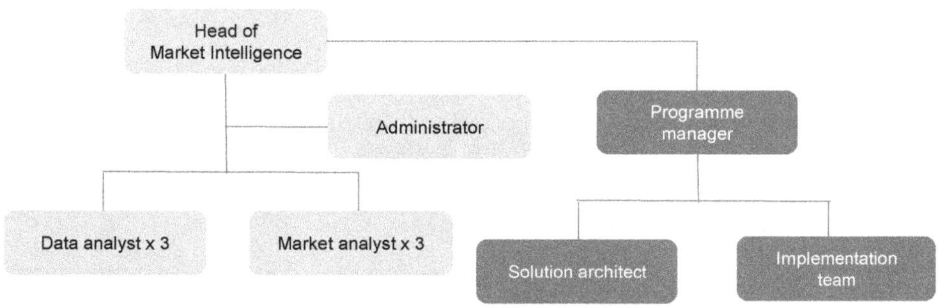

Note: Light blue denotes how the Market Intelligence Unit would be permanently structured. Dark blue designates temporary roles that may be required to put the unit in place.

The unit's permanent core staff would essentially comprise a head of unit, an administrative manager, and market and data analysts. All would require high levels of skills (Table 3.A1.1).

Table 3.A1.1. **Proposal for the Market Intelligence Unit's core staff and their duties**

Title/job	Full-time equivalents	High-level duties
Head of Unit	1.0	Responsible for overall service delivery
Administrator	1.0	Support the market intelligence team
Market analysts	3.0	Analyse data and produce reports and recommendations
Data analysts	3.0	Analyse data and develop reports and recommendations

- The Head of Unit will interact with the procurement teams to define their requirements and work with healthcare areas to agree which data can be gathered (like transaction data from local systems, i.e. purchase orders and invoice data). The Head of Unit will also need to work with healthcare areas to address issues of data quality and standards. If external market intelligence service providers are appointed by the ISSSTE, then he or she will manage them.
- The data analysts will focus on extracting internal data from the systems used by healthcare areas. Initially, their work will primarily be to process the data extracts and create data mapping tables, supported by external providers where appropriate. Once the data management arrangements have been established, the analysts can then move on to providing analysis for the procurement team.
- The market analysts will move quickly to support the procurement teams on an agreed set of requirements and expectations. Such requirements would be established on the basis of discussions between the market analysts about what is feasible and with the procurement team about what is desirable. It is important to arrive at an agreement that sets realistic expectations as to the level of detail (which may be limited by data quality) and the market analysis team's response rates.
- The role of the administrator will be to support the team and interact with healthcare areas and any external analytics providers to ensure the timely flow of information.

Altogether, though, the Market Intelligence Unit will need to draw on the high-level skills of a larger team of professionals with various roles and responsibilities – see the section on "High-level job descriptions" below.

Additional Market Intelligence Unit duties

The team could also support the co-ordination of procurement activities by, for example, creating and maintaining a contracts database. Through the business intelligence reviewed and analysis produced, the unit would be able to recommend purchasing strategies such as aggregating demand.

Building and developing the unit should be underpinned by these two questions:

- How will information from the sub-directorates be co-ordinated so that the Market Intelligence Unit provides information that meets the ISSSTE's needs?
- How will output and completed market analysis be transmitted to the sub-directorates and how will such intelligence support purchasing strategies?

One response to both questions might be to think about developing an online collaborative portal that would facilitate access to and the sharing of information and help to gather and collate needs.

The sub-directorates should provide details of their needs to ensure that analysis is focused on supporting them where they need it most. In that way, they will also help the Market Intelligence Unit to provide advice and guidance on the co-ordination of procurement activities.

Staffing the Market Intelligence Unit

To support the roll-out of the market intelligence service, additional human resources may well be required, as Table 3.A1.2 shows. They include a Programme Manager, Solutions Architect, an implementation team and staff that can be seconded from other departments.

Table 3.A1.2. **Additional staff that may be needed to roll out the Market Intelligence Unit**

Job title	Full-time equivalents	High-level duties/notes
Programme Manager	1.0	To support set-up and implementation
Solution Architect	1.0	To provide detailed technical expertise
Project Support Officer	1.0	To provide project management support
Implementation team	To be determined	For planning and implementation (Staff numbers will depend on the scale of the task and resources available)
Procurement team		
Resources from human resources		
Resources from IT	Ad hoc	To support roll-out of the activities
Resources from finance		
Resources for business cases		

- The Programme Manager will have overall responsibility for setting up and delivering the Market Intelligence Unit.
- The Solutions Architect will determine the technical infrastructure and software requirements needed to operate the Market Intelligence Service. He or she will also identify appropriate data sources and determine how data can be gathered at a central access point.
- A number of resources from other functions like finance, IT and human resources will also be required. The procurement teams may also have to contribute by buying services or solutions needed to get the unit up and running.
- One of the most important tasks in establishing the Market Intelligence Unit will be to engage with the procurement teams to identify their requirements, work with them to develop reporting and explain how it can help them. Change management, too, will be called for to introduce the new behaviours and processes that may be needed to embed the Market Intelligence Unit in day-to-day procurement activities.
- The implementation managers have a critical role to play in developing relationships and agreeing on work plans. In the future, there may also be an on-going role for a customer management function to ensure that the Market Intelligence Unit's output meets the procurement teams' requirements and delivers value.

Key deliverables

Table 3.A1.3. **List of deliverables and Forecast completion date**

Deliverables	Forecast completion date
Engage with teams across the ISSSTE to develop the requirements	2-3 months
Appoint a Programme Lead	2-3 months
Determine the requirements for the Market Intelligence Unit	2-3 months
Develop any business cases required	2-3 months
Recruitment for the programme	2-3 months
Procure infrastructure, for example business intelligence software	6-9 months
Build and develop the business intelligence solutions, including databases	4-6 months
Test solutions during development with procurement teams	4-6 months
Implement solution and deliver training	6-12 months

High-demand vacancies for high-level professionals

If the high-demand, highly skilled positions that would need to be filled to create the Market Intelligence Unit were advertised, they would read something like the profiles below.

Head of Market Intelligence Service

The Head of the Market Intelligence Service is responsible for the overall business, service delivery and management of the team. This includes setting and agreeing work plans, ensuring the timely delivery of analysis and reports, co-ordinating communications and stakeholder engagement.

- Responsibilities:
  - communicating and developing relationships with clients (sub-directorates)
  - developing and managing work plans and budgets
  - formulating analysis plans
  - scheduling and co-ordinating internal and external resources
  - overseeing projects and reviewing data quality and written recommendation reports.
- Requirements:
  - excellent organisational skills with a particular eye for detail
  - outstanding listening and communication skills, both written and oral
  - desire to learn and work with others
  - ability to develop and meet schedules
  - expertise with Word, Excel and the Internet
  - extensive market intelligence/research experience.

Market Analyst

The Market Analyst is principally responsible for interpreting data, formulating reports and making recommendations based upon research findings. To accomplish those tasks, he or she works with data analysts and with buyers to interpret data in a meaningful way and to support the development of procurement strategies. The Market Analyst applies qualitative and quantitative techniques to interpret data and produce substantiated recommendations. He or she presents findings and recommendations to the buyer.

- Responsibilities:
  - communicating with buyers to understand and document the business objectives
  - formulating analysis plans
  - working with data analysts to review information
  - analysing published data and statistics
  - assessing future trends
  - authoring reports containing actionable recommendations
  - making presentations – answering questions and instilling confidence.
- Requirements:
  - a minimum of three to five years in market research
  - one to three years of sector experience
  - strong analytic and critical thinking skills
  - good written and oral communication skills and presentation ability
  - expertise with Excel, Word and PowerPoint
  - appropriate level qualification in business, mathematics or the sciences.

Data Analyst

The Data Analyst has responsibility for ensuring the information from systems and databases flow to create a central access point and will identify, where necessary, software solutions that are required, making sure that the integrity of the available data is maintained. Data analysts will work closely with market analysts to ensure that the required information is being sourced.

- Responsibilities:
  - ensuring that data sources flow to central access points
  - building solutions for running reports both generic and bespoke
  - formulating analysis plans
  - working with market analysts to review information.
- Requirements:
  - programming skills
  - expertise in database design
  - strong analytic, critical and logical thinking skills
  - expertise with Excel, Word and PowerPoint
  - appropriate level of qualification in computing, business, mathematics or the sciences.

Solution Architect

The Solution Architect is responsible for designing and building the infrastructure that supports the collection of data. This will require evaluating the available data sources and developing the strategy and plans for collecting and analysing information.

- Responsibilities:
  - developing the infrastructure for data analysis
  - developing and managing data sources
  - formulating analysis plans
  - reviewing data sources and data quality.
- Requirements:
  - knowledge of a range of relevant solutions and systems
  - knowledge and experience of technical architecture roles
  - track record of design and delivery of integrated IT solutions
  - ability to provide advice and guidance on the design of systems architectures
  - experience in systems delivery including analysis, design, implementation and testing.

Implementation managers

Implementation managers are principally responsible for implementing the Market Intelligence Unit and its activities. They will be responsible for embedding the change management processes and developing strong communication and engagement plans with sub-directorates.

- Responsibilities.
  - communicating with sub-directorates to understand what they require from the Market Intelligence Unit
  - developing joint work plans
  - identifying where changes in process or behaviour are required
  - co-ordinating and supporting the implementation of recommendations developed by the Market Intelligence Unit.
- Requirements:
  - strong analytic and critical thinking skills
  - exceptional written, oral and presentation capabilities
  - communication and engagement skills to co-ordinate activities
  - expertise with Excel, Word, PowerPoint
  - appropriate qualification in business, mathematics or the sciences.

References

OECD (2013), *Public Procurement Review of the State's Employees' Social Security and Social Services Institute in Mexico: Smart Procurement for Health Public Services*, OECD Public Governance Reviews, OECD Publishing, Paris, http://dx.doi.org/10.1787/9789264197305-en.

Procurement, Investment & Commercial Division (2014a), "Procurement transparency", National Health Service, Department of Health, London, March.

Procurement, Investment & Commercial Division (2014b), *NHS eProcurement Strategy*, National Health Service, Department of Health, London, April.

Chapter 4.

Improving comprehensive medical services procurement in the ISSSTE

This chapter analyses procurement aspects of the supply, by external contractors, of comprehensive medical services to the State's Employees' Social Security and Social Services Institute (ISSSTE) in Mexico. The chapter makes recommendations for further action. It also provides concrete examples of criteria to evaluate bids for medical services and two case studies on the procurement of medical services, one from the ISSSTE and one from Chile.

This chapter focuses on aspects of the comprehensive medical services procured by the State's Employees' Social Security and Social Services Institute in Mexico (*Instituto de Seguridad y Servicios Sociales de los Trabajadores del Estado*, ISSSTE) which the ISSSTE has identified as requiring improvement. Comprehensive medical services are healthcare services which complement or are incorporated into those offered by the ISSSTE's medical staff. While the ISSSTE provides personnel and facilities, an external contactor supplies specialised medical equipment, goods and services together with the qualified technical personnel to operate, repair and maintain the medical equipment, and to train and support the personnel of the ISSSTE, making sure it is regularly updated. Peritoneal dialysis is also provided at the patients' homes.

Comprehensive medical services are one of the three categories of services procured by the ISSSTE from the market. The other two are:

- subrogated services – outsourced by the ISSSTE and provided on the supplier's premises, e.g. laboratory tests
- residual services, which include basic services like water and electricity, cleaning and maintenance, security and transportation (see Table 2.1 in Chapter 2).

The ISSSTE's procurement of comprehensive medical services started in 2010. The objective was to reduce the costs and improve the quality, safety and speed of healthcare in certain specialised treatments for which the ISSSTE did not have sufficient in-house capacity, or when rapidly evolving technologies made the procurement of new equipment and the acquisition of relevant medical skills too expensive. Procurement of these services aims at obtaining state-of-the-art medical services and equipment, increasing the speed of medical attention and saving on the costs that would be entailed in the provision of such services by the ISSSTE.

Currently the ISSSTE procures comprehensive medical services that fall into seven categories:

1. endoscopy of digestive tube
2. minimum invasion surgery
3. anaesthesia
4. orthopaedic endoprosthetics and osteosynthesis
5. cardiovascular surgery and haemodynamics
6. haemodialysis
7. clinical laboratories and blood banks.

Those seven categories can, in turn, be grouped into two broad classes. The first is specific medical services, like laboratory tests or haemodialysis, while the second is services that provide a medical act that is part of a more complex medical procedure – e.g. anaesthetics, orthopaedic endoprosthetics and osteosynthesis, cardiovascular surgery and endoscopy (Medesigo Micete, 2014).

Due to the medical importance and financial value of comprehensive medical services, in 2013 the management of the ISSSTE developed a strategy to make its procurement process more robust, and obtain savings as well as better and more extended healthcare services for its beneficiaries. The Secretariat General, the Administration Directorate, the Medical Directorate, the Finance Directorate, the Legal Directorate and the Delegations Directorate participated, among others, in developing the strategy.

Three actions were implemented at the same time: 1) analysis of applicable price and contract conditions and comparison with those applicable in other healthcare providers; 2) analysis of procurement results; 3) definition of a work programme to plan procurements, including initiatives aiming to promote competition, prevent bid rigging, and increase transparency and oversight through social witnesses and the ISSSTE's internal control body (*Órgano Interno de Control*).

The ISSSTE calculates that this strategy resulted in savings of MXN 262.40 million in 2013, as detailed in Table 4.1.

Table 4.1. **Savings achieved in the procurement of comprehensive medical services, 2013**

Comprehensive medical service	2013 (MXN millions)
Anaesthesia	42.80
Cardiovascular surgery and haemodynamics	32.60
Minimum invasion surgery	44.40
Peritoneal dialysis	14.40
Endoscopy of digestive system	6.70
Haemodialysis and peritoneal dialysis	55.20
Clinical laboratories and blood banks	46.40
Orthopaedic endoprosthetics and osteosynthesis	19.90
Total	262.40

Source: ISSSTE, Administration Directorate.

Procurement procedures for the services are centralised and carried out every three years. Agreements with suppliers last for those three years and are divided into regional lots. The procedure used is national public bidding, unless emergency or other special reasons dictate otherwise (see Chapter 5 on exceptions to competitive bidding).

Procurement of comprehensive medical services at the ISSSTE is standardised and planned ahead

The procurement of comprehensive medical services is one of the most standardised and closely monitored procurement activities in the ISSSTE.

Every three years, at the start of the new procurement process, medical areas identify needs that fall into the seven categories of comprehensive medical services and submit them to the Infrastructure Sub-Directorate, which groups needs by category and analyses them to verify that they are realistic. During this verification process, the sub-directorate consults with medical experts. On completion of verification, it issues, in co-operation with the ISSSTE's medical areas and experts, the terms of reference per category for the procurement of the comprehensive medical services. The transfer in 2014 of the Infrastructure Sub-Directorate from the Medical Directorate to the Administration Directorate (the central directorate in the ISSSTE organising the procurement activity), in accordance with Article 58 of the organic statute of the ISSSTE, helped optimise and speed up processes and better define the resources needed for the procurement of comprehensive medical services.

The Medical Supplies Sub-Directorate thereafter conducts market research based on the technical characteristics defined in the terms of reference. The Infrastructure Sub-Directorate takes the results of the market research and carries out a cost-benefit analysis which includes:

- a statement of the “as is” situation
- a statement of the “to be” situation
- a statement of key objectives for the service
- the description of the medical need
- the description of the scope of the service
- time parameters
- the key risks
- implications for the ISSSTE.[1]

Simply put, the process thereafter develops as follows: the Sub-Directorate of Programming and Budgeting reviews and approves the cost-benefit analysis and, once budget sufficiency has been requested and approved, and the Director General of the ISSSTE has given the project the go-ahead, the procurement procedure can get underway. It is carried out by the Material Resources and Services Sub-Directorate working together with the Infrastructure Sub-Directorate. The user areas (medical units) are consulted when bids are evaluated. The Material Resources and Services Sub-Directorate awards the contract, which is signed by the Material Resources and Services Sub-Directorate, the Infrastructure Sub-Directorate and the Director of Administration. The Infrastructure Sub-Directorate monitors the provision of the services.

The ISSSTE views the procurement of comprehensive medical services as an important facilitator in providing quality health services to its beneficiaries. It is therefore consequently seeking to improve its procurement performance, working with the OECD to identify gaps and consider ways forward.

Using valuable cost-benefit analysis more strategically

The cost-benefit analysis run by the ISSSTE’s Infrastructure Sub-Directorate (see Annex 4.A2) is a valuable tool for determining whether the service should be procured from the market or provided in-house. The analysis is detailed and all-encompassing and yields a good overview of the needs to be met, the failings to be overcome and the goals to be achieved through procurement, as well as the related risks.

The cost-benefit analysis could be enriched if, beforehand or during analysis, it further examines whether the service to be procured is a core ISSSTE competency. If it is, it should be provided in-house. If not, it can be procured from the market (Box 4.1).

The ISSSTE does not currently include the core versus non-core competency assessment in its cost-benefit analysis or in steps prior to it. It would be useful if it were carried out at the beginning of the analysis in order to procure certain services from the market. It is also worth considering whether to add to the cost-benefit analysis the core versus non-core assessment so that stakeholders – including medical areas and representatives of the ISSSTE’s beneficiaries – may give their opinion.

How procurement of comprehensive medical services can support small and medium-sized enterprises

The ISSSTE recently reached out to more suppliers than the four companies with which it had contracts in 2012. In the invitations to tender for 6 comprehensive medical services, published 13 June 2014, more than 30 suppliers participated, as shown in Table 4.2.

Box 4.1. Core and non-core competency services and procurement

A service can be described as a core competency when it:

- makes a significant contribution to beneficiaries, and
- is difficult for others (outside of the ISSSTE) to replicate, and
- secures the goals of the ISSSTE.

These services are better kept in-house so that the ISSSTE does not lose direct control over core work areas.

Non-core competency services are those that do not meet the above requirements. These can be procured from the market when the following conditions are met:

- it costs less to procure than to provide the service in-house
- the quality of service levels can be maintained or improved
- management time can be released to focus on core competency services
- service delivery risks can be maintained or improved.

Source: Presentation made at the OECD workshop on "Improving Public Procurement Practices in ISSSTE", Mexico City, 2-4 September 2014, by Steve Graham, Hadley Graham Ltd, advisors to United Kingdom's Department of Health.

Table 4.2. **Number of suppliers to invitations to tender, June 2014**

Comprehensive medical service	Number of participants
Orthopaedic endoprosthetics and osteosynthesis	4
Cardiovascular surgery and haemodynamics	3
Haemodialysis	9
Minimum invasion surgery	3
Anaesthetic	6
Endoscopy	5

This increase in the number of suppliers is the outcome of an effort undertaken by the ISSSTE's Administration Directorate in 2013 and 2014 to broaden its supply base and push down prices. One positive effect of the move is that the suppliers are smaller companies which now have direct access to procurement opportunities offered by the ISSSTE.

The ISSSTE promotes the participation of small and medium-sized enterprises (SMEs) in the procurement of comprehensive medical services by dividing each contract into regional lots. The breakdown lowers supply volumes and limits geographical areas, making procurement feasible for SMEs who often lack the capacity to respond to big, geographically dispersed contracts. Division into lots is also important because the ISSSTE accounts for a large share of the medical services market and any procurement choice it makes affects the supply base. The ISSSTE's procurements of comprehensive medical services has a particularly critical effect as contracts last for three years and, once awarded, close off that part of the market to non-participating suppliers.

For the ISSSTE to maximise the potential of the procurement of comprehensive medical services as a way of supporting SMEs, it could consider helping them through dedicated training so that if the SME is interested in bidding, it would have the required skills. Another positive step could be to reduce paperwork – within the limits of the applicable rules – for SMEs wishing to bid.

Similar initiatives have been undertaken by other OECD countries. One example is Italy, which provides training to SMEs across the country to help them participate in procurement procedures (Box 4.2).

Box 4.2. **Supplier training desks in Italy**

The Italian central purchasing body, Consip SpA, carries out procurement procedures and awards contracts for commonly purchased goods and services across the Italian public sector.

Consip has taken action to help suppliers bid for contracts by setting up supplier training desks ("Sportelli in Rete" in Italian) within the offices of suppliers' regional associations across the country. Supplier training desks provide training and assistance to local enterprises and, in particular, to micro, small and medium-sized enterprises (MSMEs) on the use of electronic procurement tools. Through supplier training desks, Consip experts train persons from the suppliers' associations who will subsequently train local MSMEs on the use of electronic procurement tools. In Italy, MSMEs take part in lower value public procurement tenders. They account for 65% of bidders in tenders with a value of between EUR 100 000 and EUR 300 000, 51% in contracts worth between EUR 1 million and EUR 5 million, and 30% in tenders with a value in excess of EUR 5 million.

Supplier training desks match Principle V of the so-called European "Small Business Act (SBA): "Adapt public policy tools to SME needs: facilitate SMEs' participation in public procurement and better use state aid possibilities for SMEs" (European Commission, 2008). It is quoted as a good practice at a European level in the "European Code of Best Practices facilitating access by SME's to public procurement contracts". It has also won the European eGovernment Awards in the category "empowering business".

This project has been well received by MSMEs. Since the beginning of the project, supplier training desks have supported more than 2 250 MSMEs and helped nearly half as many qualify for Italy's public e-marketplace (MePA) implemented by Consip for low-value purchases through e-catalogues. Around 1 000 MSMEs qualified in 2013 – 44% of the total number of firms in the e-marketplace. Tables 4.3 and 4.4 show companies' percentages of the procurement activity in the MePA in 2013.

Table 4.3. **Online enterprises active in 2013**

Size of enterprise	Online	Active
Medium	5%	6%
Micro	68%	66%
Big	2%	2%
Small	25%	26%
Total	100%	100%

Table 4.4. **Volume and value of transactions in 2013**

Size of enterprise	Volume of transactions	Value of transactions
Medium	12%	16%
Micro	54%	42%
Big	3%	7%
Small	31%	35%
Total	100%	100%

Today, more than 200 supplier training desks are in operation, providing continuous free training and assistance. The MePA has allowed thousands of SMEs to do business with the public sector.

Consip's active role in setting up an efficient e-procurement platform and commitment in establishing a collaborative partnership with suppliers has contributed to the establishment of a transparent, competitive procurement environment in Italy.

Source: CONSIP, Italy.

Helping SMEs to participate in tenders in the European Union was deemed so important that the new European Union public procurement directives contain specific rules on reducing administrative burdens for SMEs and breaking contracts down into smaller lots that allow SMEs to tender (Box 4.3). The directive encourages splitting contracts not only on a quantitative basis but qualitatively, too, to match SMEs' fields of specialisation. The ISSSTE could consider such an approach, after first assessing the SMEs that do business in Mexico.

Box 4.3. Reducing red tape in the European Union

There are more than 20 million SMEs in the European Union (EU), representing 99% of all businesses. SMEs are a key driver of economic growth, innovation, employment and social integration across the EU. Accordingly, the European Commission has taken action to ensure that its policies and programmes foster SMEs' viability by easing their administrative burdens and adapting EU rules to their needs.

In 2012, the European Commission ran its so-called "TOP10 public consultation" to find out "the top 10 most burdensome legislative acts for SMEs".

Of the 20 most burdensome pieces of legislation, procedures for the award of public contracts (public works, supply and service contracts) ranked sixth.

The new EU Directive on Public Procurement (Directive 2014/24/EU), adopted to ensure better quality and value for money when public authorities buy or lease works, goods or services, also seeks to make it easier for SMEs to participate in procurement procedures.

Rules under the new directive simplify bidding through a "European Single Procurement Document based on self-declarations as regards the personal situation and legal standing of the bidder. Only the winner of the contract will have to provide original documentation".

The European Commission believes that this new measure should reduce the administrative burden on companies by over 80%.

The new directive also encourages the division of contracts into lots to make it easier for smaller firms to bid. Contracting authorities are urged to divide large contracts into smaller or more specialised lots. Such division can be done on a quantitative basis, adapting the size of the individual contracts to the capacity of SMEs, or on a qualitative basis between different trades or project phases, to adapt the content of the individual contracts to the specialised sectors of SMEs. When a contract can be split into lots but a contracting authority decides not to, it must justify its decision.

The new directive also addresses overly demanding requirements for economic and financial capacity, which frequently rule SMEs out of bidding. It states that contracting authorities should not be allowed to require tenderers to have a minimum turnover disproportionate to the subject matter of the contract: the minimum turnover requirement should not exceed twice the estimated contract value.

Sources: European Commission (2013), "Results of the public consultation on the TOP10 most burdensome legislative acts for SMEs", http://ec.europa.eu/enterprise/policies/sme/files/smes/top10report-final_en.pdf; European Commission (2014), "Directive 2014/24/EU of the European Parliament and of the Council of 26 February 2014 on public procurement", *Journal of the European Union*, http://eur-lex.europa.eu/legal-content/EN/TXT/PDF/?uri=CELEX:32014L0024&from=EN; European Parliament (2014), "New EU-procurement rules to ensure better quality and value for money", European Parliament News, available at: www.europarl.europa.eu/news/en/news-room/content/20140110IPR32386/html/New-EU-procurement-rules-to-ensure-better-quality-and-value-for-money.

The OECD *Recommendation of the Council on Public Procurement* mentions that tender opportunities should be designed: "so as to encourage broad participation from potential competitors, including new entrants and small and medium enterprises. This requires providing clear guidance to inform buyers' expectations (including specifications and contract as well as payment terms) and binding information about evaluation and award criteria and their weights (whether they are focused specifically on price, include elements of price/quality ratio or support secondary policy objectives)" (OECD, 2015). Tender documentation should also ensure that "the extent and complexity of information required in tender documentation and the time allotted for suppliers to respond is proportionate to the size and complexity of the procurement, taking into account any exigent circumstances such as emergency procurement" (OECD, 2015).

Employing targeted evaluation criteria to procure the best solution

The system the ISSSTE usually uses to evaluate bids for comprehensive medical services is "points or percentages" (*puntos o porcentajes*), a point-based weighted evaluation of the different components in a bid.

During fact-finding for this review, ISSSTE staff and suppliers stated that it would be beneficial to design bid components and evaluation criteria so as to produce a more accurate assessment of the bidder's ability to respond to beneficiaries' complex medical needs. For example, if a supplier has to install haemodialysis devices in the ISSSTE's premises, the evaluation criteria could factor in the supplier's work methods to fit equipment and make auxiliary adjustments to the ISSSTE's building infrastructure, like wiring and treating water (Medesigo Micete, 2014). Evaluation criteria could also consider a bidder's capacity and commitment to regularly update medical and technological solutions in the course of a three-year contract. Detailed examples of evaluation criteria, developed in co-operation with peer experts for this review, can be found in Annex 4.A1.

Working with suppliers improves procurement procedures in general (see Chapter 3 on consultations with suppliers). To enhance transparency and competition for future projects, the ISSSTE could hold post-award debriefings with bidders, explaining the reasons for the award decision and discussing possible improvements. In the United Kingdom, for example, procurement personnel are encouraged to debrief each bidder after a contract has been awarded, either face-to-face, by telephone or videoconference. In the debriefing session, the evaluation process is detailed, the strengths and weaknesses of the relevant supplier's bid explained and the bidder's views, concerns or questions on the procurement process are discussed. No information is revealed about other submissions. Following the debriefing, a note is made for the record (OECD, 2007).

Monitoring suppliers' performance

According to the OECD (2014), contract performance management activities can be grouped into three areas: delivery management (ensures that what is ordered is delivered to the required level of quality and performance as stated in the contract), relationship management (seeks to keep the relationship between the supplier and the contracting authority open and constructive) and contract administration (covers the formal governance of the contract and any permitted changes to documentation during the life of the contract). By monitoring and documenting suppliers' performance, public officials are in a position to require corrective actions when performance fails to meet the contract requirements. Performance monitoring can also inform the selection of suppliers, when their past performance is assessed for award of contracts.

The Infrastructure Sub-Directorate manages and supervises supplier performance in comprehensive medical services according to the guidelines of the "General Procurement Manual", which provides templates for the different contract management tasks, as follows:

- inspect and receive goods and services
- modify contract – only when there are grounds for doing so
- apply contractually stipulated sanctions for breaches of contract
- terminate contracts (early termination)
- cancel contracts for supplier breaches of contract terms.
- enforce warranties.

The above contract management tasks are more reactive (focused on sanctions) than proactive, i.e. targeted at improving buyer-seller relationships and preventing problems. What's more, monitoring (like sanctions) necessitates a thorough understanding of the supplier's performance – such as speedy response and methods – and/or mitigating circumstances, like the ISSSTE's own delays or a sudden increase in the incidence of certain medical conditions. In that light, the medical areas would be better placed to do the monitoring. The Infrastructure Sub-Directorate does not have all the information it needs for proper monitoring as, unlike the medical areas, it does not have direct dealings with suppliers. In the last quarter of 2014, medical areas were already involved in the definition of needs, procurement processes and evaluation of bids.

The ISSSTE is seeking to improve monitoring processes by adopting performance metrics and indicators that measure supplier performance. Other OECD countries, like Italy, have also developed performance measurement indicators (Box 4.4).

Box 4.4. Consip's monitoring of suppliers

Consip, the Italian central purchasing body, has a monitoring method based on the analysis of five so-called "macro-categories".

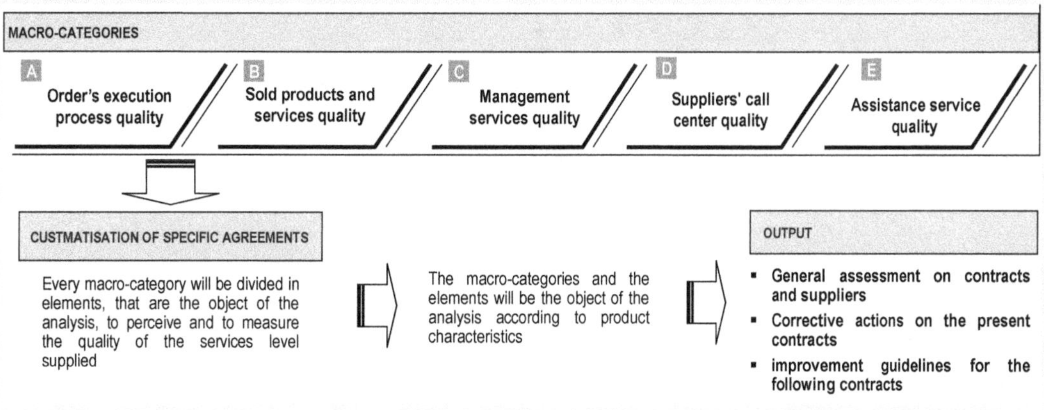

Box 4.4. Consip's monitoring of suppliers (*cont.*)

The monitoring team employs the following three tools:

- Inspections. Inspections verify suppliers' compliance with technical requirements. An external inspection body carries them out with the costs paid by the suppliers being inspected.
- Surveys. Surveys measure the buyers' perceptions of suppliers' service levels. An external call centre conducts the surveys.
- Claims. Consip collects and analyses public administration complaints to judge whether supplier performance failed to meet the agreed quality standard.

All procurement contracts factor in a specific budget for financing inspections which is included in the supplier's payment. It is proportionate of the amount of money spent as a result of the contract, the maximum amount being 0.5% of the sum spent. The supplier pays the external inspection body.

The findings of surveys and inspections are weighted to show levels of performance.

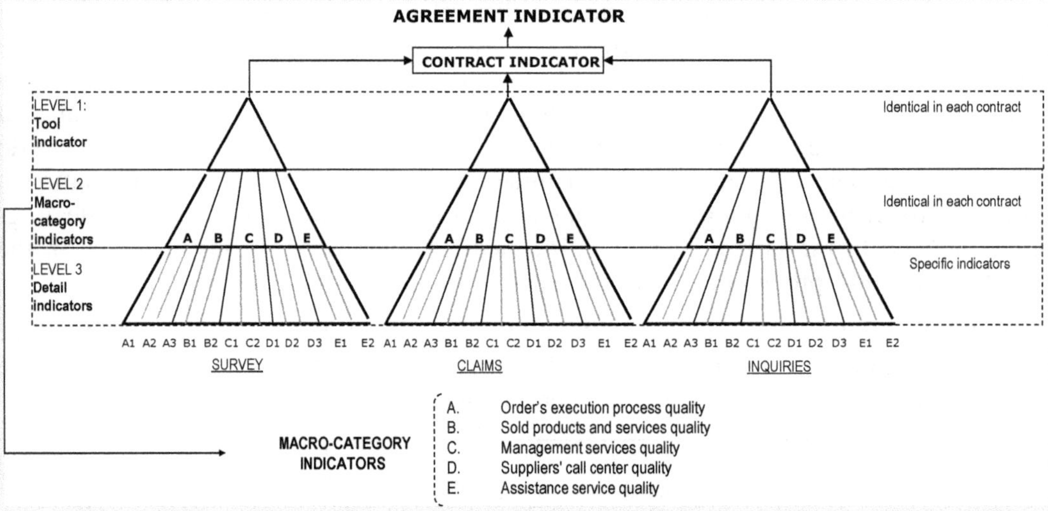

The monitoring team draws on survey and inspection findings to score each component in the indicator. Final assessment is as follows:

Score	1	2	3	4	5
Level of service % indicator	0%	25%	50%	75%	100%
Range	Alert		Warning		On target

- "Alert" when the score is equal to or lower than 50%
- "Warning" when the score is between 51% and 74%
- "On target" when the score is equal to or greater than 75%.

Source: CONSIP SpA, www.consip.it/en.

Supplier input and co-operation is necessary for fair and accurate performance monitoring. Healthcare providers, like the United Kingdom's National Health Service (NHS), ask for the suppliers' accounts payable and purchase orders for items used in the provision of the medical services. Suppliers can also be more involved in optimising services rendered. For example, it could be part of their contractual obligations to inform the ISSSTE's medical areas about volumes of use of their services (e.g. medical interventions), and whether there have been increases or decreases in those volumes, so that contracts may be adjusted accordingly. The ISSSTE should be in regular contact with suppliers and view them as partners from whom much can be learnt.

Outsourcing standard medical procedures may ease pressure on hospitals and bring savings

During fact-finding, the ISSSTE indicated that it was considering outsourcing a few medical services like haemodialysis which suppliers can provide in their own facilities. In that way, the ISSSTE does not insource external equipment and support as it does with comprehensive medical services.

The conditions to be met for outsourcing are:

- To assess the impact of new initiatives made by the ISSSTE's administration in 2014 to improve hospital management, expenditure management, hospital beds capacity, surgery management, repeat medical prescriptions to patients with chronic degenerative illnesses and follow-up medical consultations in first-level medical care centres. These initiatives are expected to free up 10-15% of capacity to care for hospital patients.
- There are medical needs.
- Cost-benefit analysis advocates it.
- There is no in-house capacity.

The outsourcing of clinical services is a relatively common practice among healthcare providers around the world. The United Kingdom's NHS has achieved savings and healthcare benefits by outsourcing certain non-core services, such as hip and knee replacement surgery (Box 4.5).

Procurement of comprehensive medical services can be consolidated with other healthcare providers

The ISSSTE may consider consolidating the procurement of comprehensive medical services with other healthcare providers, like the Mexican Institute of Social Security (*Instituto Mexicano del Seguro Social*, IMSS), to achieve economies of scale. To that end, the ISSSTE should draw on its valuable experience in consolidating purchases for medicines. The ISSSTE is already considering such consolidation of comprehensive medical services and is assessing the framework of medical coverage and healthcare protocols. Using international tenders to attract foreign suppliers may also help boost competition and secure value for money. In the OECD's 2013 public procurement review of the ISSSTE (OECD, 2013b), as well as in the OECD report on fighting bid rigging in the ISSSTE (OECD, 2013a), the OECD recommended that the ISSSTE open tenders to foreign suppliers as much as possible, for example using international tenders rather than relying on exceptions to public tendering, in cases where a national tender has been unsuccessful.

Box 4.5. The NHS outsources healthcare to make savings and focus on core services

The outsourcing of clinical services is used by public healthcare systems attempting to balance the provision of state-of-the-art specialised health services in a cost-efficient manner. The NHS has saved money and reduced pressure on hospitals to focus on complex public health issues by farming out standard medical procedures to external providers.

Successful outsourcing projects rely on principles like:

- an open collaborative relationship with the supplier
- realistic expectations and timeframes agreed in advance
- good communication and mutual understanding of needs
- embedded safety and risk management processes
- defined escalation and dispute resolution procedures being in place
- embedded informal and formal reporting arrangements
- problems tackled immediately.

Outsourcing should provide tangible, measurable benefits. A checklist of benefits should be prepared and an analysis undertaken to ensure that the benefits are worthwhile.

The checklist could include:

- reduced operating costs and capital investment
- freed-up space and resources
- improved innovation and greater value-added services
- greater service speed, quality and reliability
- greater access to specialist skills
- economies of scale.

The NHS has found that outsourcing works well for routine surgery, e.g. example hip and knee replacement surgery. Difficult cases, on the contrary, are treated better and more economically inside public hospitals.

Source: Presentation made at the OECD workshop on "Improving Public Procurement Practices in ISSSTE", 2-4 September 2014, Mexico City, by Steve Graham, Hadley Graham Ltd, advisors to United Kingdom's Department of Health.

Proposals for action

- Involve more medical areas in contract performance management and seek supplier input and co-operation for monitoring performance (immediate action).
- Assess whether a medical service is a core or non-core competency before starting the procurement process (immediate action).
- Design evaluation criteria so that they can accurately measure a bidder's capacity to respond to medical needs and risks (medium-term action).
- Consider consolidating the procurement of comprehensive medical services with other healthcare providers, like the IMSS (medium-term action).

- Train SMEs to increase their understanding of and participation in procurement (medium-term action).
- Split contracts into lots on a quantitative and qualitative basis, so that the content of each lot matches SMEs' fields of specialisation (medium-term action).
- Consider targeted outsourcing of medical services based on good examples from other OECD countries (long-term action).

Note

1. "Cost-benefit analysis of the project for the multi-annual procurement of the comprehensive medical service of cardiovascular surgery, in hospital units of ISSSTE" ("*Análisis de costo y beneficio del proyecto de contratación plurianual para la prestación del servicio integral de cirugía cardiovascular en unidades médicas hospitalarias del ISSSTE*), Infrastructure Sub-Directorate. Internal document provided by the ISSSTE. Please also refer to Annex 4.A2.

References

European Commission (2014), "Directive 2014/24/EU of the European Parliament and of the Council of 26 February 2014 on public procurement", *Journal of the European Union*, available at: http://eur-lex.europa.eu/legal-content/EN/TXT/PDF/?uri=CELEX:32014L0024&from=EN.

European Commission (2013), "Results of the public consultation on the TOP10 most burdensome legislative acts for SMEs", available at: http://ec.europa.eu/enterprise/policies/sme/files/smes/top10report-final_en.pdf.

European Commission (2008), "Think small first : A 'Small Business Act' for Europe", Commission Communication of 25 June 2008, European Commission, Brussels, available at: http://ec.europa.eu/enterprise/policies/sme/documents/sba/index_en.htm.

European Parliament (2014), "New EU-procurement rules to ensure better quality and value for money", European Parliament News, available at: www.europarl.europa.eu/news/en/news-room/content/20140110IPR32386/html/New-EU-procurement-rules-to-ensure-better-quality-and-value-for-money.

Graham, S. (2014), Hadley Graham Ltd, advisors to United Kingdom's Department of Health, presentation at the OECD workshop on "Improving Public Procurement Practices in ISSSTE", Mexico City, 2-4 September.

Medesigo Micete, J.S. (2014), Executive Co-ordinator of ISSSTE, presentation at the OECD workshop on "Improving Public Procurement Practices in ISSSTE", Mexico City, 2-4 September.

OECD (2015), *Recommendation of the Council on Public Procurement*, OECD, Paris, available at: http://acts.oecd.org/Instruments/ShowInstrumentView.aspx?InstrumentID=320&InstrumentPID=348&Lang=en&Book=False.

OECD (2014), "Towards public procurement performance indicators: First set of indicators", GOV/PGC/ETH(2014)5, OECD, Paris, available at: www.oecd.org/officialdocuments/publicdisplaydocumentpdf/?cote=GOV/PGC/ETH%282014%295&docLanguage=En.

OECD (2013a), "Fighting bid rigging in public procurement in Mexico: A Secretariat analytical report on legislation, regulations and practices relating to procurement undertaken by ISSSTE", OECD, Paris, available at: www.oecd.org/daf/competition/mexicoissste2013.htm.

OECD (2013b), *Public Procurement Review of the State's Employees' Social Security and Social Services Institute in Mexico: Smart Procurement for Health Public Services*, OECD Public Governance Reviews, OECD Publishing, Paris, http://dx.doi.org/10.1787/9789264197305-en.

OECD (2007), *Integrity in Public Procurement: Good Practice from A to Z*, OECD Publishing, Paris, http://dx.doi.org/10.1787/9789264027510-en.

Further reading

Department of Health, United Kingdom (2012), "The pathology services commissioning toolkit", available at: www.gov.uk/government/publications/the-pathology-services-commissioning-toolkit (accessed 24 February 2015).

GS1 AISBL (2014), *GS1 Healthcare Reference Book 2014/2015: 12 Implementation Success Stories*, GS1 AISBL, Brussels, available at: www.gs1hk.org/files/Publications/sector_brochures/GS1%20Healthcare%20Reference%20Book_2014.pdf (accessed 24 February 2015).

McKinsey&Company (2013), "Strengthening health care's supply chain: A five-step plan", McKinsey&Company, September, available at: www.mckinsey.com/insights/health_systems_and_services/strengthening_health_cares_supply_chain_a_five_step_plan (accessed 24 February 2015).

Annex 4.A1
Examples of evaluation criteria[1]

The first step in ensuring that quality medical services are delivered is to have a robust service specification. Output and results from market research and cost-benefit analysis should be used to inform the development of service specifications.

A service specification should include:

- A description of the nature and scope of the service required.
- The users and their needs – including level of demand – in view of health statistics.
- The overall purpose and aims of the service.
- The geographical location and spread of the service. Here, it is important to review and specify in which medical units the comprehensive medical service shall be provided and whether or how patients can be grouped per region.
- The activities to be provided.
- The standards to be achieved, which includes any national and international standards.

The specification could be based on clinical guidelines which indicate the appropriate level of healthcare and clinical practice. For example, in the United Kingdom, the National Institute for Health and Care Excellence (NICE) – a body of the Department of Health – determines the clinical guidelines for specific diseases and medical conditions that inform procurement decisions. NICE has a strong reputation for explicitly determining cost-benefit boundaries for the medical technologies that it assesses.

After the medical service has been specified, evaluation criteria may be developed. They should encompass several key areas, such as:

- organisation and management
- clinical activity
- workforce
- estates
- logistics
- IT
- transition
- finance
- legal.

Examples of evaluation criteria for key areas are given below. They are not exhaustive and it is not necessary to use them all. The ISSSTE can determine a range of suitable evaluation criteria and the weighting of each one selected.

- Example of organisational and management criteria:
  - describe the role profile for the person who has overall responsibility for the service
  - describe the organisational chart and lines of accountability
  - provide examples of successful implementations elsewhere
  - describe the method for monitoring and evaluating success measures
  - detail the key clinical and non-clinical performance indicators to be used
  - provide details of the site(s) at which parts of the service may be located[2]
  - describe the measures required to enhance the systems and processes, particularly in the event of malfunction
  - describe the actions, risks and mitigation strategies required to deliver those enhancements.
- Example of clinical evaluation criteria:
  - describe the proposed clinical service delivery model to meet the service specification
  - detail the existing volume of activity, capacity and utilisation of similar services that you provide elsewhere
  - provide flowcharts to represent the clinical pathways for this service
  - describe the time taken and service provided for each step in the pathway
  - define the person responsible for each step in the pathway
  - describe how you will ensure clinical effectiveness and compliance with standards
  - describe how you will understand and evaluate the needs of patients
  - describe how you will ensure safety
  - describe how you will improve the experience of patient and service users
  - describe your system for clinical governance and risk management
  - describe how you will maintain safe and effective services.
- Example of workforce evaluation criteria:
  - describe your existing workforce
  - describe the expected transformation plan to facilitate delivery of the service
  - describe the transitional arrangements required to deliver the service
  - provide examples of your experience in managing similar organisational change

  - provide a workforce plan with projected staff numbers and costs
  - provide your recruitment and retention plan
  - describe how you ensure that the workforce is appropriately sized and skilled to deliver the service.
- Example of estates and logistics evaluation criteria:
  - provide a map to show the geographical area to be covered by the service
  - provide details of the adjustments required at the location(s) where the service will be delivered
  - describe solutions for alternative uses and costs for discontinued service locations (particularly as the ISSSTE reserves the right to change or discontinue locations)
  - describe the logistics methodology for provision of your proposed services
  - describe methods to ensure the integrity and security of service provision
  - provide details of any subcontracts required to ensure service provision.
- Example IT evaluation criteria:
  - provide details of IT solutions required to provide the service
  - provide a timetable for the mobilisation of any new IT solutions
  - describe how IT solutions will support delivery of the service
  - describe the systems availability arrangements and standards
  - describe business continuity and disaster recovery plans
  - describe IT solutions service user training plans.
- Example of transition evaluation criteria:

  Transition evaluation criteria apply, for example, when specific parts of services will cease to be provided by the ISSSTE or where work areas within the ISSSTE need to be adjusted.

  - provide details of how the service will be transitioned to the proposed service
  - provide details of your approach to transition management
  - provide plans and costs for IT implications of transition
  - provide plans and costs for estates and logistics implications of transition
  - describe the impact on residual services
  - provide a transformation plan showing timelines and milestones
  - describe all expected and potential impacts on any retained services.
- Example of financial evaluation criteria:
  - provide a financial model for the expected volumes
  - provide a breakdown of costs by pay, non-pay, margin

  - provide a pricing model
  - describe any capital costs required to mobilise the service
  - provide a price escalation formula for the contract period of three years
  - describe any risks associated with the financial and pricing models
  - describe any risks with the transition costs
  - provide details to substantiate your financial standing.
- Example legal evaluation criteria:
  - provide evidence that you have the legal status to enter into this contract
  - confirm that you accept the draft contract documentation provided
  - confirm that you do not intend to use any sub-contractors to provide the service other than those already identified
  - provide a contract variation methodology.

Notes

1. Drawn from the OECD workshop on "Improving Public Procurement Practices in ISSSTE", 2-4 September 2014, Mexico City, with input in particular from Steve Graham Hadley Graham Ltd, advisors to the United Kingdom's Department of Health.
2. For example, in medical laboratories, ISO 15189 is used to demonstrate the competence of medical laboratories and ensure the collection of patient samples, the interpretation of test results, acceptable turnaround times, how testing is to be provided in a medical emergency, and the laboratory's role in educating and training healthcare staff.

Annex 4.A2
Case studies in comprehensive medical services

Case study 1. Cost-benefit analysis in comprehensive medical services: Cardiovascular surgery at the ISSSTE[1]

In 2013, the Infrastructure Sub-Directorate carried out a cost-benefit analysis to decide whether to procure cardiovascular surgery services through a multi-year contract or provide them using its own means (personnel, facilities, equipment and supplies, etc.). In 2014, it requested MXN 1 706 million (under the item spending code "COG 3000") for the service, to be distributed as follows:

- 2014: MXN 433 million
- 2015: MXN 606 million
- 2016: MXN 677 million.

Background

Ischemic cardiomyopathy is the first cause of mortality and morbidity in Mexico's adult population over 35 years of age, and congenital cardiomyopathy affects 8 in every 1 000 newborns, who die without treatment in their first few years of life. That rate can be reduced with adequate diagnosis and treatment.

Both ischemic and congenital cardiomyopathy require complex surgical procedures with highly technological infrastructure and specialised personnel.

In Mexico, heart surgery was first practiced in 1950, but due to its high costs few medical units provide it, even though many patients need it. In 2011, heart disease accounted for 272 420 medical appointments and 15 230 cardiovascular surgery consultations for adult patients – as well as 1 337 cardiovascular surgery consultations for children. There are 14 222 appointments for high-specialty cardiovascular surgery every year. Heart diseases cause 5.26% of deaths annually in Mexican hospitals.

Waiting time for cardiovascular surgery is between five months and two years, according to a 2001 National Institute of Cardiology study. Delays are due to insufficient infrastructure and the small number of medical units where heart surgery can be practiced. In addition, medical equipment and supplies need to be constantly upgraded to ensure patient safety.

What prevents the ISSSTE from providing cardiovascular surgery

The ISSSTE identified barriers to a better provision of cardiovascular services as falling into four categories: administrative, infrastructure, human resources and financial. Administrative barriers are related to bureaucracy, faulty processes, inadequate inventory management, and waste, misuse or reuse of supplies. Infrastructure problems include insufficient and obsolescent equipment and the inadequate geographical coverage afforded by specialised medical units. Human resources gaps are untrained personnel and lack of updated medical knowledge. Financial burdens are insufficient budgets, miscalculated demand, low maintenance and renovation budgets, and costly high-end technologies.

As a result, the ISSSTE fails to meet the needs of many patients with cardiovascular diseases which require highly specialised surgery. It therefore considered procuring cardiovascular surgery services through a multi-year contract in order to treat patients on time and with the same high standards of its second- and third-level medical units.

Procurement compared with in-house provision

Procuring rather than providing cardiovascular surgery helps the ISSSTE overcome its constraints, reduce pre-surgery hospital stays (a patient with cardiovascular problems cost MXN 1 654 a day in 2012), and saves patients travel and accommodation expenses since they can be treated in medical units near their homes. The ISSSTE calculates that savings amount to a net present value of MXN 682 million.

Comparison of equipment and facilities

Table 4.A2.1 shows a comparison between the service that could be provided by the ISSSTE in contrast with the comprehensive medical service that could be procured.

Table 4.A2.1. **Comparison of the ISSSTE's provision with the procured comprehensive medical service**

ISSSTE's facilities and resources	Supplier's facilities and resources
– The service is provided in medical units with the available physical infrastructure (cardiovascular surgery operating theatres) and with existing technical, operational and personnel capabilities. – Each unit has its own anaesthetic equipment. – The procedure requires heart and lung machines. Three machines work and two are obsolete. Other medical accessories required – e.g. pacemaker defibrillators – are obsolete too (60% are out of date). – Only one hospital has a gas meter (auxiliary equipment) in the operating theatre. The lack of such device can endanger patients. – Equipment for the activated clotting time (ACT) test is available only in two hospitals and is ten years old. – The ISSSTE has three intra-aortic balloon counter-pulsation devices.	– The service is provided in the ISSSTE's facilities with the support of the supplier, who is paid per procedure. The ISSSTE provides personnel, operating rooms, intensive care areas and auxiliary diagnostic services. For each procedure, the supplier provides: equipment, instruments, supplies, consumables, maintenance, technical staff and training to the ISSSTE's personnel in the use of equipment. – The service provision includes new anaesthetic technology and 14 heart and lung machines which are replaced every 3-5 years. – Each operating theatre has a gas meter, ACT test equipment, pacemaker defibrillator, and cellular recovery and auto transfusion equipment. – The service includes 18 intra-aortic balloon counter-pulsation devices.
The ISSSTE has to perform all the procedures included in this service according to the specific medical condition of the patient.	The contract includes a total of 48 types of cardiovascular procedures and includes all the technical staff that the ISSSTE is not able to provide.
The service is provided partially by the National Medical Centre of "20 de Noviembre".	The service can be fully provided in National Medical Centre of "20 de Noviembre" and 14 regional hospitals.

Source: Information provided by the ISSSTE.

Fully outsourcing the cardiovascular comprehensive medical services involves suppliers providing the services in their own facilities. That was not an option for the ISSSTE, as post-operative intensive care is least five days and costs MXN 250 000 per patient (plus the costs of the operating room, intensive care, laboratory services, imaging services, specialised medicines). The cost could rise by MXN 20 000 per hospital day if post-surgery complications arose and, as it does not include medical fees, could be as high as MXN 100 000 per patient in a private hospital.

Comparison of medical services

Table 4.A2.2 compares the ISSSTE's own provision of services related to the cardiovascular medical surgery to procuring these services from the market. According to the ISSSTE the main difference is one of time.

Conclusion of the cost-benefit analysis

The ISSSTE's medical units do not have sufficient medical infrastructure and personnel to provide a cardiovascular surgery service in a timely, efficient, standardised manner. Procuring surgery as a comprehensive medical service ensures that it is delivered over a sufficiently wide geographical area, offering the best technology available in a timely manner and at an affordable cost to the ISSSTE over a three-year period.

Table 4.A2.2. **The ISSSTE's own provision compared to procuring the service**

ISSSTE's medical service	Comprehensive medical service
When an ISSSTE doctor in a first-level medical unit finds signs or symptoms of cardiovascular disease, the patient is referred for a specialised medical appointment in a second- or third-level medical unit where an haemodynamic study is programmed. If called for, cardiovascular surgery is scheduled according to: – the medical unit's availability – the available stock of medicines, instruments and medical supplies, and the schedules for servicing or repairing broken equipment. The approximate waiting time for surgery is 35 days. In the event of emergency, the patient is transferred to another medical unit able to provide the service sooner.	When an ISSSTE doctor finds signs or symptoms of cardiovascular malfunction the patient is scheduled for diagnostic cardiac catheterization and, depending on results, for surgery. The approximate waiting time for surgery is seven days. In the event of emergency, surgery may be performed immediately. The service includes the support of a technician responsible for ensuring equipment is fully available in case it is needed. The technician is also responsible for cleaning and preparing equipment, the instruments and medical supplies. The service includes stock management, preventive and corrective maintenance, replacing equipment or upgrading it in the event of major technological change.

Source: Information provided by the ISSSTE.

Case study B: ChileCompra's procurement of haemodialysis and peritoneal dialysis services[2]

Background

In 2011, the number of patients in Chile who needed haemodialysis was 40% higher than the previous year. There are 182 registered dialysis centres nationwide. And although there is a regional haemodialysis and peritoneal dialysis capacity, it is in short supply and patients sometimes need to seek treatment outside of their home regions.

On March 2014, the Chilean central purchasing body, ChileCompra, launched a nationwide public tender for a framework agreement to provide haemodialysis and peritoneal dialysis for adults and 15-year-old minors. The previous framework agreement for the same type of services was with 143 suppliers and of a value of USD 219 million. The 2014 contract includes a new service: fitting adults with a peritoneal catheter during peritoneal dialysis treatment.

Defining the services

The services included in the new contract are:

- Haemodialysis. It is a treatment for End Stage Renal Disease (ESRD). The procedure can be carried out in purpose-built medical facilities and lasts four to five hours three times a week.
- Peritoneal dialysis. Peritoneal dialysis is a procedure for purging the body of toxins and eliminating liquid electrolytes in patients with ESRD. It uses the patient's peritoneum as a filter in the fluid exchange technique of cleansing the blood.
- Fitting peritoneal catheters. Peritoneal dialysis involves filling the peritoneal cavity with dialysis fluid then draining it off. The fluid is fed into the body through a tube called a catheter, that is implanted in the peritoneal cavity.

In order to define specifications for the dialysis services, ChileCompra drew on the medical expertise of healthcare specialists designated by the National Health Fund (Fondo Nacional de Salud), a public body under the Ministry of Health and visited haemodialysis centres to understand their needs.

Evaluation and award criteria

For the purposes of transparency and fairness, ChileCompra disclosed the weights of the evaluation criteria to award the dialysis (Figure 4.A2.1) peritoneal catheter contracts (Figure 4.A2.2).

Figure 4.A2.1. **Evaluation and award criteria for dialysis services**

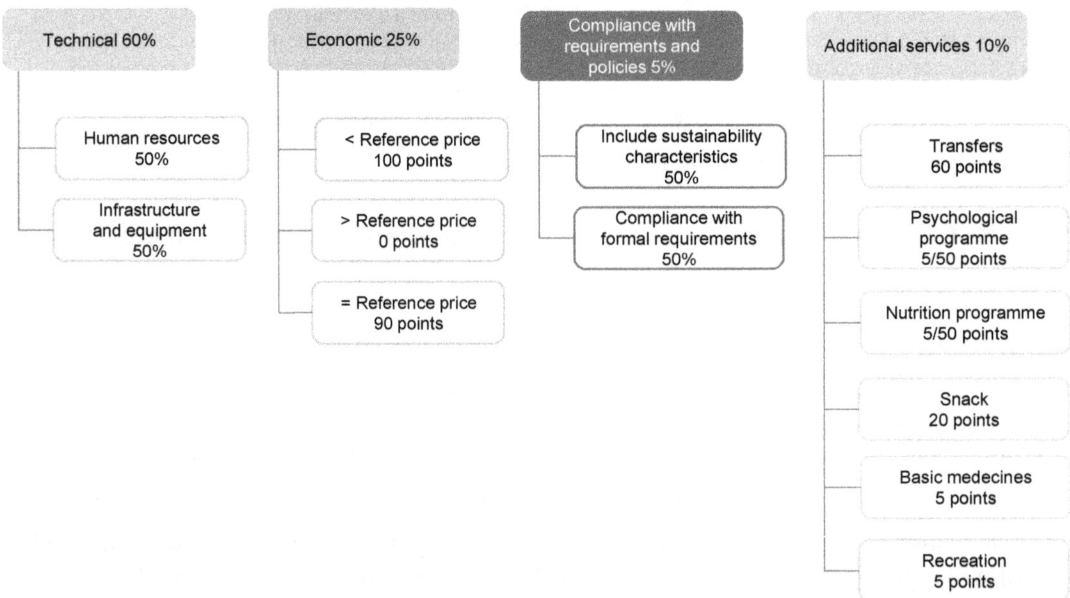

Figure 4.A2.2. **Evaluation and award criteria for peritoneal catheter services**

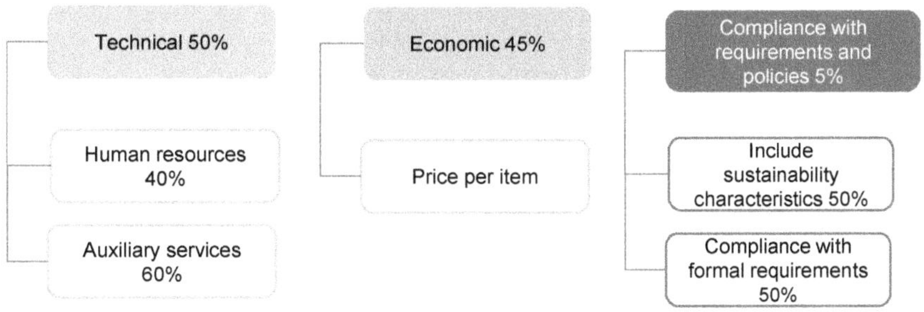

Note: To pass, bidders have to score 76 or more weighted points.

Notes

1. "*Análisis de Costo y Beneficio del Proyecto de Contratación Plurianual para la Prestación del Servicio Integral de Cirugía Cardiovascular en Unidades Médicas Hospitalarias del ISSSTE*" (Cost-benefit analysis of the project for the multi-annual procurement of the comprehensive medical service of cardiovascular surgery, in hospital units of ISSSTE), Infrastructure Sub-directorate. Internal document provided by ISSSTE.

2. Based on Ramírez (2014) and Dirección ChileCompra (2014).

References

Dirección ChileCompra (2014), "ChileCompra llama a participar en licitación de convenio marco de hemodiálisis y peritoneodiálisis adulto y menores de 15 años e instalación de cateter peritoneal" ("ChileCompra calls for framework agreement bids for haemodialysis and peritoneal dialysis for adults and 15-year-old minors and for fitting peritoneal catheters"), 13 March, available at: www.chilecompra.cl/index.php?option=com_content&view=article&id=1740:chilecompra-llama-a-participar-en-licitacion-de-convenio-marco-de-hemodialisis-y-peritoneodialisis-adulto-y-menores-de-15-anos-e-instalacion-de-cateter-peritoneal&catid=381&Itemid=1095.

Ramírez, M. (2014), former Head of Division of Framework Agreements at the Chilean central purchasing body ChileCompra, presentation at the OECD workshop on "Improving Public Procurement Practices in ISSSTE", Mexico City, 2-4 September.

Chapter 5.

The way to competition: Measuring direct awards

This chapter focuses on the use of exceptions to public procurement procedures by the central units and regional delegations of the State's Employees' Social Security and Social Services Institute (ISSSTE) in Mexico. It analyses the frequency of directly awarded contracts and the most common grounds for not opening them to competition. The chapter provides recommendations to increase competitive tendering and highlights the importance of professionalising the ISSSTE's workforce, improving tender design and collecting consistent data.

Competitive tendering enhances transparency in the procurement process and offers opportunities for doing business with the public sector. To boost competition, procurement agents should determine the procurement strategy that best serves administrative efficiency and levels the playing field for suppliers.

Competition in public procurement means that two or more bidders act independently and engage in a contest for the opportunity to secure the procuring entity's contract by offering the most favourable terms (UNODC, 2013). It is an effective way for governments to procure good supply solutions, leverage the public sector's buying power, and get value for money while ensuring that citizens' needs are served. Competition helps lower prices, and obtain better quality goods, services and works. It is also a valuable way of promoting innovation among suppliers seeking to roll out new, improved solutions.

The OECD *Recommendation of the Council on Public Procurement* encourages countries to facilitate access to procurement opportunities for potential competitors. In particular, the recommendation mentions that:

> …competitive procedures should be the standard method for conducting procurement as a means of driving efficiencies, fighting corruption, obtaining fair and reasonable pricing and ensuring competitive outcomes. If exceptional circumstances justify limitations to competitive tendering and the use of single-source procurement, such exceptions should be limited, pre-defined and should require appropriate justification when employed, subject to adequate oversight taking into account the increased risk of corruption, including by foreign suppliers. (OECD, 2015)

The ISSSTE's own commitments towards suppliers provide that it will promote free competition for all interested candidates in its procurement procedures.[1]

For all those reasons, it is worth looking at strategies for broadening the pool of potential suppliers and increasing competition for public contracts. Such strategies include facilitating bids from all over the country in public procurement procedures, encouraging the participation of small and medium-sized enterprises (SMEs), and opening up public procurement markets to foreign competition.

The ISSSTE's frequent use of exceptions to competitive tendering

The Mexican procurement legal framework establishes the use of three distinct procurement procedures:

- Public tendering (also known as "open tendering"), where public bodies call for suppliers to bid and the best offer is chosen.
- Invitations to at least three suppliers, also known as "restricted invitations". Several suppliers who meet certain prerequisites are preselected and the contract is awarded to the supplier who has the best bid.
- Direct awards, where a contract is awarded to a supplier without competition. Contracts are may be directly awarded when public tendering or restricted invitations are unsuccessful, when the value of a contract is lower than the established thresholds, or when the use of "exceptions" to public bidding is authorised.

The preference for the first approach is set out in the Mexican Constitution and restated in the Law on Acquisitions, Leasing and Services of the Public Sector (*Ley de Adquisiciones, Arrendamientos y Servicios del Sector Público,* LAASSP) in order to guarantee the best available conditions for price, quality, financing, opportunity and related requirements.

When comparing the type of procurement procedure used for goods and services between 2010 and 2013, the proportion of direct awards by the ISSSTE decreased from 54% to 44%. However, when measured in value, direct awards are more used. While in 2010 public bidding was the prevalent procedure, accounting for 81% of the value of all contracts awarded competitively, two-thirds of the contracts were awarded directly in 2013 (Figure 5.1).

Figure 5.1. **Number and value of the ISSSTE's contracts for goods and services by procurement procedure**

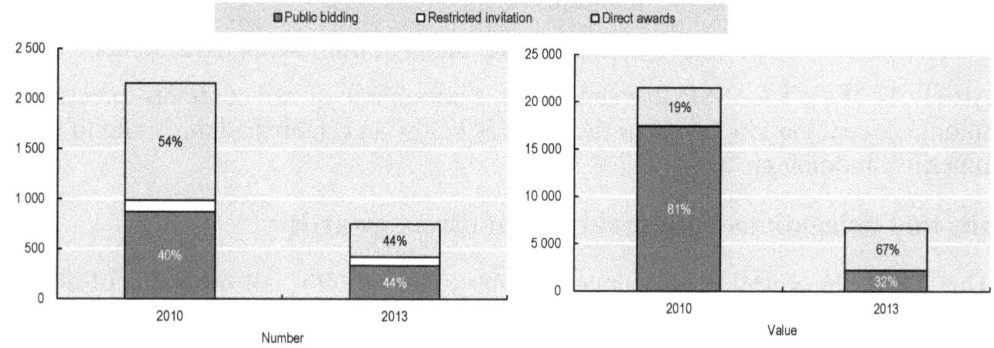

Note: Values up to June 2013.

Source: Secretaría de la Función Pública, Informe de Labores y de ejecución, 2011 y 2013, www.funcionpublica.gob.mx/index.php/temas/informes/informes-de-labores-y-de-ejecucion.html (accessed 15 October 2014).

A closer look at direct awards may help to understand why the ISSSTE has come to use them so widely, why the number of exceptions to public tendering has increased and ways to reduce them.

Article 41 of the LAASSP provides 20 possible exceptions to public biddings. Of those 20, the ISSSTE's central level and delegations used the following ones in 2013:

- Article 41. Fr. I: There are no technically reasonable alternative goods or services or substitutes products or services. There is only one potential supplier in the market, or the supplier has ownership, licensing or other exclusive rights, or copyright or art is being purchased.
- Article 41. Fr. II: The social order, the economy, public services, sanitation, safety or the environment in any area or region of the country is altered or threatened as a result of accident or *force majeure*.
- Article 41. Fr. III: Carrying out a public tendering procedure would occasion significant costs or losses.
- Article 41. Fr. V: An unplanned event or *force majeure* makes it impossible to obtain goods or services through competitive tendering within the time required –

in that event, the value of the contract or the number of items being purchased is limited to the minimum.

- Article 41. Fr. VI: A rescinded contract allows the second best supplier to be contracted.
- Article 41. Fr. VII: A public tendering was unsuccessful.
- Article 41. Fr. VIII: For the purchase or lease of a sole brand.
- Article 41. Fr. IX: Perishable goods, grains or food products are to be procured.
- Article 41. Fr. XI: For leases or services offered by rural or marginalised urban communities.
- Article 41. Fr. XIV: Services can be provided by a single specialist or technician.
- Article 41. Fr. XV: For the maintenance of goods for which it is not possible to determine the extent, the quantities or specifications.
- Article 41 Fr. XX: Specific contracts result from framework agreements.

Article 42 of the LAASSP also states that is possible to award contracts directly when the amount covers too few goods or the value is below an established threshold to warrant a competitive bidding process.

Central units and delegations both make use of direct awards

The ISSSTE's central units account for approximately 90% of the value of all of the tenders it issues through centralised procurement of goods and services. Those goods and services are medicines, medical supplies, gases used for clinical reasons in hospitals, and such non-clinical goods and services as uniforms and clothing, IT goods and services, and vehicles. In 2013, according to data provided by the ISSSTE, 63% in value of the ISSSTE's central procurement contracts were awarded directly through exceptions to public bidding (Figure 5.2).

Figure 5.2. **Types of procurement procedure used by central units, 2013**

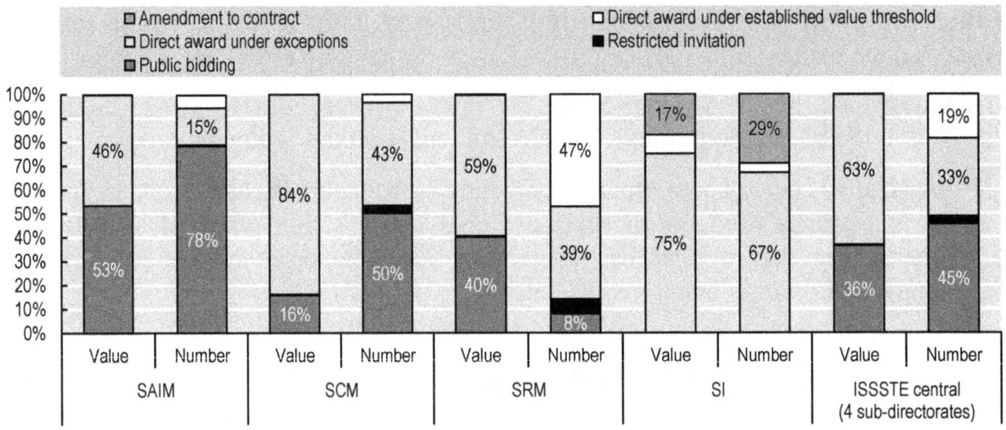

Notes: SAIM: Sub-Directorate of Medical Supplies (*Subdirección de Abasto de Insumos Médicos*); SCM: Sub-Directorate of Conservation and Maintenance (*Subdirección de Conservación y Mantenimiento*); SRM: Sub-Directorate of Materials and Services (*Subdirección de Recursos Materiales y Servicios*; SI: Sub-Directorate of Infrastructure (*Subdirección de Infraestructura*).

Source: Author's calculation based on data provided by the ISSSTE.

Some exceptions can be explained by the nature of the products the ISSSTE seeks to acquire – e.g. a patented medicine where only one supplier holds the right to sell it – by medical emergencies or epidemics, or by market opportunities for purchasing directly from one supplier only.

In 2013, delegations, too, awarded 37% in value of all procurement contracts through direct awards (Figure 5.3).

Figure 5.3. **Procurement procedures used by the ISSSTE's delegations in terms of value, 2013**

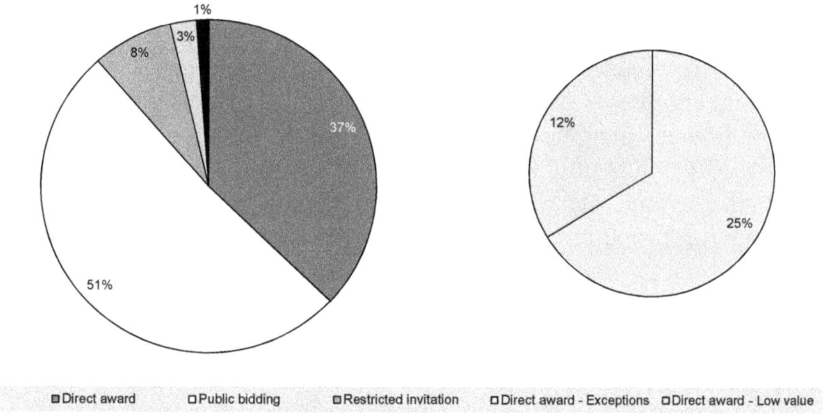

Note: No data were available for six delegations (Baja California Norte, Michoacán, Tamaulipas, Veracruz, Yucatán and Zona Norte) – information was either not provided or provided in a format that did not allow calculation.

Source: Author's calculation based on data provided by the ISSSTE.

Although 51% in value of contracts were awarded through public tenders, 37% of direct awards is nevertheless a high share. For instance, 8 delegations out of the 29 for which data were available used direct awards in more than 50% of procurements (Figure 5.4).

Figure 5.4. **Proportion of direct awards by ISSSTE under the terms of Article 41 of the LAASSP (exceptions) and Article 42 (low value), in terms of value, by delegation 2013**

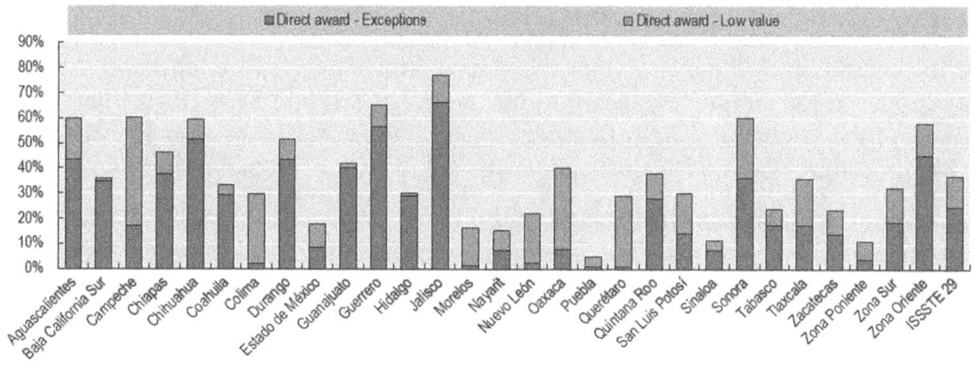

Note: No data were available for six delegations (Baja California Norte, Michoacán, Tamaulipas, Veracruz, Yucatán and Zona Norte) – information was either not provided or provided in a format that did not allow calculation.

Source: Author's calculation based on data provided by the ISSSTE.

Figure 5.4 shows that, for example, the Puebla Delegation – the one with the lowest number of direct awards – awarded only 5% of its contracts directly, while the figure for Jalisco was 77%.

Of the total of 37% of contracts awarded directly by delegations, low value accounted for 12% of them. Article 42 of the LAASSP states that low value contracts may represent up to 30% of all procurement contracts. However, Campeche (43%) and Oaxaca (33%) both exceed that threshold.

It is recommended that the ISSSTE analyse the reasons for the divergence of the use of direct awards among the delegations. A thorough examination of the reasons for using exceptions would help assess whether the facts of each case warranted them. In interviews with stakeholders – who include the ISSSTE's central units and delegations as well as external bodies, like the Ministry of Public Administration (*Secretaría de la Función Pública*, SFP) – the OECD found that direct awards can sometimes be explained by the ISSSTE's inadequate planning, both in forecasting needs for goods and services as well as in timing the procurement process, and its lack of market intelligence on the availability of products and services and Mexican suppliers' capacity to meet requirements. Such shortcoming can be remedied by improving planning processes and market intelligence levels, in accordance with the recommendations made in Chapters 2 and 3 and in the action plans proposed in those chapters' annexes.

Direct awards are principally justified using six exceptions

As Figures 5.2 and 5.3 show, 25% of delegations' contracts and 63% of the ISSSTE's central level contracts were directly awarded in 2013 through the use of exceptions to public tenders in accordance with Article 41 of the LAASSP.

The Goods, Leasing and Services Committee (*Comité de Adquisiciones, Arrendamientos y Servicios*, CAAS) is in charge of reviewing and authorising the use of exceptions to public tendering at the central level. Similar subcommittees are in place in delegations. The CAAS should carefully examine the frequency of exceptions and the reasons for using them by drawing on the insights afforded by the OECD data analysis below.

The use of exceptions at the central level

At the central level, the most widely used exceptions are Fr. I (no alternative goods, a single supplier in the market, exclusive rights, works of art) and Fr. VIII (a sole brand) of Article 41 of the LAASSP. The Infrastructure Sub-Directorate also uses Fr. III (a public tendering procedure occasions significant costs and/or losses, as shown in Figure 5.5).

According to data received by the OECD (Figure 5.6), the Sub-Directorate of Conservation and Maintenance (*Subdirección de Conservación y Mantenimiento*, SCM) has used three exceptions to public bidding in the past three years: Article 41 Fr. I, Fr. III and Fr. VII (unsuccessful public tendering) of the LAASSP. Fr. I is the most commonly used exception: the ISSSTE used it to purchase goods and services inherent to its activities, such as medical gases and rent infrastructure for its medical units. Between 2011 and 2013, the SCM's use of exceptions remained steady, with just a slight increase in 2013.

Figure 5.5. **Exceptions to public bidding used by the ISSSTE's central level, 2013**

Percentages express value of contracts

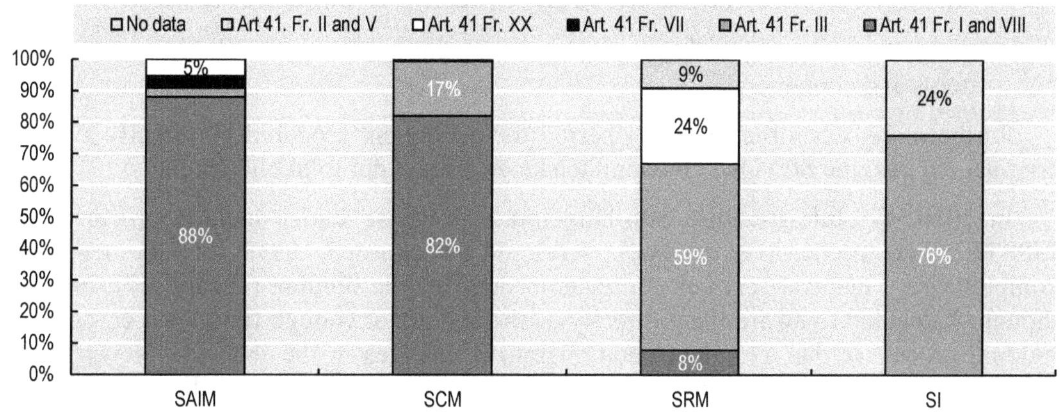

Notes: Sub-Directorate of Medical Supplies (*Subdirección de Abasto de Insumos Médicos*); SCM – Sub-Directorate of Conservation and Maintenance (*Subdirección de Conservación y Mantenimiento*); SRM – Sub-Directorate of Materials and Services (*Subdirección de Recursos Materiales y Servicios*; SI – Sub-Directorate of Infrastructure (*Subdirección de Infraestructura*).

Source: Author's calculation based on data provided by the ISSSTE.

Figure 5.6. **Use of exceptions to public bidding by the Sub-Directorate of Conservation and Maintenance in terms of value**

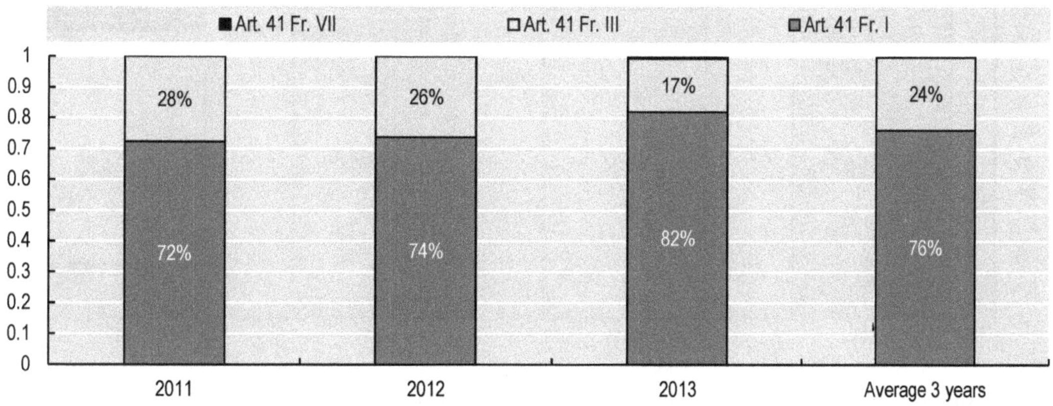

Source: Author's calculation based on data provided by the ISSSTE's Sub-Directorate of Conservation and Maintenance (*Subdirección de Conservación y Mantenimiento*, SCM).

The SCM generally procures medical gases and related equipment and services from large companies, as they have the capacity to deliver. It explains that it awards contracts directly to large suppliers because they:

- hold the exclusive rights over the brands of equipment installed in the ISSSTE's buildings (Philips, Siemens, etc.)
- provide replacement parts and service equipment installed in the ISSSTE
- are specialised and can respond in a timely manner

- comply with technical regulations; have technical, operational and financial capacity, the necessary infrastructure and trained personnel; take adequate safety measures; and provide preventive and corrective maintenance services
- have the necessary safety equipment and know-how to handle gas and related tools and containers.

Furthermore, when the servicing period for equipment procured by directly awarded contract expires, the SCM puts the maintenance contract out to public tender.

In 2010, the Infrastructure Sub-Directorate – whose duties include procuring the ISSSTE's comprehensive medical services – awarded 99% of its tri-annual comprehensive medical services contracts through public bidding (Figure 5.7). In 2013, though, it decided to award them directly as there was not enough time for a competitive bidding procedure due to internal administrative changes in the ISSSTE. Nevertheless, the ISSSTE sought to widen the supplier base for its comprehensive medical services and negotiate savings. It finally awarded its contracts directly to small companies that had previously worked as sub-contractors to the big ones. It thus managed to increase the number of its suppliers from three in 2011 to more than six in 2013 and secure significant savings.

Figure 5.7. **Use of exceptions to public bidding by the Sub-Directorate of Infrastructure**

Percentages express the value of contracts

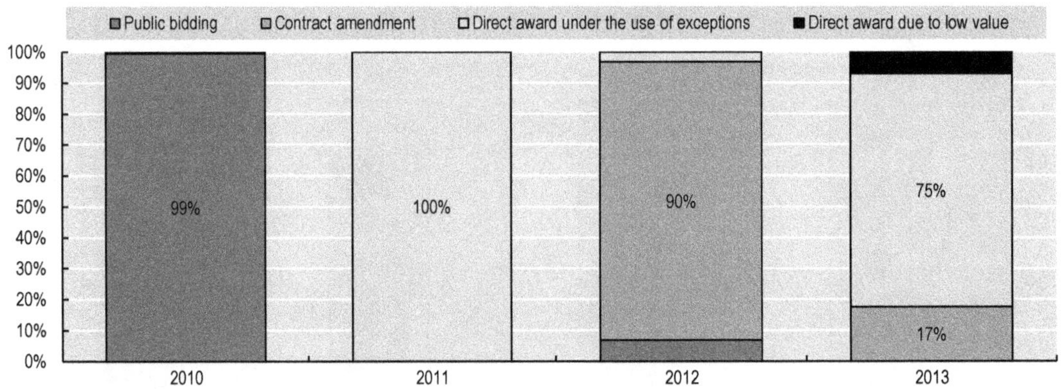

Source: Author's calculation based on data provided by the ISSSTE.

Use of exceptions at the local level

In 2013 and in order of how often they were used, Fr. III, VII, II, V, I and VIII of the LAASSP Article 41 accounted for 73% of delegations' direct awards (Figure 5.8).

According to data provided by the ISSSTE, most delegations – 20 out of 29 – used Fr. III (public tendering creates significant costs and/or losses) as the grounds for direct awards. It represented 39% of the total value of all direct awards. Fr. VII (unsuccessful public tender), with 19%, was the next most often used exception.

Figure 5.8. **Exceptions to public bidding used by delegations, 2013**

Percentages of the total value of direct awards using Article 41

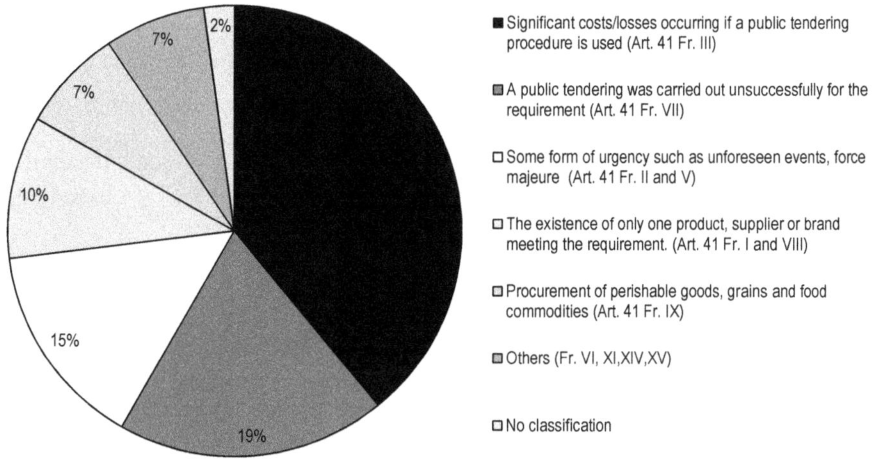

Note: No data were available for six delegations (Baja California Norte, Michoacán, Tamaulipas, Veracruz, Yucatán and Zona Norte). These delegations did not provide information or provided it in a format that did not allow calculation.

Source: Author's calculation based on data provided by the ISSSTE.

Fr. I and Fr. VIII of the LAASSP both provide "sole" grounds – sole supplier and sole brand – for resorting to direct awards (Figure 5.9).

Figure 5.9. **Delegations' use of sole source/brand exception (Fr. I and Fr. VIII), 2013**

Percentages of the total value of direct awards using Article 41

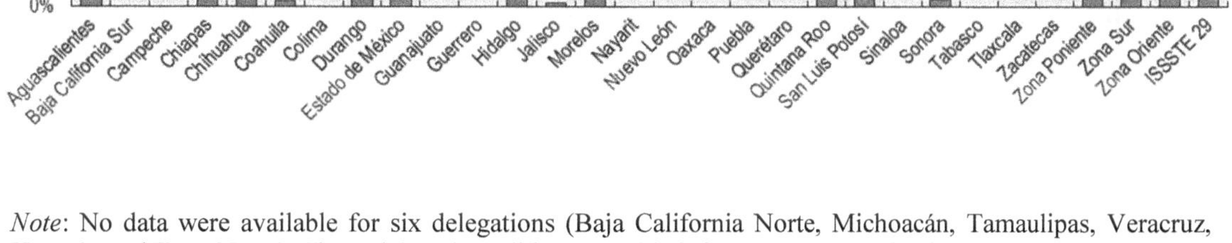

Note: No data were available for six delegations (Baja California Norte, Michoacán, Tamaulipas, Veracruz, Yucatán and Zona Norte). These delegations did not provide information or provided it in a format that did not allow calculation.

Source: Author's calculation based on data provided by the ISSSTE.

The Zona Poniente Delegation appears to have awarded all of its directly awarded contracts in 2013 using the sole-supplier exception in Fr. I of LAASSP Article 41.

Exception Fr. IX of the LAASSP allows direct awards for perishable goods, grains and food products to meet the needs of hospitals and day care centres (Figure 5.10). Some delegations argue that they have to award contracts directly to suppliers operating in the same state in order to ensure that foodstuffs are fresh and in good condition. While delivery by local suppliers makes sense, explanations for not using a call for tender are not sufficient because delegations can establish framework agreements or multi-year contracts for the provision of such goods. Contracts for perishable goods could be centralised at the regional level, depending on suppliers' geographical proximity and the type and quantities of perishables needed. Delegations that are located close to each other could make economies of scale.

Figure 5.10. **Delegations' use of the perishable goods exception (Fr. IX), 2013**

Percentages of the total value of direct awards using Article 41

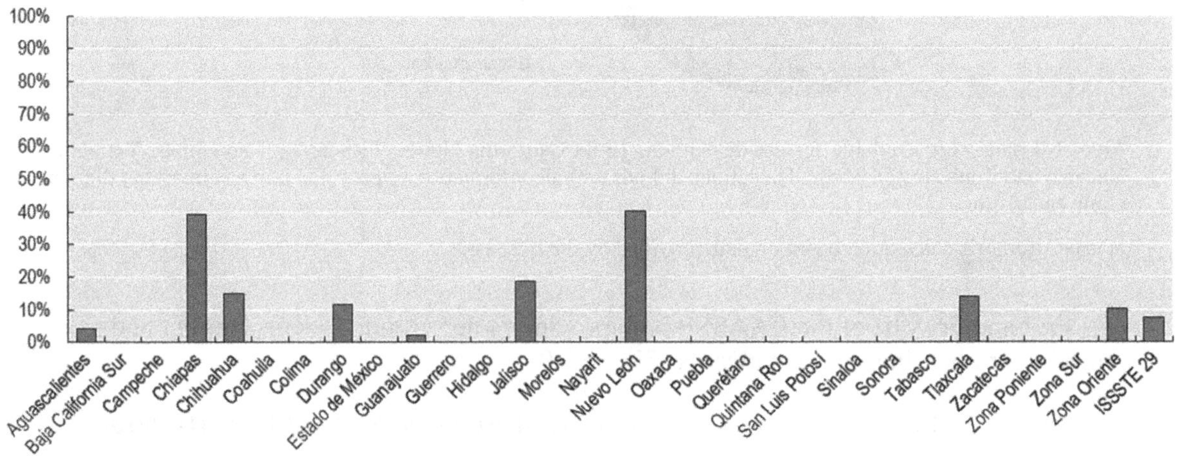

Note: No data were available for six delegations, namely Baja California Norte, Michoacán, Tamaulipas, Veracruz, Yucatán and Zona Norte. These delegations did not provide information or provided it in a format that did not allow calculation.

Source: Author's calculation based on data provided by the ISSSTE.

The use of Fr. II and V may reflect poor planning that can be remedied

Several delegations expressed concerns about the length of competitive procurement procedures. Some claimed that six months could pass between the time the winning bidder was announced and the actual signature of the contract. Such delays often stem from the fact that delegations may not use existing model contracts, but constantly (re)design contracts and ask the ISSSTE's Legal Directorate or their own legal department to review them. Recently, the Legal Directorate has created some model contracts that are being used by the delegations.

The time it takes to legally review a newly drafted contract depends on its quality and whether it needs light or substantive editing. Another factor is the workload of the Legal Directorate; there have actually been even a couple of reported instances of suppliers delivering without a signed contract in order to cover a supply emergency. And when contracts use models, the Legal Directorate still reviews them. Delays are thus caused by the replication of reviews of documents that are very similar.

Contract models should, first of all, be reviewed for their accuracy, user-friendliness and responsiveness to the commercial needs of buyers (ISSSTE delegations) and suppliers. Second, they should be updated where necessary and, third, used by all procurement units – including central ones, without requiring any modifications or check by the Legal Directorate. In the case of reasonable and justified commercial concerns that necessitate amendments to the standard contract terms, only the amendments should be vetted and approved by the Legal Directorate.

One example of a model contract for tender documents that may be used for procuring a range of goods and services comes from the NHS in the United Kingdom. The NHS "Terms and conditions for the supply of goods and the provision of services" "provides the core 'DNA' for all other sets … of contracting terms and conditions" (NHS, 2014).

As well as delays attributable to redundant, but avoidable, legal reviews, issues pertaining to planning and budget allocation issues (explained in detail later in this section) further limit lead procurement time. Indeed, the time left to run a full competitive procedure may sometimes be so short that it compels procuring entities to resort to direct awards and use exceptions to competitive tendering related to emergency or cases of *force majeure* (Article 41, Fr. II and Fr. V of the LAASSP) (Figure 5.11).

"Emergency" purchases tend to take place at the end of the fiscal year when the ISSSTE's units try to spend still-unspent monies, as they cannot carry them over into the next fiscal year. Such a practice, also found in other procurement agencies around the world, is a pseudo-emergency. Yet it enables procurers to award contracts directly when only open bidding would otherwise be possible (Kühn and Sherman, 2014).

Delegations admit that they use the grounds of emergency when they do not have enough time to carry out a public tender or respond in a timely manner to the needs of the beneficiaries. The Coahuila Delegation also mentioned that it availed itself of the emergency exception to commission equipment maintenance services and procure medicines when those acquired centrally were insufficient and medical needs had to be urgently met.

Figure 5.11. **Delegations' use of emergency and *force majeure* exceptions (Fr. II and Fr. V), 2013**

Percentages of the total value of direct awards using Article 41

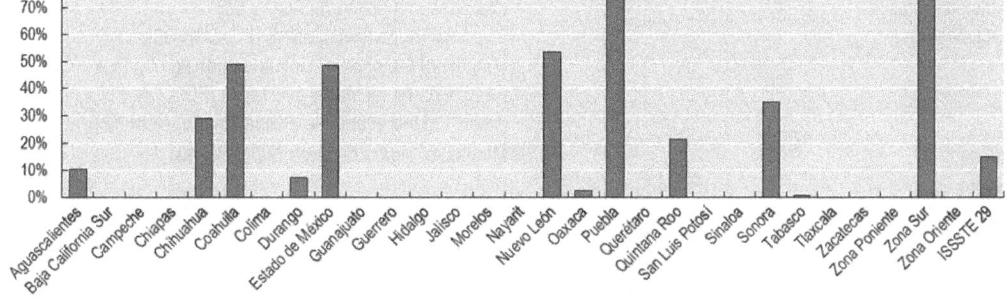

Note: No data were available for six delegations (Baja California Norte, Michoacán, Tamaulipas, Veracruz, Yucatán and Zona Norte). These delegations did not provide information or provided it in a format that did not allow calculation.

Source: Author's calculation based on data provided by the ISSSTE.

During the OECD fact-finding mission, stakeholders like the SFP and the supreme audit institution (*Auditoria Superior de la Federación*, ASF) stated that the ISSSTE's procurement planning processes were not well enough organised to allow the time to prepare and carry out a competitive procurement procedure. Some respondents also hinted that public servants were not used to planning but to working on a last-minute basis. Delegations know full well, for example, that the Annual Procurement Programme (*Programa Anual de Adquisiciones, Arrendamientos y Servicios*, PAAAS) has to be ready by 31 January each year. However, they do not draw up procurement plans that reflect their real current needs, but reuse previous ones that they modify slightly before submitting. The practice is due as much to habit as well as to understaffing or the lack of thorough data.

Room for improvement in budget allocation, procurement planning and payment approval

Feedback collected during the fact-finding mission revealed that the timing and manner of budget allocation is a recurrent challenge in the delegations. They do not have readily available funds, so, each time they want to procure, they must submit a request for endorsement of their "budget sufficiency" proving that they can commit the money corresponding to the purchase.

The contracting process, set out in the "General Procurement Manual", was adopted in 2010 by the SFP to help public bodies comply with the LAASSP (Table 5.1). This manual requires them to request "budget sustainability" (*solvencia presupuestal*) before submitting a purchase request (*requisición de compra de bienes o servicios*, RCB).

Table 5.1. **The contracting process set out in the "General Procurement Manual"**

Sub-process	Templates[1]
Elaboration of purchase request (*requisición de compra de bienes o servicios*, RCB). Involves evaluating needs based on the approved PAAAS, verifying existing contracts (including multi-year contracts and framework agreements), assessing current levels of stock, conducting market research, selecting a procurement procedure, choosing the selection criteria and procurement tools, obtaining budget sustainability (*solvencia presupuestal*) and the elaboration of the RCB.	– Purchase request form for an existing contract (FO-CON-01) – Verification of stock (FO-CON-02) – Purchase request (RCB) (FO-CON-03) – Request for market research (FO-CON-04) – Market investigation results (FO-CON-05)
Carry out selected procurement procedure – public tender – restricted invitation – direct award	– Calendar for tender procedures (FO-CON-06) – Summary of public tender solicitation (FO-CON-07) – Clarification meeting (FO-CON-08) – Checklist for reviewing offers (FO-CON-09) – Minutes of the presentation and opening of offers (FO-CON-10) – Results of the technical evaluation (FO-CON-11) – Results of the economic evaluation (FO-CON-12)
Award contract	– Minutes of award decision (FO-CON-13)
Sign contract	
File contract	

Note: 1. Format available at: www.funcionpublica.gob.mx/index.php/ua/sracp/uncp/General_Procurement Manual.html (accessed 14 September 2014).

Source: Manual Administrativo de Aplicación General en Materia de Adquisiciones, Arrendamientos y Servicios del Sector Público.

A number of delegations feel that it takes too long to have their "budget sustainability" endorsed. The result is delays in starting the procurement procedure, which in turn prompts delegations to resort to direct awards to save time. The Programming and Budgeting Sub-Directorate pointed out, however, that procurement units can start planning without their "budget sustainability" endorsement, as long as they obtain it before the tendering process (the request for bids) has officially begun. Clear guidelines from the ISSSTE's central level to the delegations on this issue would be very helpful.

In addition to the complexity of the budget sustainability procedure, delegations reported that the SSSTE's budget allocation did not guarantee that their request will be met. As explained in Chapter 2, the budget granted to the ISSSTE may be less than requested – it depends on adjustments made by the Ministry of Finance when drawing up the budget, on approval by Congress of the total federal expenditure budget in November and on other related factors. The lower the amount of funds approved for the ISSSTE, the lower the budget allocated to delegations. Delegations believe that budgets are attributed primarily according to the size of the delegation and, in particular, the number of beneficiaries that it covers. The ISSSTE confirms that the budget is indeed allocated according to:

- the number of beneficiaries
- how the budget has evolved historically
- priority projects or programmes directly approved by the Director of the ISSSTE.

However, data on beneficiaries are not reliable, patients' census reports may be inaccurate and allocation decisions may contain elements of randomness.[2] While automated data collection would improve matters (Chapter 2), delegations should also provide as much pertinent information as possible to the Programming and Budgeting Sub-Directorate when it puts together its budget request to the Ministry of Finance.

Delegations realise that it is possible – and probable – that their budget requests will not be granted in full. They could, therefore, adjust their planning accordingly, as did the Zona Poniente Delegation. It reduced its number of directly awarded contracts between 2011 and 2013 which, according to OECD interviews, was the result of good planning – it had a plan B in place, whereby it relinquished low-priority action and focused on priority ones should the total budget requested not be granted.

The ISSSTE could draw on the example of the Zona Poniente Delegation and regularly check on the percentages and reasons for the emergency and *force majeure* exceptions, used more by the delegations than by the central level. In parallel, it could meet with delegations to identify good practices for improving procurement planning and management. Good practices should be disseminated internally and externally (see Chapter 2).

Not only can the budgetary process delay the start of a tendering process (although it is possible to start planning procurements before receiving the budget), payment may also slow things down because of the *cuenta cero* (zero available cash) system. Under the system, the Programming and Budgeting Sub-Directorate must first approve all payments made by delegations (who must provide invoices). Only once it has received the funds it requested can a delegation pay its supplier.

Delegations used to have autonomous budgets. The *cuenta cero* system was put in place by the ISSSTE's central level to control units' expenditure and ensure that suppliers are paid in a timely manner and that funds are used efficiently. The largest delegations – like those of the State of Mexico, Zona Norte and Oriente – agree that the measure has contributed to better organised, more timely payments, since it obliges delegations to plan payment more effectively. However, other delegations have argued that *cuenta cero* has restricted their capacity to face emergencies, as approvals can be lengthy and squeeze the timeframe for directly contracting and paying suppliers. According to the Programming and Budgeting Sub-Directorate, approval generally takes 72 hours but can be as long as 5 days at the end of the year, when requests from delegations under pressure to use the unspent part of their budgets flow in.

Although the *cuenta cero* system applies to the payment of suppliers, and not contracting *per se*, a clarification of the timelines and procedures involved in approving and transferring funds to delegations would be helpful.

Direct awards may stem from the complexity of the law

Article 41, Fr. III states that a contract may be directly awarded if a public tender creates significant costs and/or losses. It accounts for an average of one-third of the total value of direct awards (Figure 5.12).

Figure 5.12. **Delegations' use of the Fr. III exception, 2013**

Percentages of the total value of direct awards using Article 41

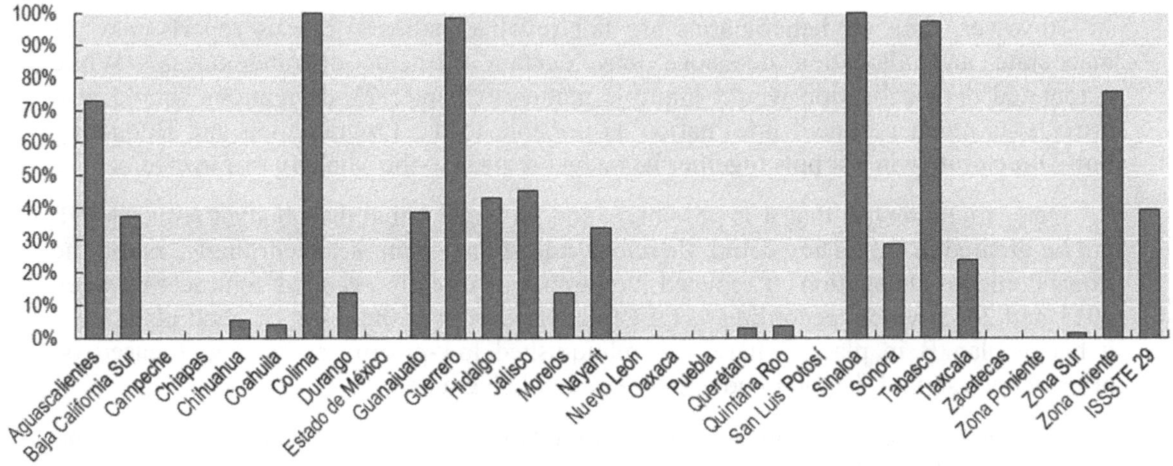

Note: No data were available for six delegations (Baja California Norte, Michoacán, Tamaulipas, Veracruz, Yucatán and Zona Norte). They did not provide information or provided it in a format that did not allow calculation.

Source: Author's calculation based on data provided by the ISSSTE.

Some delegations make use of Fr. III as follows. If during the market intelligence phase a procurement unit finds that a supplier's price is higher than the price obtained in a previous public tender, it may award the contract directly to the supplier who had offered the lower price. However, competition is one of the principles of the Mexican procurement legal framework which does not encourage direct awards and admits them only in exceptional cases. Open competitive bidding should be the rule, particularly as market intelligence only provides an indication of price. Indeed, stakeholders interviewed by the OECD (who included suppliers) mentioned that suppliers may deliberately quote a high price in response to the request for estimates phase of market research. They do so as not to lower the procurement reference price and avoid being pressured into making even lower bids when the actual procurement process gets underway.

A further incentive for awarding contracts directly is the complexity of Mexican procurement rules. To comply with them, procurement officers have to follow several administrative procedures at once. They are sometimes tempted to save themselves time, bureaucracy and inconvenience by directly awarding contracts to suppliers whom they already know and have proven themselves in previous bids.

Clear guidelines, possibly from the SFP and perhaps with added guidance from the ISSSTE, would help shed light on how Fr. III should and should not be used.

The ISSSTE can overcome challenges

Full-time, skilled staff and training to support effective competitive procurement procedures

As Chapter 3 pointed out, the ISSSTE's market research can be perfunctory and not afford a full overview of markets. Not all delegations feel equipped to carry out market research and sometimes they try to avoid it. The shortfalls of market intelligence are exacerbated by the ISSSTE's limited staff and skills capacity and the absence of appropriate training. Central directorates, the ISSSTE's internal control body and delegations all highlight low staffing and skills levels and the fact that that procurement staff are overburdened with paperwork and therefore not wholly dedicated to the procurement activity.

According to information provided by the ISSSTE for the first OECD review, approximately 600 officials work in procurement. The fact that some units are reportedly understaffed suggests that the problem is one of poorly planned and distributed staffing across the organisation. The fact-finding mission for this report found that staffing decisions are taken at the central level on the basis of proposals from the delegations, but without any real communication between the delegations and the Administration Directorate on staffing needs and priorities. Furthermore, there is little provision for transferring or reallocating staff to the units where they are needed the most, which prevents any results-oriented distribution or efficient management of human resources.

Like many other OECD countries, Mexico suffers from a shortage of full-time procurement officers that are exclusively dedicated to public procurement activities and not to other administrative tasks, and that are recognised as specialised professionals (Figure 5.13).

Staff could be distributed more effectively on the basis of good and open communication between human resources departments and areas in need of support from people with a grasp of procurement. It would also be possible to improve the knowledge and skills of procurement staff through continuous training.

To date, procurement training has been provided chiefly by Ministry of Public Administration (SFP), especially on the use of the Mexican e-procurement system, Compranet. The classroom training takes place in Mexico City, while local training is still relatively limited, although the SFP does have plans to bring in-person courses to different cities. The ISSSTE provides some training to personnel involved in procurement planning. Nevertheless, its internal control body, central units and delegations concur that trainings should be increased and enhanced since "those that exist are limited to detailing what is stated in the procurement law and regulations but do not provide examples or guidance on operational problems or challenges such as price negotiation or market research"[3].

Figure 5.13. **OECD countries that recognise procurement as a specific profession, 2010**

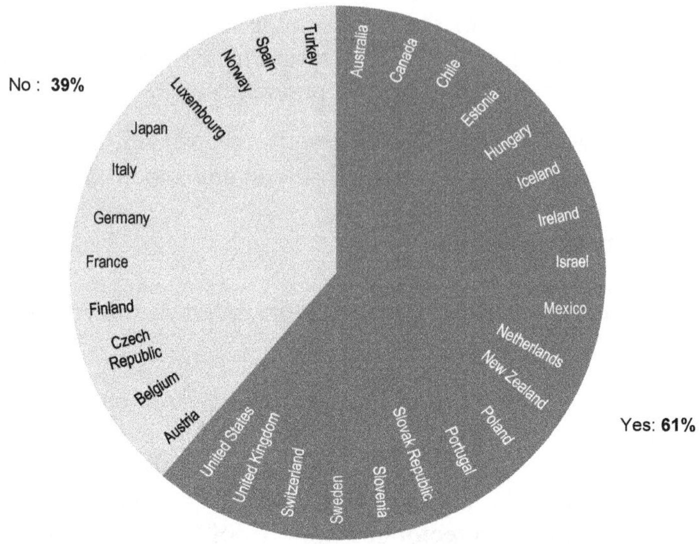

Source: OECD (2013a), *Government at a Glance 2013*, OECD Publishing, Paris, http://dx.doi.org/10.1787/gov_glance-2013-en.

The SFP is developing training that goes beyond Compranet and offers procurement officials operational information. The ISSSTE could benefit from training initiatives currently led by the SFP and tailor them to its own needs, implementing ISSSTE-specific internal capacity building, like workshops, conferences, online courses and webinars. The dissemination of materials for the purposes of such capacity-building activities and resources is as vital as the activities and resources themselves, since they materials will ensure knowledge transfer and sustainability of results.

Experienced procurers from central areas and delegations could do the training, focusing on practical issues related to planning, budgeting and ways of avoiding overreliance on direct awards. ISSSTE-specific training courses could also be prepared and conducted in conjunction with international organisations or training bodies, or leading Mexican universities and institutes. The ISSSTE has co-operation agreements with the Autonomous National University of Mexico (*Universidad Nacional Autónoma de México*) and the National Polytechnic Institute (*Instituto Politécnico Nacional*) on procurement good practices and could develop courses and materials with them.

Streamlined, functional specifications could reduce reliance on exceptions

Under the terms of Article 41, Fr. VII of the LAASSP, a contract may be awarded directly if a competitive bid was unsuccessful and as long as its terms and requirements remain unchanged. During the OECD fact-finding mission, it was reported that public tenders may be unsuccessful because the bids received do not meet the terms of the tender documents or because no bid is received. The ISSSTE's delegations make use Fr. VII as shown in Figure 5.14.

Figure 5.14. **Delegations' use of the unsuccessful bid exception (Fr. VII), 2013**

Percentages of the total value of direct awards using Article 41

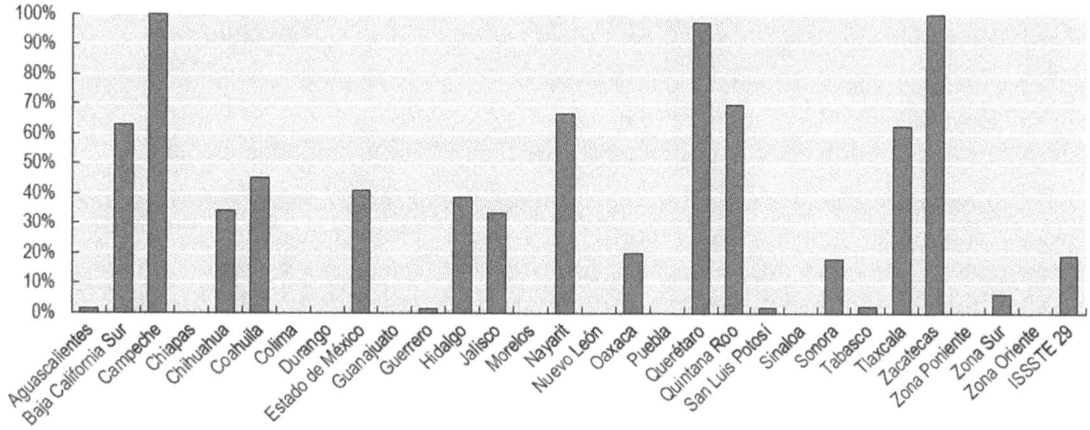

Source: Author's calculation based on data provided by the ISSSTE.

The OECD's first public procurement review of the ISSSTE found that that specifications were restrictive (OECD, 2013c) and sometimes difficult for suppliers to meet. They may be one reason for unsuccessful procedures. Another reason may be that the ISSSTE's *Institutional Catalogue of Healthcare Supplies* is not updated in a timely manner, leading some ISSSTE areas to request products that no longer exist.

Specifications should be as open as possible and based on functional and performance terms rather than solely on technical descriptions in order to encourage effective competition (OECD, 2008). The importance and difficulty of adequately translating an organisation's needs into clear functional or performance characteristics are often underestimated, not only by user areas but by procurement units as well. Nonetheless, functional requirements – which focus on results and not on compliance with rigid tender terms – can greatly contribute to achieving the best value and reducing the number of tender procedures that are declared unsuccessful and lead to direct awards. Moreover, functional requirements allow potential suppliers to offer valid alternatives, thereby increasing the level of competition, promoting innovation and offering better supply conditions.

During the first OECD procurement review of the ISSSTE, delegations reported that drafting specifications is challenging, as requesting areas identify their needs late and there is little time to analyse demand requests and supply solutions and to draft, in consequence, effective specifications. Matters are compounded by a lack of knowledge of the various solutions available on the market – which links back to the need to improve market intelligence in the ISSSTE – and the inadequate guidance in drafting tender specifications.

In order to translate needs into specifications that serve the institute's goals, procurement agents should describe them in functional terms. Practical tools (such as checklists, best practices and templates) and training in how to prepare specifications would help. For standard goods and services, a clear description, which ensures that what is bought is what was needed, may suffice. To that end, the ISSSTE could consider putting in place a regular update of the *Institutional Catalogue for Healthcare Supplies*.

Standardised technical specifications for the most common products would also be helpful as long as it was regularly updated to keep pace with the supply market.

Consistent data across the ISSSTE could reduce the use of exceptions

As detailed above, to reduce the extensive use of exceptions to public tendering, the ISSSTE should regularly monitor the use of exceptions in order to identify persistent problems and opportunities to improve procurement planning and management.

Currently the ISSSTE lacks the tools to consolidate data rapidly and accurately into organisation-wide statistics and reports and to take action accordingly. The ISSSTE's procurement units use different codes and formats, which are sometimes inconsistent even within the same unit. For example, it emerged during fact-finding for this review that few delegations were able to provide the information in the format requested. The spreadsheets provided by the delegations exhibited significant disparities in the value of contracts awarded over the period 2011-13 and the use of exceptions to public tendering. Also, several codes sometimes designated the same exception.

In order to ensure the compatibility of procurement data and facilitate their consolidation, the ISSSTE could consider limiting and harmonising the number of codes used in the various procurement units. For example, standard tools like spreadsheets with harmonised, fewer codes and formats and basic functionalities that prevent or highlight deviations from the established standards would strongly improve the efficiency and effectiveness of the data collection process.

The ISSSTE could consider implementing a standardised classification model for identifying products (that matched the codes used by manufacturers, retailers or service providers). For example, the McKinsey report, "Strength in unity" (Ebel et al., 2012), identified recurrent savings of USD 4.9 million and USD 8.1 million for a 600-bed trust based on full implementation of global GS1 standards[4] (NHS, 2013).

Table 5.2. **Examples of codes used to designate the exceptions**

Adjudicacion Directa Articulo 41	Article 41 – no classification
Adjudicacion Directa Articulo 41 Fr. I Adjudicación Directa Art. N°41 Fr. I Adjudicacion Directa Art. N° 41 Fr. I	Article 41-Fr. I
Adjudicacion Directa Articulo 41 Fracc III Adjudicacion Directa Aticulo 41 Fr. III Adjudicacion Directa Articulo 41 Fr. III Adjudicacion Directa Art. N° 41 Fr. III Adjudicacion Directa 41 Fr. III Adjudicacion Directa 41 Fracc III Adjudicacion Directa Art. N°41 Fr. III	Article 41-Fr. III
Adjudicacion Directa Art. N°41 Fr. V Adjudicacion Directa Articulo 41 Fr. V	Article 41-Fr. V
Adjudicacion Directa Art. N° 41 Fr. IIv Adjudicacion Directa Aticulo 41 Fr. VII	Article 41-Fr. VII

Source: Based on information provided by the ISSSTE.

The immediate benefit of using a unified product classification is that the same understanding of exactly what products are needed will be shared across the ISSSTE. If the same classification is also used by suppliers and a single nomenclature is eventually used for all purposes and all products, then all procurement buyers and vendors will share the same understanding of needs. The issues of imprecise or inaccurate specifications, non-compliant bids and unsuccessful processes will be no more.

The absence of appropriate software prevents the efficient collection and consolidation of data. A sophisticated information management system for all procurement activities would help the accuracy, scope and timeliness of data (see Annex 2.A1). During the fact-finding for this review, the OECD found that most delegations and central areas did collect data, since they were able to provide the data requested. However, the data were not standardised or consolidated.

Information is extracted from the system and consolidated, albeit on an irregular basis. An example of such information is data on the monitoring of particular targets as part of specific initiatives. Nevertheless, data are not consistently collected in such a way as to be able to assess results over time and quickly identify, for example, positive or negative trends on the use of exceptions. The ISSSTE could gain a clearer view of what is spent, understand buying patterns and forecast supply requirements if it established a common coding system such as the NHS has done (Box 5.1).

Box 5.1. National Health Service's procurement strategy promotes greater transparency on hospitals' supplier expenditure

The NHS currently spends GBP 4.5 billion annually on clinical supplies and services. In 2013, it outlined a new procurement strategy which it hopes will result in GBP 1.5 billion of "procurement efficiencies" over a three-year period.

Data is at the core of the strategy which is – through the development, procurement and implementation of a single, best-in-class NHS Spend Analysis and Price Benchmarking Service – to streamline the data collection and benchmarking process and enable NHS trusts to frequently and cost-effectively compare prices across a wide range of goods and services.

Accurate master data used consistently across the supply chain provides the foundation for procurement efficiency. A common language, backed by a common messaging standard, enables trusts and their suppliers to capture and share procurement data using the same barcode-driven technology that is used by retailers and industry to eliminate errors and waste in the supply chain.

Master data provides the key to analysing and sharing procurement expenditure. Visibility of spend is essential to understanding buying patterns and forecasting supply requirements, thus enabling trusts to secure better deals from their suppliers. Benchmarking between trusts will drive lower prices, releasing savings to the front line.

The essential building block for improving data for the longer term is the adoption by both the NHS and its supplier base of GS1 as the supply chain coding standard.

As part of this strategy, the NHS will:

- mandate through contracts the use of GS1 coding for the NHS
- create a single NHS GS1 data pool for the NHS to use in its systems
- centrally invest in enabling product information management and messaging technologies
- create a single "data warehouse" for NHS procurement data
- define standards to ensure interoperability between e-procurement systems

Box 5.1. National Health Service's procurement strategy promotes greater transparency on hospitals' supplier expenditure (*cont.*)

- establish standards for datasets and classification
- put implementation support arrangements in place for trusts to draw upon.

Implementing the e-procurement strategy, which includes the adoption of GS1, will enable trusts to share, compare and be transparent with their procurement information. This will not only help to hold the public service to account, but will increase visibility of opportunities for small and medium-sized enterprises, therefore supporting the economic recovery.

The NHS will therefore explore opportunities to:

- increase transparency by requiring all providers of NHS healthcare – through the NHS Standard Contract – to publish all procurement data, including opportunities, expenditure and contracts on their websites and Contracts Finder (an online tool that helps information about contracts with the government and its agencies)
- develop, procure and implement a single, best-in-class NHS Spend Analysis and Price Benchmarking Service to streamline the data collection and benchmarking process, and enable trusts to frequently and cost-effectively compare prices across a wide range of goods and services
- implement a dashboard of procurement performance metrics to support internal management and governance, enable public reporting and facilitate the identification and exchange of good and best practices.

Source: NHS (2013), "Better procurement, better value, better care: A procurement development programme for the NHS", National Health Service, Department of Health, Crown copyright, London, available at: www.gov.uk/government/uploads/system/uploads/attachment_data/file/226835/procurement_development_programme_for_NHS.pdf (accessed 17 October 2014).

On the basis of past OECD recommendations to gather consistent procurement data and reduce reliance on direct awards (OECD, 2013b; 2013c), the ISSSTE has started to work towards these goals in a pilot data collection project. The ISSSTE's central areas and delegations can still work together to better plan, avoid urgent requests, improve tender specifications and train procurement agents so that they can successfully carry out their tasks.

E-catalogues of products and services with standard characteristics are also helpful buying tools, in particular for purchases of small quantities. E-catalogues also allow extracting data on what is being procured by calculating types and quantities of products and services bought from them. They are used by many OECD countries. For example, the Portuguese Shared Services of the Ministry of Health developed an e-catalogue for commonly bought health products and services (Box 5.2).

Box 5.2. **Portuguese Shared Services of the Ministry of Health's e-catalogue promotes standardised purchases**

The Shared Services of the Health Ministry in Portugal (Serviços Partilhados do Ministério da Saúde, SPMS) is a public entity created in 2010 which works under the Ministries of Health and Finance. Its aim is to centralise, optimise and rationalise the procurement of goods and services for the national health system of Portugal. As part of its activities, the SPMS procures health goods and services, usually through framework agreements which are made available to public buyers.

In order to allow public buyers to place purchase orders for products or services easily and even in small quantities, the SPMS has developed an e-catalogue, which covers almost all medicines which have received marketing authorisation in the European Union, as well as medical equipment like catheters, gloves, pacemakers, stents, healthcare dressings. Buyers can search the e-catalogue for a particular product or service among a predefined list of various products and services with agreed specifications and prices, place an order for it directly with the supplier and follow up on the order until product delivery. More details on the e-catalogue can be found at: www.catalogo.min-saude.pt/caps/publico/default.asp?idioma=EN.

Source: Presentations made at the OECD workshop on "Improving Public Procurement Practices in ISSSTE", Mexico City, 2-4 September 2014, by Joana Candeias, Senior Officer at the Direction of Central Purchase of Health Goods and Services of the Shared Services of the Ministry of Health, Portugal.

Proposals for action

To reduce the use of exceptions, the ISSSTE could:

- Start in-house training by experienced ISSSTE procurement professionals to share practical ways of overcoming challenges and securing competition for contracts, strengthening current training initiatives (immediate action).
- Educate user areas (medical units) and procurement areas in the strategic importance of planning ahead for procurement processes (immediate action).
- Implement standard data collection tools common for all procurement units, like a spreadsheet with harmonised, and fewer codes and formats, as a step before introducing a comprehensive ISSSTE-wide procurement database (immediate action).
- Promote the use of functional tender requirements focused on results and not on compliance with specifications (immediate action).
- Regularly examine the use of the exceptions to competitive tendering in order to identify opportunities for curbing direct awards (immediate/medium-term action).
- Benefit from training and materials developed by the SFP and tailor them to the ISSSTE to strengthen internal capacity, possibly in conjunction with international organisations or training bodies, or leading Mexican universities and institutes with which the ISSSTE has co-operation agreements (immediate/medium-term action).
- Develop checklists and templates to facilitate the drafting of tender specifications (medium-term action).

- Regularly update the *Institutional Catalogue for Healthcare Supplies* (medium-term action).
- Consider implementing a standardised classification model for identifying products together with a classification system used by suppliers to ensure common understanding (long-term action).

Notes

1. The ISSSTE's commitments to its suppliers (*compromisos del ISSSTE con sus proveedores*), available at: www2.issste.gob.mx:8080/index.php/compromisos-issste-provedores.
2. Statement by various delegations during the fact-finding mission.
3. Statement during the fact-finding mission.
4. For more on GS1 standards, see: www.gs1.org/healthcare/standards.

References

Candeias, J. (2014), Senior Officer at the Direction of Central Purchase of Health Goods and Services of the Shared Services of the Portuguese Ministry of Health, presentations made at the OECD workshop on "Improving Public Procurement Practices in ISSSTE", Mexico City, 2-4 September.

Ebel, T. et al. (2012), "Strength in unity: The promise of global standards in healthcare", McKinsey & Company, October, available at: www.gs1.org/docs/healthcare/McKinsey_Healthcare_Report_Strength_in_Unity.pdf.

Kühn, S. and L.B. Sherman (2014), *Curbing Corruption in Public Procurement, A Practical Guide*, Transparency International, available at: www.transparency.org/whatwedo/publication/curbing_corruption_in_public_procurement_a_practical_guide.

NHS (2014), "The NHS terms and conditions for the supply of goods and the provision of services: Guidance", Department of Health, Crown copyright, March, available at: https://www.gov.uk/government/uploads/system/uploads/attachment_data/file/417479/NHS_TC.pdf (accessed 24 February 2015).

NHS (2013), "Better procurement, better value, better care: A procurement development programme for the NHS", National Health Service, Department of Health, London, available at: www.gov.uk/government/uploads/system/uploads/attachment_data/file/226835/procurement_development_programme_for_NHS.pdf (accessed 17 October 2014)

OECD (2015), *Recommendation of the Council on Public Procurement*, OECD, Paris, available at: http://acts.oecd.org/Instruments/ShowInstrumentView.aspx?InstrumentID=320&InstrumentPID=348&Lang=en&Book=False.

OECD (2013a), *Government at a Glance 2013*, OECD Publishing, Paris, http://dx.doi.org/10.1787/gov_glance-2013-en.

OECD (2013b), "Fighting bid rigging in public procurement in Mexico: A Secretariat analytical report on legislation, regulations and practices relating to procurement undertaken by ISSSTE", OECD, Paris, available at: www.oecd.org/daf/competition/mexicoissste2013.htm.

OECD (2013c), *Public Procurement Review of the State's Employees' Social Security and Social Services Institute in Mexico: Smart Procurement for Health Public Services*, OECD Public Governance Reviews, OECD Publishing, Paris, http://dx.doi.org/10.1787/9789264197305-en.

OECD (2009), "Enhancing Integrity at Each Stage of the Procurement Cycle: A Checklist", in OECD, OECD Principles for Integrity in Public Procurement, OECD Publishing, Paris, http://dx.doi.org/10.1787/9789264056527-8-en

UNODC (United Nations Office on Drugs and Crime) (2013), "Good practices in ensuring compliance with Article 9 of the United Nations Convention against Corruption: Guidebook on anti-corruption in public procurement and the management of public finances", United Nations Office on Drugs and Crime, Vienna, available at: www.unodc.org/documents/corruption/Publications/2013/Guidebook_on_anti-corruption_in_public_procurement_and_the_management_of_public_finances.pdf.

ANNEX A

Actions to promote transparency and efficiency in ISSSTE's procurement system

In order to move towards the implementation of the recommendations proposed in the OECD study, the ISSSTE has established a series of actions to promote transparency and efficiency in its procurement system. Each of these actions is part of the agenda that has been built by the Institute, which is immersed in a process of continuous and deep transformation. The agenda rests on four pillars:

a) A user-friendly and safe ISSSTE, where the beneficiaries have certainty about the healthcare network that assist them with quality and kindness.

b) An effective ISSSTE, which incorporates best practices, innovative protocols, and trains highly specialised staff to meet the needs and the demographic and epidemiological profile of its beneficiaries, ensuring the adequate supply of medicines.

c) A digital ISSSTE, which transforms the bureaucratic window into a new mechanism of electronic interaction with the intensive use of information technologies, and no longer the face-to-face procedure with its beneficiaries, enabling them to handle administrative procedures and services online.

d) A sustainable ISSSTE, which becomes sustainable in the long-term by capturing efficiencies, generating savings and releasing capacities.

The actions developed by ISSSTE on the following three areas are as follows:

I. Strengthening planning and co-ordination

II. Improving market intelligence

III. Improving procurement of comprehensive medical services

IV. Boosting competition for contracts and limiting direct awards

Action plan

	Recommendations OECD	Actions at the ISSSTE
	I. Strengthening planning and co-ordination	
1	Develop an explicit, performance-based procurement strategy, including a long-term vision for procurement, sequencing actions and timelines, as well as detailed monitoring and adjustment strategies.	The procurement of medical supplies for 2016 will be determined based on actual consumption in the medical units and patient registries for highly specialised drugs, not only at the request of the units, thereby improving inventory management with transparency and the participation of civil society via social audit.
2	Establish a comprehensive database that incorporates all the procurement-related information, building on current initiatives, to put together a reliable patients' registry for those requiring high-specialty medicines and a data set for procurement contracts in central units.	In this regard, a procurement database was developed by central areas, where all 2014 and 2015 contracts are uploaded; eventually it will include the entire Institute and is expected to be operational in the medium-term, according to budget availability. Additionally, all procurement procedures are recorded in COMPRANET as required by the law, which is the online procurement governmental information system for leasing, acquisitions and services of the Federal Public Administration.
3	Institutionalise internal good practices beyond specific persons or ISSSTE units and reinforce communication between central and decentralised areas leveraging on web-based tools and meetings.	Since the beginning of 2015 the Institute has increased the meetings with its delegates in the country, where they were informed about issues related to the budget and some indicators about procurement of supplies, security and cleaning services, allowing to show them comparisons between procurement and the national average. Through the Delegation Advisory Councils, the Institute tracks the results of tenders for each delegation and the spending of their budget on local public procurement. Concerning internal practices and new tools, ISSSTE developed the Counter for Medicine Vouchers in the Comprehensive System of Medicines Supply to improve the operation of hospital pharmacies. This aims at providing beneficiaries the medicines that are not available in the pharmacies of medical units through the issuance of a Medicine Voucher that can be used in one of the exchange centers that will be established.
4	Establish procurement performance indicators to measure efficiency and outcomes.	Available information will be analysed in all administrative units in order to determine the feasibility of developing uniform performance indicators, in coordination with the relevant areas on the matter and in the framework of the lines of action of the Programme for a Modern and Friendly Government 2013-2018 through key indicators, medicine supply boards, and monitoring of failures.
5	Establish a coordination unit for procurement, subject to the required resources and authorisations.	This recommendation will be assessed with the Ministry of Finance and Public Credit and the Ministry of Public Administration to develop the structure, the allocation of human resources, and the budget availability.
	II Improving market intelligence	
6	Develop a market intelligence methodology and plan, assessing the required human and material resources throughout ISSSTE and including method variations according to the degree of critical importance or complexity of procurement.	This is a medium-term project that starts with the understanding of the daily dynamics of the operations of public procurement areas, their staff and the analysis of different strategies to interact in a competitive market that requires advanced and deep knowledge from agents, suppliers, and users of goods and services with different capacities and supplier logistics systems, supply and distribution on time and subject to budget availability.
7	Formalise the Market Intelligence Unit in the Medical Supplies Under-Directorate, depending on available human and financial resources and the required authorisations.	This recommendation will be assessed by the Ministry of Finance and Public Credit and the Ministry of Public Administration for the development of the structure, the allocation of human resources and budget availability.
8	Work with other healthcare institutions to pool and share knowledge.	Joint work with healthcare institutions is being carried out, mainly on health supplies, in order to strengthen the work of the areas involved. During the current administration, concrete progress has been achieved on consolidated purchases and institutional collaboration with the Coordinating Commission for Negotiating the Price of Medicines and other Health Supplies, to standardise policies and generate savings in key acquisitions, highlighting important economies in the purchase of medicines.
9	Consult suppliers, online or through traditional means, on the development and structure of good OECD procurement practices.	This recommendation will be assessed with the Ministry of Finance and Public Credit and the Ministry of Public Administration to develop the structure, the allocation of human resources and budget availability.
10	Select people with the appropriate skills to create an informal network of procurement officials in ISSSTE. Rely on the market research unit specialists from the Medical Supplies Under-Directorate to train the network members.	Work will continue by carrying out workshops to explain the methodology to conduct market research, by approaching agencies and research centers and sharing experiences and best practices. Additionally, there is a strategic planning framework approved in the Institutional Programme 2014-2018 and regulatory reform has been undertaken following the adoption of a new Organic Statute and the modernisation process of information technologies. This will result in improving the quality of the public procurement process, impacting for good spending efficiency and the quality of services.

	Recommendations OECD	Actions at the ISSSTE
	III. Improving procurement of comprehensive medical services	
11	Consider consolidating the procurement of comprehensive medical services with other healthcare providers, such as the Mexican Institute of Social Security (*Instituto Mexicano del Seguro Social*, IMSS).	The analysis for procurement of comprehensive services was completed, but because of the validity and specific characteristics of the existing contracts, it is not possible in the short term to implement this consolidation until the standardisation of coverage and protocols. There is work to align the procurement of comprehensive services with the needs and profiles of ISSSTE beneficiaries. This is done through market analysis and by comparing prices offered to other health care institutions, which aims at keeping quality standards and achieving opportunity in the supply of comprehensive services, as well as generating savings for the Institute.
12	Involve more medical areas in contract performance management and ask suppliers for their cooperation in monitoring performance.	The procurement of comprehensive services in the last quarter of 2014 involved the participation of the medical areas of the Institute to define requirements and procedures, as well as to clarify and evaluate proposals. The cooperation between technical and specialised medical staff and procurement experts allowed to generate savings and improve monitoring and supervision.
13	Design evaluation criteria to accurately measure bidders' capacity to respond to medical needs and risks.	As best practices are incorporated, closer supervision of procurement processes and results is achieved. It is also feasible to define criteria for the assessment of needs and capacities to meet the supply of goods and services in the medium-term.
	IV Boosting competition for contracts and limiting direct awards	
14	Promote in-house training by experienced ISSSTE procurement professionals from the central areas and delegations, to share practical ways of overcoming challenges and tested solutions for securing competition for contracts.	In the second half of 2014 a procurement workshop was carried out, with the participation of the ISSSTE decentralised administrative units, central procurement units, and OECD experts, as well as representatives from Chile and Portugal, who analysed framework contracts, regulatory frameworks, and the incentives to promote healthy competition among bidders, ending up in a renegotiation with major contractors. In the framework of the Programme for a Modem and Friendly Government, the Ministry of Public Administration promotes permanent training and the improvement of the COMPRANET system.
15	Implement standard data collection tools for all procurement units, such as a spreadsheet with fewer and harmonised codes and formats, as a step before introducing a comprehensive ISSSTE-wide database.	Currently, the ISSSTE is working on a pilot project for the development of a procurement database for central areas. This pilot is estimated to be tested in the medium-term.
16	Train user (medical units) and procurement areas in the strategic relevance of procurement processes.	The Institute regularly provides training about procurement to the personnel involved in the planning process of purchases, in order to develop capacities.
17	Regularly analyse the use of exceptions to competitive tendering in order to identify opportunities to contain direct awards.	There is a review process of all reforms to the legal framework, rules, and processes to increase competition and transparency in public tenders.
18	Leverage on training and materials developed by SFP and adjust them to ISSSTE's needs in order to strengthen internal capacities. This could be done through a joint effort with international organisations, major universities, and institutes with which ISSSTE has signed cooperation agreements..	The ISSSTE has several agreements with the National Autonomous University of Mexico (UNAM) and the National Polytechnic Institute (IPN), for the delivery of courses, workshops, and trainings to strengthen the institute's practices in public procurement.
19	Implement a standardised classification model for identifying products, aligned with suppliers, to facilitate mutual understanding.	-The tender process for distribution of medicines and health supplies was improved, as well as for supply according to the needs of medical units based on the Programmed National Demand. This facilitated the optimisation of resources by decreasing the risks related to expiration and unnecessary stocks. There is work to update the Basic Basket of Medicines and identify equivalence that may diversify the supply of products, without threatening the health and quality of care received by patients. These initiatives are the basis to build a model for the standard classification of products, with specifications, supply cycle, and contractual terms, aligned with institutional regulations and policies.

Source: Information provided by ISSSTE as of 30 September 2015.

ORGANISATION FOR ECONOMIC CO-OPERATION AND DEVELOPMENT

The OECD is a unique forum where governments work together to address the economic, social and environmental challenges of globalisation. The OECD is also at the forefront of efforts to understand and to help governments respond to new developments and concerns, such as corporate governance, the information economy and the challenges of an ageing population. The Organisation provides a setting where governments can compare policy experiences, seek answers to common problems, identify good practice and work to co-ordinate domestic and international policies.

The OECD member countries are: Australia, Austria, Belgium, Canada, Chile, the Czech Republic, Denmark, Estonia, Finland, France, Germany, Greece, Hungary, Iceland, Ireland, Israel, Italy, Japan, Korea, Luxembourg, Mexico, the Netherlands, New Zealand, Norway, Poland, Portugal, the Slovak Republic, Slovenia, Spain, Sweden, Switzerland, Turkey, the United Kingdom and the United States. The European Union takes part in the work of the OECD.

OECD Publishing disseminates widely the results of the Organisation's statistics gathering and research on economic, social and environmental issues, as well as the conventions, guidelines and standards agreed by its members.

OECD PUBLISHING, 2, rue André-Pascal, 75775 PARIS CEDEX 16
(42 2015 27 1 P) ISBN 978-92-64-24988-2 – 2016

www.ingramcontent.com/pod-product-compliance
Lightning Source LLC
Chambersburg PA
CBHW061215240926
51846CB00006B/1233